Over the last two hundred years some important ways of understanding theatre history have been undervalued or ignored by
scholars. Leading theatre historian Jacky Bratton employs new
approaches to examine and challenge this development, and to
discover how theatre history has been chronicled and how it is interpreted. Using a series of case studies from nineteenth-century
British theatre, Bratton examines the difference between the existence of 'the drama' (plays and play literature) and 'the stage'
(performance, theatre building and attendance). By rejecting literary history, Bratton experiments with other ways of analysing
the past, and the ways that have actually seemed relevant to the
people on stage. This book suggests new histories: of theatrical
story-telling, of performing families and of the disregarded dramatic energy of Victorian entertainment. As a result, we gain a
new perspective on theatre history, not only for the Romantic
and Victorian periods, but for the discipline overall.

JACKY BRATTON is Professor of Theatre and Cultural History
in the Department of Drama and Theatre at Royal Holloway,
University of London. Professor Bratton has written widely on
Victorian theatre and literature as well as on performance history, including melodrama, music hall, and on the contribution
of women in the theatre.

New Readings in Theatre History

Theatre and Performance Theory

Series Editor
Tracy C. Davis, *Northwestern University*

Each volume in the Theatre and Performance Theory series introduces a key issue about theatre's role in culture. Specially written for students and a wide readership, each book uses case studies to guide readers into today's pressing debates in theatre and performance studies. Topics include contemporary theatrical practices; historiography; interdisciplinary approaches to making theatre; and the choices and consequences of how theatre is studied, among other areas of investigation.

Books published

Jacky Bratton, *New Readings in Theatre History*
Tracy C. Davis and Thomas Postlewait, editors, *Theatricality*

New Readings
in Theatre History

Jacky Bratton

Professor of Theatre and Cultural History
Royal Holloway, University of London

CAMBRIDGE
UNIVERSITY PRESS

PUBLISHED BY THE PRESS SYNDICATE OF THE UNIVERSITY OF CAMBRIDGE
The Pitt Building, Trumpington Street, Cambridge, United Kingdom

CAMBRIDGE UNIVERSITY PRESS
The Edinburgh Building, Cambridge, CB2 2RU, UK
40 West 20th Street, New York, NY 10011–4211, USA
477 Williamstown Road, Port Melbourne, VIC 3207, Australia
Ruiz de Alarcón 13, 28014 Madrid, Spain
Dock House, The Waterfront, Cape Town 8001, South Africa
http://www.cambridge.org

First published 2003

Printed in the United Kingdom at the University Press, Cambridge

Typeface Plantin 10/12 pt.   *System* LATEX 2ε   [TB]

A catalogue record for this book is available from the British Library

Library of Congress Cataloguing in Publication data
Bratton, J. S. (Jacqueline S.)
New Readings in Theatre History / Jacky Bratton.
    p.   cm. – (Theatre and performance theory)
Includes bibliographical references and index.
ISBN 0 521 79121 9 – ISBN 0 521 79463 3 (pb.)
1. Theatre – Great Britain – History – 19th century.   2. Theatre – Great
Britain – History – 18th century.   3. English drama – 19th century – History
and criticism.   4. English drama – 18th century – History and criticism.
I. Title.   II. Series.
PN2594.B73   2003
792′.0941′09034 – dc21   2003048478

ISBN 0 521 79121 9 hardback
ISBN 0 521 79463 3 paperback

Facts, like stones, are nothing in themselves; their value consists in the manner they are put together, and the purpose to which they are applied.

(Bulwer Lytton, *England and the English*, 1833, p. 78)

Euripides in his *Helena* says – 'Nothing is more useful to mankind than a prudent mistrust' – a maxim particularly applicable to the history of the stage.

(John Genest, *The English Stage*, 1832, vol. 3, p. 307)

Contents

Illustrations

Illustrations reproduced by permission of the V&A Picture
Library.

Acknowledgements

This book has been an extraordinarily long time in the making. It has survived three life-threatening illnesses (one of mine, two of my partner's) and seven years' headship of the Department of Drama and Theatre at Royal Holloway, University of London. I'm not sure which has been the more distracting. During that time it has of course been many times transformed, and parts of it have been aired at conferences in many places; the input of others has been invaluable. In the later stages I have received the financial support of the Arts and Humanities Research Board, for which I am most grateful. During the writing friends and colleagues have discussed the work with me on many occasions: I would particularly thank Richard Cave, David Mayer, John Earl, Frances Dann and Kate Newey for their interest and input, and Tracy Davis for her inspiring editorial responses. Also during the long writing, postgraduates have become colleagues and friends, and have helped me in many ways with my work, and with their new visions of theatre history as we might make it together. I would particularly like to thank Dr Gilli Bush-Bailey for her co-teaching, thinking and inspiration, and Dr Ann Featherstone for the immense amount of work she has put into this book as my research assistant, as well as for her unique and ever-challenging excitement about nineteenth-century entertainment.

This book is dedicated, however, to Jane Traies; without whom . . .

Part I

Background

1   Theatre history today

For more than a decade now theatre history has been, rather belatedly, coming to self-consciousness about knowledge. We still do not well know what we are supposed to be doing, what we can seek to know, what, in fact, we are talking about. There have been huge claims for the centrality of the discipline to the liberal education; and simultaneously the discovery by academic and professional institutions that fewer and fewer people are interested in it in its established form.[1] This uncertainty may or may not be linked with a more general concern about the fate of theatre itself, loudly asserting the vital importance of live performance in a world of increasingly virtual reality. Our realisations of doubt seem to trail a long way behind the theoretical disputes in wider historical studies, where the death and rebirth of narrative, for example, appear to have happened before anyone in the backwater of theatre seriously considered that one might do without it.[2] But since the 1980s academic theatre history has been increasingly uneasy, and there is no longer any consensus about such a shared endeavour, its terms of reference or its historiography. Spats take place. Despite many years of the digestion of Foucault and Derrida, not to mention writers more closely interested in the field, like Greenblatt and Orgel, it was still possible in 1999 for the respected theatre historian Robert D. Hume to refer to New Historicism as 'an unfortunate complication'[3] and to assert a version of the credo of the positivist which he calls 'Archeo-historicism' in the face of the widely held consensus about the non-neutrality of facts.[4]

Robert Hume is by no means alone in maintaining an antiquarian interest in the stage. At the opening of the twenty-first century many disparate, sometimes mutually discrediting, activities are going on. On the one hand, major undertakings in documentary history still roll forward. Scholars under the aegis of the Records of Early English Drama still cull materials from medieval documents and present them as self-verifying facts.[5] The continuation into the next century of the massive calendar of eighteenth-century performances, *The London Stage 1660–1800*,[6] is still projected, as *The London Stage 1800–1900*, and has produced one publication, *The Adelphi Theatre Calendar, Part 1, 1806–1850*[7] as an earnest of its intent to list every performance in every theatre as its predecessor did (or asserted that it did – in fact *The London Stage* fails to include most performances in taverns, public halls and other spaces, or indeed in theatres beyond the patent houses). Computer technology seductively offers new possibilities of the comprehensive publication of data: the Adelphi microfiche have been translated into an on-line database; many other initiatives are beginning. On 10 June 2002, for example, at the London Theatre Museum, *Backstage* was launched, an on-line catalogue, reaching right down to the names on the playbills, that covers the theatre holdings of a large number of British libraries.[8] Beside the work of compilation, that of synthesis and definition moves slowly forward. Attempts – to which this book is in some ways related – are being made in many countries of Europe to write national theatre histories.[9] Books have appeared which question the grounds on which such histories are being written, and either, as in Thomas Postlewait and Bruce A. McConachie's *Interpreting the Theatrical Past*, suggest ways to use new historical methodologies, or, as in the ingenious structure of Simon Shepherd and Peter Womack's *English Drama, a Cultural History*,[10] offer contextualisation of their own history by reviewing the constructions of previous writers alongside their own new interpretations. Meanwhile, books about the much more developed field of performance theory now often contain some move towards the inclusion of a theorised theatre history; and the first volumes of new kinds of history, taking up the most obvious developments in historical writing – feminist, *annaliste*, New Historicist or cultural/anthropological studies, for example – have been published.[11] So developments in historiography and performance theory are at last beginning to filter into examinations of long-past theatre events, and from that a new hybrid, which might become a historiographically challenging and exciting new mode, begins to emerge. But no new direction or set of procedures has so far been agreed; the performance falters; and the audience is becoming impatient.

Binary thinking in the twentieth century: theatre as 'ritual and revelry'

My first intention is to move backwards, and consider the historiography of the theatre as shaping the peculiar situation not only of the discipline today, disputatious, excited and unsettled as it is, but also the current state of the theatre, its equally troubled object of study. I hope to approach British theatre history by examining how it came to be written as it is, considering the forces that determined and shaped it in the nineteenth century, as part of the hegemonic battle for possession of the stage itself; and then to suggest a new historicising of the field, undertaken from a different position. One cannot, of course, change the course of past events, and reverse the direction taken by theatre performance and reception within western culture; but it is my hope that an understanding of the cultural determination of one influential and sometime highly regarded national theatre and its history will enable a clearer understanding of why theatre and its historical study are where they are today.

Underlying the organisation of the field of theatre history is, unsurprisingly, a series of binary assumptions. On the institutional level, the calendaring activities mentioned above are the legacy of the first mode of academic study of theatre history, which is usually fathered upon Max Hermann. His Theaterwissenschaftliches Institut in Berlin, founded in 1923, set out the model for the rigorous study of documented facts about the material remains of theatrical life – theatres or their ruins, promptbooks, designs, bills, costumes and so forth. According to its dogma, history lies in the artifactual record; nothing can be known without sufficient factual documentation.[12] This principle is still powerful, and is restated in Hume's 1999 volume cited above: he maintains strongly that satisfactory 'archaeo-historical' work is entirely dependent upon the first-hand study of adequate amounts of primary documentary evidence.[13] The work done under its banner is indeed rigorous; to see this rigour at work one has only to consult the 1987 Society for Theatre Research edition of the first book that offers detailed British theatre facts,

John Downes's *Roscius Anglicanus* of 1708, which Hume edited with Judith Milhous. The editors were expressly intending 'to help the reader follow Downes without being misled'.[14] Every date, every name has been checked against other sources; no page of the text is without a substantial footnote, many of them containing more words than those of the original text. But beyond such facts, one might learn very little about Downes, or directly about his colleagues the actors, the plays or the culture in question from this book. The binary observed in this model of theatre history is a strict divide set up between this 'scientific' activity, susceptible of concrete proofs and never venturing beyond demonstrable facts, and the critical activities of students of the drama, who interpret and study the written texts in the light of the facts generated elsewhere. The theatre historian is expressly debarred from considering the plays that were put on by the people she or he studies, except in clearly limited and defined, factual ways.

The many distinguished archaeo-historical writers have not undertaken this work, of course, with the intention of belittling the study of the play text. Rather the reverse. Intent upon establishing an academic discipline that could be respected in its own right, the objective of *Theaterwissenschaft* is that its products should be of use to the wider world, providing a secure knowledge on which critical, aesthetic and conceptual responses to literature could be based. However, as the title of Hume's book, *Reconstructing Contexts*, makes clear, this effectively sets up the discipline as the lesser term in a powerful binary: it is merely context to the text of literature. Thus the study of the theatre is always at the service of the written drama, its *raison d'être*. As I hope to show, this is a debilitating assumption; and, moreover, it has unintentionally given rise to much tedious and inferior work by lesser hands, which cannot claim any function beyond the gratification of an impulse to unearth, hoard and dispute over the detritus of the past. No knowledge *need* be dull; but exemption from the obligation to be critical, imaginative, alert to implication and synthetic of ideas in one's research has led too many scholars to an intellectual inertia, and the antiquarian pursuit of relics for their own sake.

The obvious conceptual challenge to *Theaterwissenschaft* comes, of course, from the direction of post-Modern and

post-structuralist thought, which questions the distinction between text and context, as well as the nature of fact, proof
and evidence assumed in its quasi-scientific foundation. Again,
the mainstream of historiographical revisionism has been there
ahead of us, and one may find much recent work on the nature of historical truth, its rejection and reclamation, stemming
from such moves as the questioning of 'grand narratives' in Jean-
François Lyotard's *The Postmodern Condition* in 1984[15] and moving on through an intricate and protracted debate which is not
(of course) susceptible of closure. In this line of thought theatre
history is especially susceptible to challenge, but at the same
time, it seems to me, potentially especially well equipped to
find constructive responses. The susceptibility stems from the
consciousness, shared by even the most stubbornly myopic antiquarians, that our study is of something which is always-already
irrecoverably lost. While political life, for example, was played
out at least partly in documents that have been archived, poems,
novels and play texts are still in the library, and local identity
inheres in surviving rivers, houses, families, the theatrical performance is in essence evanescent, gone for ever. Joseph Roach
notes theatre historians' tendency to strike notes of 'irretriev-
able loss' about the 'fragility of their subject', to express 'self-
consciousness about the perceived contradiction of writing the
history of so notoriously transient a form'.[16] But the same writer,
in his path-breaking cross-disciplinary study *Cities of the Dead:
Circum-atlantic Performance*,[17] shows that the subject of performance, if adequately theorised and imaginatively extended, offers wonderfully suggestive ways of dealing with its own absences.
He begins with a quotation from the *annaliste* medieval historian
Jacques Le Goff: 'Today documents include the spoken word,
the image, gestures':[18] what better than the theatre to provide
a wealth of such documentation. In the course of his book,
amongst many other things, Roach interprets a British theatre
history even older than *Roscius Anglicanus*, James Wright's 1699
Historia Histrionica. Milhous and Hume dismiss Wright's work as
dilettante, containing only 'some useful scraps of information',[19]
but to Roach it is 'an exemplary meditation on popular performance as a measure of epochal memory'[20] and takes a place in
his synthesis of cultural history alongside slave dancing places,
effigies of Elvis Presley and the funeral of Thomas Betterton.

Popular performance: 'theatre of pure diversion'

Roach's invocation of 'popular performance' points to another important binary, and one with which I shall be particularly concerned: that between high and low, elite art and 'the popular'. Tracy Davis argues that her fundamental reinterpretation of nineteenth-century theatre history in economic terms is necessary because it is still the case, in both Britain and America, that 'theatre with "enlightened" goals is cast as the "other" to commercialized entertainment'.[21] I would reverse the terms, and so the emphasis: the British critical assumption is still that commercialised entertainment is the Other of the art of theatre. This impacts upon current thinking about the arts in fundamental ways; and it interacts significantly with the historiography of theatre. Whatever the minor byways pursued by antiquarian theatre historians of subsequent generations, the *Theaterwissenschaft* exclusion of the text from consideration did not mean – why should it? – that the interest of the historian should challenge the standing of the texts of high art. As Marvin Carlson points out:

Traditional theater history developed in the shadow of European high culture of the late nineteenth century and almost universally accepted the values of that culture. Theater history was by no means considered a study of the phenomenon of theater in all periods and cultures, but a study of the production conditions of the already acknowledged major periods and accepted canon of European literary drama. The Greek and the Shakespearean theater were thus considered favored topics for historical investigation (as they still are), while the rich tradition of popular and/or spectacle theater, even in Europe, was ignored as undistinguished, decadent, or generally unworthy of critical attention'[22]

The effect of this binary on, especially, the attitude to women in the theatre was wonderfully vividly expressed in 1931 by Rosamund Gilder, in a work whose recovery of important female contributions to past performance is still not superseded. It is, however, deeply embedded in the values of cultural hierarchy, and her language is richly suggestive of the effects of that tradition, even as she tries to break away from it and give proper attention to women in the theatre. She discusses women's exclusion from Greek Golden Age performance, and adds:

[w]hile the official Greek theatre, forgetful of its sources in the cyclic
dance and the dithyramb in which women had taken part, closed its
doors to feminine participants in its elevated mysteries, that other
theatre, forever effervescent at the heart of humanity, the theatre of
pure diversion, continued its unfettered course. Ever since Eve invented
costume, and, coached by the Serpent, enacted that little comedy by
which she persuaded Adam that the bitter apple of knowledge was sweet
and comforting, there has been something satanic in the very nature of
theatre. Born of ritual and revelry, it is at once the child of God and
the offspring of the Devil. We see it simultaneously reflecting the no-
blest aspects of the mind of man, stemming from his aspiration toward
beauty and goodness and blossoming in the highest forms of art, and
at the same time we find it creeping up from the gutter, befouling the
image of its creator and reducing him to something a little lower than
the beasts. In this double aspect it very fairly mirrors the larger human
scene, and not least of all in its attitude toward woman. When, as in
Greece, the nobler aspects of the theatre were closed to her, she came
in, as was to be expected, by the Devil's way.[23]

In such self-deprecatory terms Gilder outlines the history of the
feminised Other set up by the theatre of male genius, of moral
and sacred high art. She is concerned with the low estimation of
women involved in theatre, but without challenging the binary
thinking that has placed them in the inferior position.

The abjection of the 'theatre of pure diversion', and often all theatre whatsoever, is set out and explored at length in another classic text, Jonas Barish's *The Antitheatrical Prejudice*. Barish traces
the prejudice he describes through its long philosophical and political history, but in the end sees it as a pathology, 'tenacious,
elusive and protean in its own right, and springing, as it seems,
from the deepest core of our being', an affliction which he sees
as yet undefeated, since while 'the public may have lost much of
its old suspiciousness of the theater' '[t]he theater remains suspi-
cious of itself'.[24] In British scholarship explanations are always
more likely to be sought in culture, and especially in class, than
in psychology. With the new popularist turn of scholarship in the
1960s that became British cultural studies, the binary between
sacred and profane art and the prejudice against entertainment
and feigning were read as hierarchical, a matter of high and low.
Hence there was a deliberate reaction, a move away from the
prejudged, exclusory history of drama towards the study of 'folk'

performances, customs, festivals, street theatre and the spectacular and musical theatres of 'the people'. In nineteenth-century
history, music hall and melodrama became the focus of work that
attempts to recuperate or to understand these commercial entertainments in relation to a 'little' or 'popular' tradition deriving
from broadside ballads, street singing and tavern culture, or to
place them in a social-historians' context of class definition rather
than in the history of performance.[25] The obvious problem here,
of course, is that to invert a binary of this sort is not to abolish
it; but also, and more damagingly still, the definition of 'popular
culture' has become increasingly problematised as attempts have
been made to theorise it within a more sophisticated cultural
analysis. A single entity called people's theatre has tended to
vanish into ideological smoke, leaving popular theatre history
without a coherent field of study.[26] But the implications of this
particular binary opposition remain and are, I will argue, at the
root of much of the hegemonic work done by modern theatre
history ever since it was invented.

That invention predates the twentieth-century *Theaterwissenschaft* movement; its British manifestation came into force at
an easily pinpointed moment, the early 1830s, in the midst of
change and modernisation on a very large scale. It was, indeed,
one cultural aspect of the British response to the second wave
of revolutionary change that was sweeping the rest of Europe.
The British political outcome was the reformation of the parliamentary system, which was thought at the time to have staved
off revolution; but many cultural changes were also part of that
defensive response to the revolutionary impulse. It is my argument that at this particular point theatre history became a part of
the hegemonic negotiation taking place at many levels in British
culture, and that there was a vested interest in its reinvention in
a particular mould – many of whose lineaments have survived
until today, to the detriment not only of the historical study, but
also of its object of contemplation, theatrical work itself.

The birth of our grand narrative

It was in the 1830s that the field became defined and its procedures set up so as to mark limits to what theatre is, and to
establish it in a system of difference – text and context, high

and low, the written drama and the materiality of the stage. In a simple bibliographical sense this is very clearly the case, in that a flood of writings about theatre history began around the turn of the nineteenth century and came to a high-water mark with publications in the early 1830s. It is from these historians – Edward Malone, John Payne Collier, John Genest – that we have derived our sense of the shape and meaning of the British theatre.[27] Their books, multi-volumed, scholarly and obviously representing a serious investment not only of publisher's cash but also of cultural capital, time and status, are the first works about which the questions of intention, ideological determination and the cultural work being done by theatre history can be asked and answered in detail. They formed part of a heated debate in their own time, which amounted to a struggle for mastery of the stage. The success of certain historians and their allies in that debate has shaped and conditioned the British theatre. That success has arguably been a malign influence on the practice of theatre, its cultural work, even its funding and its training practices; it has certainly distorted our understanding of the development of theatre in Britain, and so poses a major challenge, standing in the way of a new understanding.

One may see this continuing legacy in the way that the institutions of the British 'National Theatre' are apparently set upon a foundation divided against itself on complex class lines – and also the lines Gilder calls the gulf between 'the child of God and the offspring of the Devil'. The battles are perpetual. The Royal Opera House, excitedly exposed to popular view in 1990s TV documentaries about mismanagement, is controversially funded from the taxes and the entertainments of the poor – the National Lottery. The Royal National Theatre is vilified by the critics for recharging its box office by staging spectacular revivals of American musicals. The resemblance to the disputes of the 1830s is startling. That link is also to be observed in the hostility of the 'writers' theatre' at the Royal Court to the spectacular West End, which in turn anxiously defines 'the fringe' and assigns to it inferior venues, small pockets of civic funding and minority audiences. History and heritage are repeatedly invoked by all sides, and university drama departments, amateur theatrical groups and educational and regional projects are all contenders not only for recognition, public money and/or respect, but for possession of centre stage, the right to make their voices heard, their definitions stick.[28] All these disputes are in some sense the legacy of conventional theatre history that began in the nineteenth century.

The melodramatic 'Decline of the Drama'

The continuing strength of the received way of reading theatre history can be gauged from the difficulties critics, performers and historians still have when they attempt to recuperate anything from the early nineteenth-century stage. A clear example is the problem of 'melodrama'. Much has been written about the mode, or modality, or genre, or dramatic form that goes by this name, and it is undoubtedly a successful and dominant organising principle in much contemporary dramatic fiction on TV and film. It has been argued to exist in the highest reaches of the drama – the plays of Ancient Greece and the Renaissance[29] – but it is the characteristic dramatic form of the nineteenth century, and so it is caught in the inescapable trap of being the form of the drama in decline. 'Melodrama' is bad drama; it is the word used whenever a critic, trained or untrained, wishes to indicate that they think poorly of the art of the enacted fiction they are discussing, to deny it the universally praiseworthy character of being 'realistic', 'true to life'.[30] Melodrama is the play not disguised as literature; theatre allowing its falsity and allure to show; the Devil's way.

We may see the linkage of this to theatre history. Pre- and early twentieth-century accounts of melodrama and of the theatre which spawned it are obviously part of the Modernist project, the moment when the 1830s attempt to take possession of the stage for a particular class fraction finally came to fruition, with the importation of the plays of Ibsen and all that stood for. The followers of William Archer believed in the Decline, indeed the Death, of English Drama before their own arrival: '[we] are pretty safe, then, in setting down the twenty-five years between 1810 and 1835 as the winter solstice of the English drama'. Archer was aware, in a way, that he was carrying a programme begun in the 1830s to its logical conclusion, and observed that '[t]he period was more or less conscious of its own degradation', citing a *Blackwood's* article by 'the Shakespearean scholar, Harness' in 1825 on the subject of the 'ignoble' modern playwrights.[31] He had many followers; Augustin Filon, for example, announced 'had I not had his books as a guiding thread, I should have hardly ventured to risk myself in the labyrinth of theatrical history' where there is nothing but 'Theatrical "Reminiscences" . . . crowded with fictitious anecdotes'.[32] Structuring his account of the stage around the plays he read, he found that the most ambitious of the 1830s dramatists – Bulwer Lytton – wrote 'literary melodrama; a detestable combination'.[33] Like most others, he accounted for their poverty as the fate of the dramatist in a situation where 'the new public which filled the theatres was gluttonous . . . [m]asterful, clamorous, ill-bred, uncouth . . . [t]he barbarians had begun to arrive; it was the first wave of democracy before which the *habitué*, the playgoer of the old school, was forced to flee'.[34]

Given the elitist slant of this received history, it is not surprising that the foundational recovery work on melodrama was the product of the 1960s. Michael Booth was an enthusiast for melodrama who opened the eyes of a whole generation of theatre scholars. However, his analysis relies on a late Victorian aesthete, Jerome K. Jerome, for a typology of melodramatic characters, which inevitably belittles them, seen as they are through the condescendingly reversed telescope of a class-hostile intellectual sophistication.[35] To Jerome, melodrama was a joke; and most of the 'recuperative' studies of the subject that followed Booth condescended to be amused in the same way, where they were not led into even less helpful judgements by 'taking the plays seriously' in anachronistic critical terms. The recovery of contextual study followed, with the comprehensive work of Martin Meisel's hugely impressive *Realizations* as its exemplary text. After reading through this discriminating, meticulous and highly documented and illustrated study of the pictorial stage and its centrality in Romantic and Victorian culture, it comes as something of a shock when the last word goes to W. B. Yeats and his utter rejection of all stage effect that compromises or competes with the poet's verbal text; but the implicit explanation follows – 'the cinema took over the popular audience that had earlier supported the nineteenth-century pictorial stage'.[36] What belongs to 'the popular audience' is not art.[37]

Writers coming from the literary field and not concerning themselves with how melodrama actually played may cope better with finding ways to free it of the stigma of its history in the theatre. Peter Brooks's *The Melodramatic Imagination* is a groundbreaking text[38] in seriously theorised reading; but he is ultimately writing about the novel, his approach is psychological and semiotic, and he dismisses all stage melodrama after the 1820s as the form in decline, in theatrical hands. The latest major study is by Elaine Hadley,[39] who sketches this very history of the term and its critics before embarking on her examination of nineteenth-century culture's 'theatricalized dissent' with only one chapter on the theatre. Most of us whose focus is the history of the theatre can still be found joking, apologising, and explaining melodrama away; and every attempt I have ever seen to revive texts labelled 'melodramas' on the professional stage was similarly crippled by apologetic self-consciousness.[40] This attitude to the nineteenth-century stage presents itself, therefore, as a historical problem.

The problem, and how to tackle it

Hume prescribes such a problem as the starting point for scholarly investigation: 'A scholar needs to start by explaining the current state of understanding, and then tell us what is wrong or inadequate about it. What evidence is left out of account? What is misinterpreted? How can we improve our understanding?'[41] I would push this further, with Peter Burke, and seek for 'an approach to the past which asks present-minded questions but refuses to give present-minded answers; which concerns itself with traditions but allows for their continual reinterpretation; and which notes the importance of unintended consequences in the history of historical writing as well as the history of political events'.[42]

The problem can be restated through two paradoxical perceptions. The first is that the already canvassed observation made early in the nineteenth century and echoed by commentators and historians ever since – that the century suffered from 'the Decline of the Drama' and that its theatrical culture was disastrously undermined by a lack of good writing for the stage – was set running while the stage itself, the theatres built, memorable performances given and numbers of people seeing shows and professionally appearing before the public grew spectacularly.[43] Worth and value and cultural significance were said to have disappeared from a theatre that was thriving, multiplying and serving ever-increasing numbers of spectators. Secondly, in a period where the received history denies any serious involvement of women in writing for the stage and lists only isolated examples of women in management, a period which habitually used the word 'actress' as a facetious synonym for 'prostitute', research today constantly turns up women whose contribution to theatre was substantial, innovative and decisive, but whose stories were not remembered or were inaccurately recorded.[44] I would like to establish what the connection might be between these two paradoxes; and that speculation begins with a reappraisal of the early writers of British theatre history, and the crucial period of theatrical development during which they wrote.

In the rest of Part I I will therefore argue for the dating of current theatre historiography from the first third of the nineteenth century, showing first that a different kind of historicisation, in the hands of theatre people themselves, preceded that period. Chapter 2 deals with that historical vision. Chapter 3 offers a contextualising materialist overview of the state of London theatre in the 1830s, and simultaneously attempts to model a new way of telling such a story, by means of the intertheatrical reading of contemporary playbills. Chapter 4 then examines what happened in theatre politics in the years of Reform, 1830–2, the moment when the previous historical practice was successfully challenged and discredited. It attempts to decode the assumptions and hegemonic processes at work in the creation of the modern history of the stage. I consider only the case of Britain – largely, indeed, London – because the historical practice then founded was constituted explicitly as nationalistic, concerned with issues of the formation of a new national identity. The concept of 'the National Drama' stems from the eighteenth century,[45] but took on a new force in the political arguments of the first half of the nineteenth. On a philosophical level what can be said to have happened is that around 1800 the idea of 'literature' came to depend upon a aesthetic of autonomy: the artist was envisaged as a unique and self-justified creative spirit. Such a conception of the necessary conditions for art results in a distrust of the theatrical as undermining the artistic autonomy attributed to the writer. Such a polarisation can be seen as the philosophical justification of the reified separation of text and context in *Theaterwissenschaft*: the dramatist is the creative artist, the theatre should serve his genius.[46] In ideological terms a group of politically engaged writers, most obviously exemplified by the Radical Member of Parliament, novelist and would-be dramatist Bulwer Lytton, made a bid for control of the public sphere which included the voice of the stage, as part of the Radical turn of the 1830s. Their case was substantiated by an appeal to history, in the pursuit of which a history of the stage since the medieval–Elizabethan point of origin was written – a history which was not substantially challenged until very recent years, and has still not been overturned in respect of its analysis of its own period. And it was a necessary condition of the successful hegemonic control of the theatre that there was a binary division set up between 'the popular' and the theatre of art; that women's work within the public space should be disguised, discounted or appropriated to male control; and therefore entertainment, embodied as female, became the Other of the 'National Drama' of male genius. It will be the work of the case studies in Part II to make approaches to theatre history that challenge and deconstruct (rather than simply overturn) this binary Modernist history.

2 British theatre history: 1708–1832

In this chapter I seek to uncover the historicising of theatrical life that existed before the early nineteenth-century hegemonic appropriation of the story of the British stage. My argument is not that no history had previously been written. The unique poignancy of the theatrical experience, which comes from the intensity of its presence and hence the sense of loss when it is over, has evoked a wish to capture those stories, to pass on our individual sense of that magic, for many generations. The political turn of the 1830s discredited and soon eclipsed a long-established tradition of theatre history, which I seek to recover, at least in outline, below.

The librarians and the tribal scribes

The first books about the history of entertainment in Britain are the two volumes already mentioned: James Wright's *Historia Histrionica*, 1699, and John Downes's *Roscius Anglicanus* of 1708.[1] Wright was a barrister, antiquary and book collector; he was therefore an interested hanger-on, outside the working life of the theatre. The point of view of his account is that of the audience; it is given voice by two theatrically inclined figures he invents, for whom he writes, appropriately, a dialogue. The first is Trueman, a theatre buff who recalls the players 'before the wars' and compares them with the first post-Restoration generation. The other, Lovewit, acts as stooge and prompt, and is the youngster eager to be inducted into the mysteries of the stage, for whose admiring ears the basic theatrical dispute – whose generation of great actors was the greatest – can be told over. *Roscius Anglicanus* is very different. John Downes was the prompter at Lincoln's Inn Fields, and is the first of a long line of theatrical

professionals turned historian. In his book the main interest is
not anecdotal or aesthetic but factual and practical: detailed particulars of plays and cast lists and takings that only he and his
friend Charles Booth with the King's Company[2] at the other theatre had at their command. From these books stem two distin-
guishable, though sometimes intermingled, branches of writing,
contributing the two main elements present in varying proportions in each subsequent history, forming a kind of traditional
account of the British stage. A rich tradition ran unbroken from
them to work that was still being undertaken and elaborated
in the early nineteenth century: the annals of the London stage.
The men involved in compiling, altering, correcting and adding
to it had no notion of offering the public their own original ideas
or analysis, and claimed only to be adding more information to
a received text, the body of theatre lore, as more years passed
by. Sometimes they express a preference for the plays and the
theatre practices of a particular period – normally the period of
their own young manhood – and some plume themselves on having unearthed more facts and better stories, or corrected details
which their forebears mistook, or on acknowledging sources that
others had used silently; but that is as far as their critical and
scholarly principles extend.

They produced works which we may place on two main stems.
One is the playlist, whose central information is about the published play, authors, dates of publication and/or first performance, and, in the more sophisticated instances, about editions
of printed texts. These books function as 'companions to the
playhouse', a useful reference for playgoers keen to buy play-
books for their libraries and wanting to know a little more about
the authors of revivals they might see performed. They often
include an introductory section outlining 'the rise and progress
of the British Stage', but their meat is an alphabetical series of
entries about dramatists, and a second (or an integrated) list of
play titles. The central text here, many times reprinted, rewritten,
corrected and added to, was known by the eighteenth and nineteenth centuries as *Biographia Dramatica* or simply *BD*.[3] This was
an indispensable tool in the library, and it was the practice of antiquarians and collectors to annotate their copies with notes of
their own purchases of old books, and to make their observations
to add to its bibliographic completeness. Some copies, including

one now in the British Library,[4] were bound up with lined blank sheets for notes in every opening; some have survived with annotations by eighteenth- and nineteenth-century scholars such as Charles Burney.[5] John Payne Collier, the leading historian of the new school, whose work will be considered below, records working with a very important *Biographia*. In his *An Old Man's Diary, Forty Years Ago* (a curious volume, privately printed and published in 1871 but masquerading as a diary of 1832 and the first six months of 1833)[6] he describes his employment in that year by the Lord Chamberlain, the Duke of Devonshire, who told him that he

> wanted to put the whole of his English Dramatic library, ancient and modern, under my care, and he showed me John Philip Kemble's Catalogue, which had been sent to him with the Plays, and which I saw at a glance was the *Biographia Dramatica*, by Stephen Jones, 8vo, 1812, with manuscript notes. As J. P. Kemble obtained the Plays there enumerated, he had put a cross against each in the margin of the book, and marked under the particular edition in his collection. This book the Duke wished to be my guide in procuring plays.[7]

Over the ensuing weeks the Duke and his excited librarian sat and copied Kemble's annotations into Collier's own interleaved copy of the book, so that they could keep track of their proceedings. Meanwhile Devonshire raided the auction houses for Shakespearean quartos and Collier lectured him on the history of the stage, and warned him that the Kemble collection he had acquired was inferior, since it was not made until 'Garrick, Steevens and Malone had secured nearly all the rarest and most valuable productions.'[8] These lists, tending to privilege the written text, were tools of the bookseller and the wealthy antiquarian, and the gentleman scholar, as is clearly the case here. Their relation to the collections of Garrick and John Philip Kemble might suggest that they were also the amusement and perhaps the tool of the highest level of theatrical management, who might be said to use them not only to annotate their valuable acquisitions but to secure and authenticate their control of the repertoire of the London stage.

The other stem of scribal history is the accumulating account of the British stage, whose main text is the book often referred to by the accumulating names of its authors and revisers – 'Victor

Oulton etc etc' (see below, p. 32) – but formally entitled *The History of the Theatres* or *An Annual Register.*[9] This is a genre which has little to do with expensive book-buying, and one whose focus might be said to be on a more democratic form of expertise. The compilation of annals – a serial account, year by year, of happenings in the world of the scribe, whether on an international, a national or a local level – is a basic and primitive form of historical writing. The effort to link events, creating some sort of reflexive chain or set of relationships, transforms such a compilation into a chronicle, effecting an enormous historiographical step. Writers who undertake such work are rarely as self-conscious as were the seventeenth-century erudites Mabillon, Tillemont and Muratori cited by Hayden White, who deliberately resorted to annalistic writing in order the free their accounts of the bias they deplored in their religiously or patriotically partisan contemporaries; in the twentieth century, of course, the title of the journal *Annales* has invoked that practice in an even more challenging historiographical move.[10]

But these British theatre annalists were in no way sophisticated or self-aware historians. The knowledge they offer is more at home in the pit, or even in the theatre tavern, than in the library. The books contain annual entries of performances, debuts, premieres and so on at the several theatres of London and also often of Dublin, with, in addition, information and anecdotes about the playhouses and their various people, rather than biographies of playwrights. Sometimes as a gesture to completeness they include a brisk summary survey of early times, often borrowed from a scholarly source. Dodsley's *Old Plays*, 1744, for example, was raided early on in the evolution of both strands of this writing and contributes a few paragraphs on British drama before Shakespeare to several compilations.[11] The praise heaped upon Shakespeare and his times is automatic and fulsome, but not protracted, since most share the view of *Egerton's Theatrical Remembrancer* that their task is to trace 'the gradual and progressive Advancement of the Theatre, from its rude Beginning to its present State of Excellence, chronologically digested',[12] and therefore naturally concentrate upon its more excellent years – those within their own recall, or that of recent generations. The assumption is that Shakespeare is the exemplary dramatist, but that it was on Garrick's stage that his work came to its proper home and finest flower. Importantly, the 'chronological digest' is substantiated – often doubled or trebled in extent – by the addition of anecdote; there are certain famous stories that are everywhere repeated, and others are added from the knowledge or the assiduous collection of individual writers, becoming in turn fodder for later versions and copies of the book.

The writers of these composite texts had a great deal in common. The major contributors are men of the theatre: John Downes (d.1712), William Rufus Chetwood (d.1766), David Erskine Baker (d.1767?), Benjamin Victor (d.1778), Thomas Davies (d.1785), Walley Oulton (d.1820) and Francis Godolphin Waldron (d.1818). A related but lesser figure who published biographical anecdote rather than annals was Ralph Wewitzer (d.1825),[13] and a more significant writer who resembles these but whose *Complete History of the English Stage*, published 1797–1800,[14] is not in the annal form and has perhaps more in common with Collier's writing, was Charles Dibdin the elder (d.1814). Booksellers and publishers – for example Egerton, Isaac Reed and Steven Jones – contributed to, corrected and reprinted the playlists, but in the main the field, especially the stem recording the cumulative annals of the stage, was dominated by the professional men of the theatre listed above. Their careers as actors were either very brief – Downes was 'spoil'd . . . for an Actor' by the sight of the King and the Duke of York in the audience at one of his first appearances,[15] and Victor similarly failed on stage – or were very undistinguished: Waldron aspired no further, in twenty-seven seasons at Drury Lane, than playing Second Gravedigger and walking in processions. Baker, Davies and Waldron married women who were better and more successful performers than they were themselves; Wewitzer was the most useful actor amongst them, performing hundreds of tertiary roles as foolish foreigners or eccentric Jews at Drury Lane between 1791 and 1819. Dibdin, on the fringe of the category, was of course a much more distinguished performer. Chetwood, Victor, Baker, Oulton, Wewitzer and Dibdin all wrote pieces for the stage – songs, farces, ballad operas, prologues – useful materials to oil the wheels of the theatre business. Several also wrote other antiquarian, money-making or hack publications, Baker producing a poem about Ossian, Waldron editing Chaucer, Oulton penning a guide to Margate and editing a short-lived periodical. Interested in the press, Chetwood, Davies and Waldron took up bookselling as a day-job. More importantly to their role as historians, several of them did their major theatre work in management. Downes was prompter at Lincoln's Inn Fields from the late 1660s to the reorganisation in 1706; Chetwood was prompter at Drury Lane 1715–21 and at Lincoln's Inn Fields 1722–41, and instructed actors in this capacity; Victor managed under Thomas Sheridan in Dublin and then was treasurer at Drury Lane from 1759 until his death in 1778; during his long and inglorious career at Drury Lane Waldron prompted as well as acting minor roles, and was the administrator of the pension fund which Garrick set up for the company; in the off-seasons he played at the Theatre Royal, Richmond, once attempting unsuccessfully to buy it, and he managed a company performing at a Hammersmith inn.[16]

These, then, were men with some sort of literary bent or sideline, who spent their time around the theatres, often for very long periods. Managements succeeded or failed, and actors had their moments of fame, but these inconspicuous servants of the stage watched them all come and go. Unnoticed by the public, they occupied good places from which to observe the scene – and to make use of what they saw in various ways. The central, the most symbolically significant of the places that they occupied, one that most potently combined their theatrical and their literary or sub-literary expertise, was the role of prompter.

The prompter

The prompter was the keeper of the book. In post-Restoration days this was literally the case – it was his responsibility to keep, and to give out, the written text. Receiving the play (if it were new, the author's manuscript, or if it were a revival in a manuscript or printed form that was already annotated by himself or previous incumbents of his place) he would become its custodian, recreator, and intermediary to the actors and the crew. As still happens, he made a prompt copy for his own use, in which to record entrances, exits, cuts and business, as well as his own cues for ringing for music, whistling for scene changes, sending the call-boy for performers from the green room or a porter for those still in their homes in the neighbourhood. But he also copied out lines and cues for each performer, and enclosed each part in covers; he saw to the binding of the scores. Having dispensed the lines, he heard actors rehearse them; this might even have included teaching them verbatim to illiterate performers, and it certainly in some cases – the notable example is Chetwood – meant more in the way of actor training than simply listening to the words. And, of course, when they acted the play, he supplied words to those who lost them in spite of all his previous care. As the theatres grew in scale during the eighteenth century the prompter became a department head, with a regiment of copyists, runners and hands to carry out his instructions. Sheridan is reported to have said, about the esteemed Drury Lane prompter Wrighten who died in 1793, that 'he thought an intelligent prompter of the greatest importance to a well-regulated theatre: a stage-manager was only required for *state days* and *holidays*, but a steady prompter was the *cornerstone* of the building' (emphasis original).[17]

During the early 1730s there appeared a theatrical periodical called *The Prompter*, edited by Aaron Hill, who was also a writer of stage entertainments and lessee of the Opera House, 1710–11. The journal gave a critical view of the London stage and up-to-date news and gossip about plays and players. The figure after whom it was named is described in slightly awed tones by an observer who found him

standing in a Corner, and attentively perusing a Book, which lay before him; he never forsook his Post, but, like a General in the Field, had many Aid de camps about him, whom he dispatched with his Orders; and I could perceive, that tho he seemed not to command, yet all his Instructions were punctually complied with, and that in the modest Character of an Adviser, he had the whole Management and direction of the little Commonwealth.[18]

It is interesting that the writer notices the book that the prompter commands before he mentions the people who are at his beck and call. This view of theatre as 'the little Commonwealth' in which everyone is obedient to the common good is of course romantic, and not all representatives of the management were popular figures. James Winston, the Drury Lane manager under Elliston whose unpublished work as the last of the tribal scribes will be discussed below, was certainly cordially hated. In 1806 the *Satirist* depicted him as a 'universally disliked tyrant' in the workplace, and Alfred Bunn ungratefully annotated a letter from him, in which Winston had offered him help, with the information that he was 'facetiously called "A stage Screw"' and 'had a pettifogging miserable mind, universally detested'.[19] But Winston was not a magus-like prompter, rather the powerful and ruthless sub-manager. In a ideal position to accumulate the materials of his history, he was free, once the curtain rose at Drury Lane, to spend his time alone in his office arranging his collections; he did not participate in the performance, but wielded his power over the lives of most of the company from a distance. But there was no such reason to dislike the minor actors, husbands of actresses, and sundry lowly hangers-on who wrote the eighteenth-century histories, who had no power at all, and were no doubt tolerated for what they contributed to the common good; while the prompter–historians, especially, were at the centre of the organism, and on their personal participation, their coolness, their wisdom and knowledge of the ropes and of the book, the actors depended for their success on the night.[20] A doggerel verse by the born actor John O'Keeffe expresses this perfectly:

> Rehearsal's call'd, and, from the first to last,
> The prompter on the stage at table sits:
> He vers'd in works of great and little wits,
> What safe and dangerous can with art contrast.
>
> Thro' dressing-rooms is heard the warning call,
> 'First music, gentlemen; first music, ladies':
> 'Third music!' that's the notice to appal;
> Like summons from Lord Mayor, or huffing cadies:
>   [caddies, i.e. messengers]
> The call-boy is this herald's appellation.
> The curtain up, the prompter takes his station.
>
> 'Tis not alone with art to throw the word,
> If actors in their parts should make a stand;
> To prompter many duties more belong,
> Than biding in the wing with book in hand.
> Of their go-off, come-on, he points the sides,
> By margin letters of P.S. O.P.   [prompt side, opposite prompt]
>
> Stage properties, stage business, music, band,
> Of stage arcana the prompter keeps the key.
> He writes the playbills out, pens paragraphs,

Marks forfeits down for every stage neglect.
The audience gone, he, ere the lights are out,
Of all new scenes tries every new effect:
And, from eleven o'clock, perhaps till three,
He in his duties all that time must spend;
And then from six to twelve o'clock at night,
Upon the stage the Prompter must attend.'[21]

There from the inception of each production, there to publish the day, write the critiques, issue the terrifying and exhilarating summons to appear before the public, still at work after the audience are gone, making everything happen before, during and after the performance, the prompter is in power, because he can tell everyone from the author to the actors and the scene-painters *what will work.* He is 'vers'd in works of great and little wits / What['s] safe and dangerous can with art contrast', and this because, in a vital (if inharmonious) line, 'Of stage arcana the prompter keeps the key.' And he who 'keeps the key' in the form of the book – the book of the present production, and also the tradition, memory and record of all the productions that have gone before – is naturally in a position to become the scribe, annalist, chronicler and repository of the stories, the historian. He is the man who makes, as Kipling (that great aficionado of the esoteric knowledge) has it, the tribal lays.

Scribal practice: the stories of the stage

Kipling declares that all one-and-twenty ways of making such lays are right, and there is certainly a sense of indifference to rules and formal requirements in the ways these scribal records are put together. One may, however, discern two main elements that seem to be part of the theatrical account, present in varying proportions in each book. There is firstly a kind of detail, more or less minute, that is recorded entirely for its own sake, almost as if it were produced out of a hat with a triumphant air of conclusive satisfaction (though it may also provide a jumping-off point or peg for the other element of the discourse). These factual statements begin with lists of plays mounted, sometimes year by year or company by company, or both, and are provided with two kinds of detail: who appeared in what roles, and what was the box-office success. The third detail, the date of the

performance, which subsequent historians have regarded as a
sine qua non, seems to be of least import in these pellets of owlish
information, which possibly points to their writers' vital difference from *Theaterwissenschaft* historians who have mined their
books for facts. The second sort of material is the other form of
information that was available to the prompter, the manager or
the theatre factotum who had spent thirty-five seasons at Drury
Lane: the good story. Both these are 'arcana', that is, 'inside information'. The detailed stuff comes from the working practice
of the writer, his custodianship of the daily records of the theatre and his acquaintance with others in similar positions in rival
houses: these are the 'tricks of the trade'. The other ingredients
are the tales he can tell because he has rubbed shoulders with
the great, seen them drunk and sober, listened to their excuses
and complaints, and yarned with and about them over a bottle:
the 'secrets of the stars'. The balance between the two kinds of
information in the published works is partly, no doubt, temperamental or related to the particular opportunities of each writer,
but it is also to do with the steady establishment of a body of received wisdom, in a recognisable form – a tradition both written
and oral in the telling of theatrical tales, the *textus receptus* of the
story of the stage.

Some writers were, of course, better at the task, or took it
more seriously than others; the eighteenth-century habit of creating books to pay off one's debts rather than from any pressing
need to communicate operated in this field. Chetwood, for example, speaking of himself in the third person in the preface to
his anonymously published *The British Theatre* as the source of 'a
considerable fund of theatrical history', lamented that he was unfortunately now in jail and likely to die there from indigence.[22]
His approach is particularly antipathetic to the modern historian. Flourishing his claim to the status of man of the theatre,
he dedicates his *General History of the Stage* (1749) to Garrick,
John Rich and Thomas Sheridan, the Theatre Royal managers
for whom he has worked, claiming to 'have disciplin'd some of
your troops'.[23] He starts with a brief, rather waggish pretence
of a history of the Classical stage, laced with Latin quotations
which he then translates for those who, he says, are like himself –
unable to read Latin. By page 15 he has arrived at Britain, where,
he states blithely, 'I need not say, that the *theatre* in *England* came

in with the Reformation' because Queen Elizabeth encouraged it. To illustrate this period he lists plays, in a scholarly manner – but only those of Thomas Heywood, which he boasts of having read himself, before diverging into footnotes about the foundation of Dulwich hospital, Shakespeare's supposed paternity of Davenant and Davenant's loss of his nose (to syphilis). He adds some genuinely interesting practical remarks about acting – the use of the hands, the voice – which substantiate reports that he was acknowledged as a teacher by major actors including Macklin. Then he arrives at his own time in the theatres of Dublin and London and records a handful of plays with dates and cast lists, before suddenly throwing up the endeavour on page 59: 'I shall leave this last Quarter of a Hundred years to the memory of others, that I may sooner get to the conclusion of my little *History*, and fall upon the *Memoirs*' and, accordingly, the rest of the 256 pages consists of the 'notes antient, modern, foreign, domestic, serious, comic, moral, merry, historical, and geographical, containing many theatrical anecdotes' that his title page promises. Lowe, in his magisterial academic bibliography of stage history published in 1888, remarked that this book 'has been abused in unmeasured terms',[24] and from a modern historian's point of view it is easy to see why. Chetwood is a very poor witness, declining to be bothered to tell us dull dates and details within his own immediate knowledge, much more concerned to reveal the secrets of which he has heard tell, to puncture the reputations of the self-aggrandising or to let his readers in on the dirt. Sometime this is scurrilous, ill-natured or misogynist, as in his objection to Madame Violante's muscular legs; elsewhere his writing is simply in the journalistic mode of amazing the readers with his strange but true revelations, like the story of the young actor who came back from the dead, to find himself laid out naked with a bowl of salt perched on his stomach.[25]

It is also a part of the tradition of such publication that it automatically opened the author to criticism from those he spoke about or claimed to correct. The tale-teller holds an equivocal position even within his own circle: most professional groups reinforce their communal identity by swapping gossip about their compeers, but few people care to hear their own mishaps recounted as anecdotes, even within the private world of their trade. The old actor yarning for pints in the theatre tavern, like the

off-stage mimic, has to be careful to judge his audience of professionals and hangers-on. Almost all we know about Downes
as an individual, for example, comes from a hostile lampoon in
which it is said that he

> attested with Oaths what no matter of fact is,
> As he gave strange Accounts of both Farces and Plays,
> And brag'd of things done, in *Hart's* and *Mohun's* days

in order to sponge for food and drink.[26] Chetwood sweeps away
'the rest of the Stage Historians, who have hitherto appeared in
Print' as 'abounding with Errors', and Egerton similarly rejects
all but one of his predecessors as 'each being compiled, as it
seems, from the other', and therefore being 'grossly erroneous
and imperfect'. Oulton sets out not only to correct Victor but
to purge his style 'of its egotism and prolixity', while Davies is
dismissive of *Roscius Anglicanus* as a 'fragment' requiring 'careful
searching' and Waldron presents his edition of the book with
apologies for the faults he could not eliminate from his original.
Jones, in his edition of *Biographia Dramatica*, finds it hard to
speak of Chetwood 'with any temper', not for numerous faults
arising from neglect or ignorance, which are 'pardonable', but
rather for the 'wantonness of his invention' in citing dates and
titles for books that never existed.[27]

It is important, however, to recognise Stephen Jones's com-
plaint as more than a display of bad temper or an attempt to
puff his own work. A split between the bibliographical and the
theatrical branches of the scribal tradition becomes very clear
by the nineteenth century; a divergence that is ideological, and
based on status. To Jones in 1812 Chetwood's perceived transgression is documentary – he is dismissed from the historians'
ranks for the 'forging' of dates for Shakespearean quartos. Over
the ensuing twenty years the insiders of the theatre, whose expertise was manifest as access to secrets they could both reveal
and personally swear to be true, were to be challenged and eventually driven from the ground by writers outside the arcana, who
served the booksellers and collectors, and whose criteria of value
in a story were quite different. An indicative confrontation takes
place when Collier, as he recorded in his self-serving and suspect retrospective diary for 1832, went with the Duke of Devonshire to see Charles Mathews's collection of theatrical portraits.
Collier is ironical about the pictures and their attributions,

but the Duke was too polite to express an opinion, and took the shew-
man's [sic] word. Mathews and his wife . . . were quite upon their hind
legs. Winston, the Secretary of the Garrick Club, of which the Duke is
President, happened to come in: his father had been an actor, but of
small repute, and he was well versed in all the transactions of the stage
during the last thirty or forty years.[28]

Collier's disdain for the actors bleeds value from their knowledge
of their own business: the great comedian Mathews is a 'shew-
man', a lying denizen of the fairground, before the Duke, and his
club secretary, Winston, is given a small-time-actor father – of
whom there is no evidence anywhere – to account for his expertise in the modern theatre. Elsewhere in the diary Collier records
jousting with Winston in the public rooms of the Garrick Club
as to which of them knows more about actresses who have married into the aristocracy, and dismisses him as no better than a
lying old woman as a witness to the career of Sarah Siddons: 'Mrs
Hatton (Anne of Swansea), with whom I formerly corresponded,
used to tell astounding and incredible stories of her sister, Mrs
Siddons: so did Winston, Secretary of the Garrick Club, neither
credible nor creditable, and I disbelieve them all.'[29]

James Winston

Winston is one of two known theatre historians from within the
profession who collected their materials during the first quarter of
the nineteenth century, but, in the increasingly antagonistic and
denigratory atmosphere of the times, never published their work.
The other is the actor O. Smith (properly Richard John Smith)
whose collection has now found its way into the British Library
in twenty-five quarto volumes. Besides these volumes, Smith also
appears to have owned and augmented a cuttings collection first
assembled by Joseph Haslewood, which includes handbills for
two more projected histories of the stage.[30] Smith's story is that
he was contracted by a bookseller to produce a history, but in
1829 decided the man was not going to do him justice, and so
he put his work aside in manuscript. He also, at that point, made
a breakthrough into success as an actor, in the company at the
Adelphi where he played melodramatic villains with great éclat
for the rest of his career. He therefore left the ranks of the
minor player–tribal scribe, or at least was able to avoid the risk
of publishing his collected stories for a few guineas.

The case of James Winston's work is worth considering closely, to pin down the supersedure of the history produced by the tribal scribes in the first third of the nineteenth century. Winston published only one book, *The Theatric Tourist*, in London in 1805. At that time he had already collected much more material than went into this slender volume, and he continued to amass more throughout his life; but nothing further was published. His take on the subject is clear from the mountains of materials he collected, which were sold and dispersed round the libraries of Britain and America on his death in 1849.[31] It appears that he saw himself as following – either unquestioningly or ironically – in the tradition of the annalists. But while they were happy to publish their books with little thought beyond the profit and the consequence that might ensue, Winston seems to have had grave difficulties in bringing his work to the public. His research is monumental, but it is largely unpublished, and mostly not even prepared for the press. It is difficult to say whether this failure was temperamental, or due to the hostility to which his old-fashioned approach exposed him. Perhaps he was not a mere annalist; it may even be the case that he had a sophisticated and ironic view of the world he observed so closely. There is no suggestion in the form in which he made and ordered his notes that he would have written his history up in such a way as to argue for development or decline in the British theatre world. Either he did not wish to do so, or he found it impossible. His passion seems to have been a voracious appetite for stories, reports, facts and quasi-facts, items of information that he could order and record, rather than evaluate or use to prove any point. He sets down side by side the mundane and the extravagant, equally laconically. He apparently values everything that comes his way: gossip and rumour about the stars, details about box receipts, the complaints of the cleaning staff at Drury Lane are all written down without comment. The only work he did publish, *The Theatric Tourist*, and the working materials for it that survive, show an avidity for detail that goes beyond all usual textual sources, and overwhelms the bounds of publication. Winston had been a strolling player, and so visited numerous provincial theatres, and he travelled with a sketchbook and measuring tape.[32] He recorded each ex-barn and tiny playhouse on a series of circuits. In the four notebooks he compiled as he travelled there are 340 pages filled with sketches, anecdotes and general theatrical 'information', as well as entries for 280 theatres from Sadler's Wells to rural Shropshire, even two theatres in America. Not content with his own observations and much copying from Tate Wilkinson and other sources, he embarked upon a nation-wide correspondence with provincial managers.[33] Some of his letters soliciting information and urging managers to consult local antiquaries and any other authorities survive, together with responses from sixty-three places. He found, however, that the process of putting all this into publication filled him with 'great anxiety,' and the printed *Theatric Tourist* never progressed beyond the representation of twenty-four theatres, less than 10 per cent of its projected scope.[34]

A similarly voracious, and perhaps finally prohibitive, desire to be exhaustive is evident in all his amassed material. Winston bought an interest in the Haymarket theatre in London and became acting manager there from 1805, and immediately began to save and accumulate routine letters from performers.[35] He eventually mounted them, together with other biographical items, in scrapbooks: there are five that survive on Elliston, seven on Edmund Kean, three on Garrick, one on John Bannister and his wife Elizabeth Harper, one on Catherine Clive, three on John Philip Kemble, and there were many more.[36] Similarly he amassed materials under the headings of individual London theatres: the Adelphi scrapbook survives, as does that for the Royalty; there is a calendar for the Haymarket, 1720–1800, and no fewer than twenty-seven volumes on Drury Lane. Three of these are a cash record of receipts and performances, 1772–1826; the other twenty-four are scrapbooks and an accumulation of loose papers.[37] Before they are swamped by the working documents of his own stint as acting manager at the theatre, these materials are ordered with Winston's characteristic method. He set up books in chronological order from 1660 onwards and pasted in material in the right place as it came to hand. He collects everything – the death of a long-serving dresser alongside Sheridan's receipts for his fire insurance premium and a newspaper biography of Thomas Holcroft; ephemera like bills for goods or services and tickets are pasted in, or sometimes described and copied, when he was unwilling to purchase the originals. He also took notes from published works and manuscript collections that came in his way, and added an abbreviated source ascription to each separate item so that he could cut up his sheets of notes and paste them into the appropriate scrapbook page. In other volumes the management of his materials becomes even more complex. The most finished state of his work was perhaps represented by 'the two volumes of Lord Chamberlain Coke's papers, which cannot be touched as they form a very complete history of the stage of that period 1710–1810', and from which, therefore, he was unwilling to extract autographs to exchange with his correspondent, the collector C. B. Smith.[38] The 'papers' he refers to were, presumably, transcriptions, intermingled with collected contemporary letters, since it was these latter in which Smith was interested. Whether or not the volumes were as 'complete' as Winston boasted, they do not seem to survive. A more characteristic state of affairs exists in the surviving sixteen volumes labelled 'Dramatic Register', covering the period 1300–1803 and the four 'Diaries' that follow on from that date to 1830. Volume 2 of the Register begins with a title page: 'A / Dramatic Register / Containing a Summary Account / of Every / Public Place of Amusement / where / Theatrical or Vocal / performances have been introduced; / But more particularly / An Accurate Account / as far as it can be ascertained / of every / Dramatic Performance / from the most remote period to the present time'.[39] The format of the majority of these volumes is the same: the recto, right-hand page is divided into two columns and records performances at Drury Lane and Covent Garden. The facing verso has notes about these and other theatres, anecdotes about actors and other memoranda; in the 'Diary' volumes these are set out in annotated form for transfer to other files; some are crossed through, presumably after he had copied them to their next destination.

Winston made no move so far as we know to publish his Register; but another MS volume[40] seems to suggest he had at least imagined a step towards that. It is provided with a very neat, pseudo-printed title page reading 'A History of the London Theatres from the Year 1805 to the present time being a continuation of Victor Oulton etc etc.' and follows the arrangement of contents in the publication he indicates; it peters out into scrappy notes at the point where he had in fact the most material, in the period of his Drury Lane management. Winston may have been kept from publishing his history by a combination of many difficulties: he told a correspondent that he only had time to work on his 'collections' after the curtain had risen at Drury Lane; he was clearly a squirrel rather than a beaver, collecting being his passion, rather than building an edifice from what he brought together; he might never have been satisfied that he had enough information, or been able to fit it all into the compass of a synoptic view. He seems to have been the kind of man for whom the computer database would have been a perfect tool, or rather, perhaps, an end in itself.

But at least part of his problem was that he stood at the end of a tradition – the line of 'Victor Oulton etc etc', as he said – and the writing of history was moving elsewhere. He was widely known in London for his collections, but he was not regarded with respect; references to him compound academic suspicion and class contempt. Macready, the aspirant gentleman leader of the stage, referred to Winston in his diary as 'impertinent' and 'vulgar'; and referred to his collection as 'a picture of the miserable weazel creature who could give his time to such a little work – scraps of calumnious anecdote, false assertions, adverse criticisms, and notices from Messrs Theodore Hook – as *unprincipled* a villain as ever lived . . .'[41] Winston was in fact both better and worse born than Macready, the provincial theatre manager's son, since he was probably the natural son of an aristocrat, and enjoyed to a certain extent the money and connections that went with his shady position.[42] This made him exactly the kind of dubious creature whom Macready, passionate about respectability in the theatre, would most deplore. To Collier, with more precise reasons for dislike and distrust, James Winston was the current representative of a kind of credulous, cynical, gossiping, inaccurate theatre history with which he and his own circle did not wish to be associated.[43] Collier was a scholar and a gentleman; Winston was a paid professional man, a tribal scribe; and his days were over.

John Genest

The supersedure of an amassing, compiling, annalist approach by one with more sophistication – and with an axe to grind – is not a simple matter of a gentlemanly, educated takeover of ground previously occupied by squabbling amateurs. One set of annals

was published in 1832; it came not from within the theatre, nor
from anywhere within the London cultural field. It was written
by an educated and disinterested gentleman, had none of the perceived faults of its predecessors, being preternaturally accurate
and completely independent in its views; but it was a complete
failure. Modestly called *Some Account of the English Stage, from
the Restoration in 1660 to 1830*,[44] it was published with no name
on the title page by the Rev. John Genest, a retired Cambridge
man for many years curate in a remote Lincolnshire village. It is
an extraordinary book. Genest must be presumed to have been a
complete outsider not only to the London theatre scene but also
to the councils of Reform in politics, scholarship and theatre;
he worked in isolation, slowly, and he thought and published to
please himself. His work is described by Lowe in 1888 as 'the
only complete history of the stage since the Restoration . . . the
work of a Bath clergyman, who must have devoted his life to it.
No words can do adequate justice to the honest and thorough
nature of the work; and its value cannot be over-estimated. Yet
it fell dead from the press . . . It was for many years a drug in the
market but is now becoming one of the most valued of theatrical
books.'[45] It takes the form of an annual register, offering precise
dates, descriptions and detailed critical opinions on plays and
their reception, as well as cast lists, at the Theatres Royal and the
fairground booths in London, Bath and Dublin, together with
trenchant and sometimes detailed reviews of theatrical publications, and notes of events from the burning of the theatres to
charity benefits to the auctions in which he bought playbills to
help in his labours.

Genest's principles are naively scholarly: 'The manner, in
which some of the articles in the B.D. [*Biographia Dramatica*]
have been compiled, is truly ludicrous' he notes in his first
volume – because the editors repeat the blunders of their predecessors and have *not read* all the plays they list.[46] Their transgression is in not checking what could be checked and therefore
corrected, and in not acknowledging their sources generously
and in full: his prefatory remarks are short, but one of the points
he makes at length is the shabbiness of Davies's appropriation
and subsequent denigration of Downes.[47] He himself discusses
Downes and each of his informants fully as he goes along, and
points out errors, but with the gloss that '[i]n compiling a history

of the stage, it is almost impossible not to make mistakes' and that it is comforting 'to persons of inferior abilities' like himself to find that others sometimes 'blunder as grossly as themselves'.[48] A Greek tag from Evagrius is offered on the title page begging pardon for anything overlooked or inaccurate in his history, 'compiled from all quarters'. Equally striking is his openness and critical tolerance in the discussion of the plays and performances he describes, a freedom of comment which he justifies in quite a different vein, with a quotation from Tacitus, to the effect that in critical opinion 'every body has a right to think for himself and to say what he thinks'.[49] He is capable of pronouncing Settle's *Empress of Morocco*, one of the most vilified plays of its period, of 'considerable merit' because it is 'never dull', and a song of Aphra Behn's 'very indecent' but also 'very good'.[50] Thus his work is ahead of its time, or rather, it is independent of the ideological battle that was joined in London at the moment it was published. It had to wait for the triumph of nineteenth-century historical scholarship to be recognised as 'the basis of most exact knowledge concerning the stage. Few books of reference are equally trustworthy, the constant investigation to which it has been subjected having brought to light few errors and none of grave importance.'[51] Sadly it is unlikely that modern taste will ever recognise its forerunner in his dry, humorous and intelligent commentaries; but certainly his ten volumes were entirely unacceptable in 1832, of no use to either side in the war for possession of the stage.

Thus the histories used and augmented by generations of theatre people and those interested in their doings were quite suddenly, and comprehensively, discredited. Such work has not, in fact, ceased to exist – I consider some of its fruits in chapter 5 below – but it has been contemptuously talked down, displaced from academic consideration. The writers who contributed to and were championed by the 1830s movement to reform the theatre began to construct its history upon a very different basis.

3   Theatre in London in 1832: a new overview

In order to understand what happened to theatre historiography in the 1830s it is necessary to offer an overview of the theatrical situation at the time. Obviously this is a rather touchy under-taking, in the context of questioning the basis upon which such history can be written.[1] The summary that follows has there-fore two purposes. It aims to give some account of developments in London theatre leading up to the 1843 Theatres Regulation Act,[2] focusing upon years of the First Reform Bills, 1830–2, when developments concerning the stage interacted with public excitement over parliamentary reform. In a conventional way, this account will draw upon contemporary newspapers and pe-riodicals, biographical and autobiographical writing, documents in the Lord Chamberlain's collections, and my own reading of some of the plays staged in those years. But I am also concerned to reread these facts, and to launch the new perspectives illus-trated later in this volume. Eschewing the received teleological assumption that this period was the nadir of theatrical life, the starting point for a long upwards struggle from darkness into light, I have included a much wider variety of venues in and around London than is usually surveyed, and I have accepted, or at least sought to understand, the claims made for these places and their entertainments by their creators, and the pleasures de-rived from them by their audiences. In reading this wider field, I have deployed a new theorisation of the transactions in the theatre: a concept I am calling intertheatricality. I have sought to ground that concept materially by a focus upon the primary source that best represents these transactions: the bill of the play. This move, the development of a new conceptualisation coupled with a focus upon a specific kind of evidence, is the model for the case studies in Part II.

Intertheatricality

Richard Schechner offers a typology of the elements of theatre. He envisages four realms – drama, script, theatre and performance – in which the *drama*, which is a written text or score, and the *script*, which is 'all that can be transmitted from time to time and place to place' and can be taught by one person to another, form one dyad, while *theatre*, 'the event enacted by a specific group of performers' and *performance*, 'the whole constellation of events, most of them passing unnoticed, that take place in/among both performers and audience from the time the first spectator enters the field of performance . . . to the time the last spectator leaves', form another.[3] He remarks that among the world's cultures, 'only "modern drama" since the late nineteenth century has so privileged the written text as to almost exclude theater-performance altogether'.[4] The opposition to this damaging bias, he suggests, has been an avant-garde interest in non-western performance. But I would like to look back from a twenty-first century perspective to reread what was actually happening before that late nineteenth-century point, and de-emphasise the dyad script/drama, to rediscover a more comprehensive way of reading theatre, that continued to exist for the majority of audience members and performers outside the ambit of literary-critical self-consciousness and the emphasis on the writer.

I also seek to enlarge the significant area for consideration beyond the limits Schechner sets to performance, which he defines within a relatively narrow timespan, that is, from the moment people arrive at the venue until they leave. I want to look beyond the specific occasion to include an awareness of the elements and interactions that make up the whole web of mutual understanding between potential audiences and their players, a sense of the knowledge, or better the knowingness, about playing that spans a lifetime or more, and that is activated for all participants during the performance event. This is my field of study, the intertheatrical, so-called by analogy to the intertextual, in which no writing or reading is isolated from the other writing and reading within its culture. An intertheatrical reading goes beyond the written. It seeks to articulate the mesh of connections between all kinds of theatre texts, and between texts and their users. It posits that all entertainments, including the dramas, that are

performed within a single theatrical tradition are more or less in-
terdependent. They are uttered in a language, shared by successive generations, which includes not only speech and the systems
of the stage – scenery, costume, lighting and so forth – but also
genres, conventions and, very importantly, memory. The fabric
of that memory, shared by audience and players, is made up of
dances, spectacles, plays and songs, experienced as particular
performances – a different selection, of course, for each individual – woven upon knowledge of the performers' other current
and previous roles, and their personae on and off the stage. The
single night in the theatre is a point of crystallisation in a continually moving, dissolving and re-forming pattern, most elements
of which are, as Schechner suggests, not only unrecorded but
unremarked, though not uninfluential. There is thus a collabo-
ration in the creation of a particular theatrical experience, taking
place first in writing, casting, rehearsal and designing and then
anew, afresh each night in front of a new audience. This creative
process has many more elements than any set of conventions deployed in the written medium, and they are in many hands. The
immediate problem of attempting to invoke such a perspective
historically is, of course, how we may access more of the web
than was written down by the dramatist and the critic. My first
suggestion for a new reading of nineteenth-century London performance culture in this way is that we read individual theatre
events, rather than just the plays and other entertainments that
happened within them, by a new approach to the playbill.

The reading of the playbill

Playbills are the essence of theatrical antiquarianism. They are
the solid, comfortable, substantive stuff of theatre history. Long
ago they have been extracted and calendared, charted and published, in many substantial volumes from which one may learn
exactly how many times each Theatre Royal gave *A School for
Scandal* or *A New Way to Pay Old Debts*, where and when a van-
ished host of performers made their London debuts and in which
roles they appeared. From them we know the companies, the
plays, the thousand performances of Hamlet and the evanescent
appearance of farces that did not make it to author's benefit on
the third night. The body of theatre history hangs upon these

bones; its face, its gestures are familiar to us from these types and borders. A real theatre historian can tell[5] from the evolution of the types and the changing appearance of the royal arms what period any bill belongs to, and not only at the legitimate London houses, for their style reverberates through the announcements of the provincial and minor stages, only slightly lag of their brothers. In every metropolitan and provincial library, local record office and private collection lie the enticing bundles of bills: pasted into leather-bound volumes as they are at the Garrick Club, or enclosed in acid-free envelopes; meticulously electronically catalogued, or ignorantly summed up on old index cards. However provided, they make the true researcher light up with desire. This is the real stuff: the man in the pit electrified by Kean, enticed by Jordan, awed by Siddons or thundered at by Forrest, held this flimsy page in his hand, on the very night that it records. It is from this source, more than any other, perhaps, that our conviction that we feel we know what happened in the theatrical past ultimately stems.

And yet playbills are really a very unimaginatively used resource. They have normally been treated as a simple source of extractable factual information. The most scrupulous historians remind us that the plays advertised did not always happen, and sometimes performances took place that were not listed; but these are otherwise no more than the basic primary sources, against which such things as memoirs are tested and corrected. To some extent the form of the bills has been noted, giving us an understanding – at least a formal recognition – of the context of performances. The evolution of the playbill, both the piece of paper and programme of events it represents, is being chronicled; but I would say that, unlike the history of the changes in staging and theatre design, the part it plays in the dramatic experience has not been recognised. My contention is that in the playbill we have not only evidence for what was performed by whom and when, but also for those most difficult and evanescent aspects of theatre history – the expectations and disposition of the audience, their personal experience of theatre. The important thing from this point of view, though, is *not* to extract, precisely *not* to seek for particular names and count productions of individual plays: it is to read the bill whole, and understand that every element on it is a signifier which, like all signifiers, has a meaning only as part of a system of relationships. In that way the old resource may become the starting point of an intertheatrical conceptualisation of theatre history. This is what I shall exemplify in the course of the overview that follows.

Theatre in London in 1832

The patent houses

More than thirty theatres operated in London in the early 1830s.[6] There was a range of official ways in which they were permitted to operate, expanding the original royal permission for playhouses. Many public houses and tea gardens applied for a magistrate's licence for entertainments, music and dance – at Michaelmas 1832 fifty-four applied to the Middlesex sessions alone, twenty-one of these being new applications; a similar number probably applied to Surrey, south of the river, and no doubt many more places put on shows without any official sanction whatsoever.[7] This entertainment boom had been under way since the 1790s; it served a rapidly growing city that was not only a major port and manufacturing centre but also the capital, with all that that implied of clerks, merchants, businessmen, professionals of all sorts and pleasure-seeking visitors from home and abroad. The archaic and unsatisfactory laws governing theatre building and public performance and the censorship of plays were about to become part of the cultural crisis of the times. There were complex regulations and privileges dating back to 1660, when King Charles II granted exclusive rights to two of his courtiers to recruit companies of players, erect playhouses and perform plays old and new. The original patents had undergone many vicissitudes; by this date only Covent Garden still operated under the original grant, while Drury Lane was obliged to obtain another in 1816 to run for twenty-one years at a time. Both these old houses had been demolished or burned down repeatedly, and at every rebuilding – the most recent was in 1809–12 – they emerged with a heavier burden of debt to add to their accumulated rents, expenses and customary charges. At least a thousand people were constantly employed at Covent Garden, giving the theatre a weekly expenditure of around £1,200 before the cost of mounting plays.[8] Attendance at these huge, ill-lit and ill-regulated places was an expensive and increasingly difficult business. Payment at the door – 3s in the pit, 7s for a box seat and 1s in the gallery – was only the first of several official and unofficial exactions an inexperienced playgoer could fear from servants, touts and hangers-on of the theatre, whether or not he was interested in the services on offer, which notoriously included the sexual. Large, noisy auditoria with poor sight-lines did not encourage the chamber play, and for maximum profit shows with a wide appeal were often mounted, to the disgust of some critics. At Covent Garden the Kemble family management was coming to a sad end. Sarah Siddons died in retirement in June 1831, and Charles Kemble, the current manager and lessee, put his twenty-two-year-old daughter Fanny centre stage to inherit her aunt's mantle, and, they hoped, her following. Fanny's play *Francis the First*, composed when she was seventeen, was staged in March 1832, and she played in it and in Sheridan Knowles's *The Hunchback* to a very mixed reception. But the end came quickly, with bailiffs in the theatre and father and daughter sailing for America to recoup their family fortunes.[9]

The state of the bill at the patent houses by the early 1830s has been regarded as obvious evidence of 'the Decline of the Drama'.[10] Take the example reproduced as plate 1 from near the beginning of the 1831–2 season. The conventionally worded and type-set announcement that at the 'Theatre Royal, Drury Lane. | This Evening, Monday, Nov. 7, 1831, their Majesties' Servants will act the Tragedy of | Macbeth', with Macready and Miss Phillips in the leading roles, is sandwiched between italics, pointing fingers and exclamation marks above and huge block capitals below, proclaiming that a spectacle called *Hyder Ali, or the Lions of Mysore*, designed to showcase the animal-training act of Henri Martin, patronised in Paris by King Louis-Philippe, and now mounted behind bars on the classic stage in London is 'the Most Gorgeous Spectacle ever produced'. The small compass devoted to Shakespeare and the additional line announcing that the overture to *Macbeth* by Spohr will be played are dwarfed by four times as much excited description of the spectacle; the bill concludes with trailers for the rest of the week, during which the lions will share the stage with Mrs Wood (late Miss Paton, a young woman with a scandalous history) singing in Auber's opera *The Love Charm, or the village coquette*, which will then be

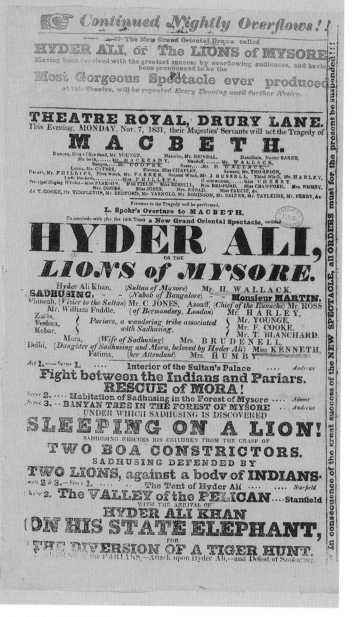

1 Playbill for Theatre Royal, Drury Lane, 7 November 1831

Scene 3. .... PALACE of the SULTAN from the GARDENS. .. *Stanfield*

Scene 4. .. **THE ARENA AT MYSORE** .. *Marinari*

IN WHICH IS EXHIBITED,

A Terrific Combat with Sadhusing & a Lion.

Scene 5. .... The CURTAIN APARTMENT in the PALACE .... *Marinari*

Scene 6. .... THE ENTRANCE TO MYSORE .. *Marinari*

WITH A SPLENDID

TRIUMPHAL PROCESSION!

IN WHICH WILL BE INTRODUCED, THE TROOPS OF HYDER ALI KHAN,

With the Standards and Banners of Bangalore, Myconda, Chitteldroog, Bednore, Chinapatam, Coorg, Henloore, Maggeri, Mailootta, Ramajeri, Severndroog, & Seringapatam.

AMBASSADORS, OFFICERS of STATE, and of the HOUSEHOLD.

Dancing Girls, Singing Girls, Ladies of the Court and of the Harem, Eunuchs, Slaves, &c.

HYDER ALI and DELHI

ON AN ELEPHANT!

THREE MILITARY BANDS!

SLAVES BEARING PRESENTS FROM CONQUERED STATES.

Mr. FUDDLE & FATIMA on an ELEPHANT

Bodies of Jahrejahs, Mahratta Troops, the Pariar Tribe, and Household Guard.

SADHUSING BORNE BY 20 SOLDIERS,

With the Conquered Lion at his Feet!!!

Mrs. WOOD, late Miss PATON

Continuing to be received with the utmost enthusiasm by crowded Audiences, will have the honour of appearing (for the 3rd time) To-morrow Evening, in Auber's New Opera of

THE LOVE CHARM,

Or, THE VILLAGE COQUETTE.

Which was again received by a brilliant and overflowing house, with every possible demonstration of public favour, and will be repeated

EVERY TUESDAY, THURSDAY, and SATURDAY, UNTIL FURTHER NOTICE.

To-morrow.... The last New Opera of **THE LOVE CHARM.**

Signor Furbaroso, Mr. Seguin (*who was received with great favor on his 2nd appearance*),

Fanfaron de Joli-Cœur, Mr. H. Phillips,   Guillaume, Mr. Wood,

Terezine, Mrs. Wood.   Jeannette. (2nd time) Miss Pearson.

And **CHARLES XIIth.** [which was received on Saturday Evening with great Applause.]

Charles 12th. Mr. Warren, Major Vanberg, Mr. Cooper. Triptolemus Muddlework. Mr. Harley,

Adam Brock, (2nd time) Mr. Wallack   Eudiga (2nd time) Miss Pearson

Wednesday.... will be produced, (on a scale of great splendour) the Operatic Play of

The EXILE, or, The Deserts of Siberia.

WITH NEW SCENERY, MACHINERY, DRESSES, AND DECORATIONS.

Daran, Mr. Macready,   Count Ulric, Mr. Cooper, Count Calmar, Mr. Templeton,

Governor of Siberia, Mr. W. Farren, Baron Altradoff, Mr. J. Russell.   Servitz, Mr. Harley,

The Czarowitz, Miss M. Chaplin,   Yermak, Mr. Younge,   Wezen, Mr. Brindal,

Elizabeth, Mrs. Faucit, Sedona. Mrs. Brudenell,   Alexina, Miss Phillips, Katharine, Miss Pearson.

In the course of the Play will be introduced,

The GRAND PUBLIC ENTRY INTO MOSCOW, & the CORONATION of the EMPRESS ELIZABETH.

After the Play, will be produced [FOR THE FIRST TIME] a Classical Entertainment, entitled

THE DAYS OF ATHENS.

IN WHICH THE CELEBRATED

Mr. DUCROW,

Will have the honour of making his 1st Appearance at this Theatre these three years.

Thursday.... The New Opera of The LOVE CHARM, or, The Village Coquette.

Friday ...... A popular Play, and other Entertainments.

Saturday .... The Opera of The LOVE CHARM, or, The Village Coquette.

CHINA.   No Money to be Returned.   J. TABBY Printer, Theatre-Royal, Drury Lane.

succeeded by a new spectacle, an operatic play 'on a scale of great splendour' with lots of new scenery, and, on the same night, the beginning of the engagement of 'the celebrated Mr Ducrow', the equestrian star.

The manager responsible for this exciting array of attractions was Alfred Bunn. He had just taken over for the leaseholder Captain Polhill, theatrical amateur and later MP, after a season managed by the musician Alexander Lee. The gutter press openly accused rich men like Polhill of maintaining an interest in the theatres only because they were 'Serails des Milords': *The Satirist* was convinced that the singer Miss Pearson owed her leading roles at Drury Lane that season to the fact that she was Polhill's mistress, and asserted that it was a clash between her and Lee's mistress, the more established singer Harriet Waylett, that caused Lee to give up the management. Bunn, Polhill's next choice, had a lurid marital, amorous and financial history of his own, but he attended strictly to the best financial interests of the theatre: he imported the lions, he probably suborned *The Satirist* to speak well of them, and all the world came to see them.[11]

The tragedian Macready's resentment of his place, and the place of the legitimate drama, in Bunn's bills was widely known and shared by the great majority of newspaper critics.[12] Drury Lane is obviously, from the evidence of such bills as this, locked in a hegemonic struggle between art and entertainment; but what might we conclude about its activities if we sidestep the self-righteous construction Macready and his literary supporters put upon the situation? What are the possible implications of a mixture of either Shakespeare or modern opera with dramatised lion-taming or horse-riding as a single night on the stage? Who came to such a motley event? Who would not come? Critical opinion[13] was that the major theatres were failing to cater for them, and the constituency they represented – the cultivated playgoer. Instead, spectacle and opera were mounted to attract more people, and the investment they required meant that the same pieces were played for longer. But *Macbeth* is still on the bill; did the critics and the spectacle-seekers all attend both pieces, together? It seems that there was not one audience involved here, but several. We are looking at a developing fragmentation of taste; the large audience for the 'National Theatre' is splitting up, and will, inevitably, begin to dispute domination of the territory. Historians have begun to reappraise received opinion about this change, which until recently tended to echo Filon's disgusted sense of an invasion by barbarian hordes and a heroic but unsuccessful stand by the defenders of literature.[14]

Fashionable nights

There was a second London centre of legitimate theatrical entertainment, located so as to serve the leisured classes whose haunts were St James's and Mayfair, amidst the expanding world of gentlemen's clubs, fashionable venues like Almack's, and high-playing gaming houses such as Crockford's. Here a further patent for the legitimate drama had been granted to the Little Theatre in the Haymarket, to open during the summer months when the 'winter theatres' were closed, but that too had lapsed and been replaced by an annual licence. Also in the Haymarket stood the King's Theatre, London's Italian Opera House, which customarily gave opera and ballet from April to July, and was let between-times for other fashionable entertainments such as oratorio, and the visits of French dramatic companies.

A Haymarket bill suggests none of the sensation-seeking of the Drury Lane example. The full night's offering would often be as long in each place, but the usual Haymarket configuration was of three plays – a comedy or a drama plus two farces. These were normally all assumed to be equally attractive, and, crucially, to need no advertisement beyond a plain list in plain type. Plate 2, the bill for Monday 12 July 1830, is as near as they came to puffing – a small headline telling us that 'Mr. Kean will perform King Lear This Evening; being *POSITIVELY* the *LAST NIGHT* of his Engagement in London, previous to his departure for America' – and, as we now know, his fairly imminent departure for another world. The announcement at the foot of the bill that 'The New Petite Comedy, called Separation & Reparation . . . will be repeated Every Evening', '(this Evening excepted)' tells us that Kean's farewell is cutting across the regular round of performances. His Lear – as we see from the cast list, substantively in Tate's text – is supported by William Farren's Primrose in J. B. Buckstone's *Popping the Question* and another one-act farce. It is a night they expect a full house – 'no orders whatever will be admitted' – but they are making only a minimum of fuss. Such

Theatre Royal Hay-Market.

Mr. KEAN

will perform KING LEAR THIS EVENING; *being POSITIVELY the LAST NIGHT of his Engagement in London, previous to his departure for America.*

This Evening, MONDAY July 12, 1830.

Will be performed, Shakspeare's Tragedy of

KING LEAR.

King Lear,   Mr. K E A N,
(Being POSITIVELY the LAST NIGHT of his ENGAGEMENT.)
Duke of Burgundy, Mr. CATHIE,   Duke of Cornwall,   Mr. GALLOT,
Duke of Albany, Mr. W. JOHNSON, Earl of Gloucester, Mr. THOMPSON,
Earl of Kent,   Mr. WILLIAMS,
Edmund,   Mr. BRINDAL,   Oswald, Mr. WEBSTER,
Edgar,   Mr. C O O P E R,
Physician, Mr. COOKE,   Captain of Guard, Mr. C. MORRIS,
Herald, Mr. FENTON, Edward, Mr. COVENEY, Old Man, Mr. M. BARNETT
First Ruffian, Mr. LODGE,   Second Ruffian, Mr. MOORE,
Regan,   Mrs. W. CLIFFORD,
Goneril,   Mrs. T. HILL,   Aranthe, Mrs. NEWCOMBE,
Cordelia,   Miss F. H. KELLY.
After which, a Comic Piece (in One Act) called

Popping the Question!

Mr. Primrose,   Mr. W. F A R R E N,
Henry Thornton,   Mr. COOKE,
Miss Biffin,   Mrs. GLOVER,
Ellen Murray, Mrs. NEWCOMBE, Miss Winterblossom, Mrs. TAYLEURE,
Bobbin,   Mrs. H U M B Y.
To conclude with the Farce of

Modern Antiques.

Mr. Cockletop,   Mr. W. FARREN,
Frank,   Mr. VINING,   Joey,   Mr. WEBSTER,
Napkin,   Mr. COVENEY,   Hearty,   Mr. W. JOHNSON,
Thomas,   Mr. C. MORRIS,   John,   Mr. BISHOP,
Mrs. Cockletop, Mrs. W. CLIFFORD,   Belinda, Mrs. ASHTON,
Mrs. Cammomile, Mrs. COVENEY,   Nan,   Mrs. T. HILL,
Flounce, Miss BARNETT,   Betty, Mrs. W. JOHNSON.
STAGE MANAGER MR. P. FARREN.   VIVANT REX ET REGINA!

BOXES 5s.—PIT 3s.—FIRST GALLERY 2s.—SECOND GALLERY 1s.
Doors to be opened at Six o'Clock, and the Performances to begin at Seven.
☞ Places for the Boxes to be taken of Mr. MASSINGHAM, at the Theatre, Daily, from Ten till Five.
N. B. PRIVATE BOXES may be had Nightly, and Free Admissions for the Season, on application at the Box-Office.

NO ORDERS WHATEVER WILL BE ADMITTED.

A New Drama, (in Two Acts,) called

THE FORCE of NATURE.

will be produced on FRIDAY July 16:
THE PRINCIPAL CHARACTERS:
Philip,   Mr. W. F A R R E N,
Frederick, Mr. COOPER,   Count de Beauvais, Mr. VINING,
Countess D'Harville,   Mrs. FAUCIT,
Matilda,   Miss MORDAUNT.

⁎⁎⁎ On Wednesday and Thursday Evenings next, there will be no Performance.

⁎⁎⁎ The New Petite Comedy, called

SEPARATION & REPARATION,

encreasing nightly in attraction, will be repeated Every Evening till further notice,
(This Evening excepted.)

To-Morrow, The CLANDESTINE MARRIAGE; Lord Ogleby, Mr. W. Farren, Lovewell, Mr. Cooper, Brush, Mr. Vining, Sterling, Mr. Williams, Sir John Melville, Mr. Brindal, Mrs. Heidelberg, Mrs. Glover, Miss Sterling, Mrs. W. Clifford, Fanny, Miss F. H. Kelly, Betty, Mrs. Tayleure, with SEPARATION AND REPARATION, and JOHN OF PARIS; John of Paris, Mr. Vining, Pedrigo Potts, Mr. J. Reeve, Princess of Navarre, Miss Turpin.
On Friday, The PADLOCK; Leander, Mr. Horn, Mungo, Mr. Webster, Don Diego, Mr. Gallot, Leonora, Miss Turpin, Ursula, Mrs. Tayleure, with (never acted) a New Drama in Two Acts, called The FORCE OF NATURE, SEPARATION AND REPARATION, and THIRTEEN TO THE DOZEN; Simon Knippenclipper, Mr. Webster, Maurice Holster, Mr. J. Reeve, Bridget, Mrs. Humby.

2 Playbill for Theatre Royal, Haymarket, 12 July 1830

bills as this, for one of Kean's late appearances, are often found to have been preserved as souvenirs;[15] but the theatre does not need to tell its patrons in bold type that this is a special night.

As usual here, the bill says nothing about scenery or spectacle; the novelties are strictly those of text or acting, catering for the conservative playgoing public represented by the critics. Such a public knew how to read this bill, and, indeed, how to consume the products it represents: if they came to witness the last days of a tragic star, they might well not have stayed for two farces after *King Lear*; on the other hand, they might choose to do so, if they pleased. The price of the ticket was not important to them, and in any case many audience members entered at will on a season ticket. If they had come on the evening before to see the new comedy, they might equally not have chosen to stay late for the two farces. The intertheatrical experience was individualised as well as shared; but the proprietor could rely on these people to know what to do, how to behave, and how to interpret a reserved and cryptic bill. They might indeed be indifferent to the waning pretensions of a passé cockney performer, and only turn up, late in the evening, to be amused a little by the dull, gentlemanly comedian Farren,[16] whose father before him had taken similar roles and whose brother Percival was stage-manager. Their time was all their own.

A similar set of aristocratic assumptions operated at the Opera House, where boxes were taken for the season by ladies of fashion, and the Members of Parliament joined them there after the House rose; both theatres continued to entertain their patrons until it was time for the night houses and gambling clubs, in the early morning. The Opera House was part of the international circuit: in the early 1830s the diva Pasta, the queen of Romantic ballet Taglioni, and the virtuoso violinist Paganini were its passing stars. Exclusivity and complicity characterised both Haymarket theatres. The grand new Theatre Royal's stately boredom and the Opera House's decrepit interior, extortionate charges, worldly-wise, indeed downright lubricious patrons and appalling drains were, they felt, nobody's business but their own.[17] On the other hand when in 1832 Cooke's circus in Great Windmill Street off the Haymarket converted itself into a theatre called the Albion and the Westminster Subscription Theatre opened in Tothill Street south of St James's Park, their pretensions to a foothold in this world were met with vitriolic class abuse from the fashionable satirical sheet *Figaro in London*.[18]

The West End

Covent Garden and Drury Lane could not defend themselves so easily as the Mayfair theatres from encroachment and threatening competition. They stood in a busy market district near the intersection of the town and the City, a maze of old streets and alleys that was the traditional centre of the arts in London, the home of publishing and the press as well as the theatres, but by this date packed, insalubrious and, at night, actively dangerous: the criminal quarter of St Giles was nearby, and brothels and pornographic print-shops lined the streets that led to the theatres. Every kind of entertainment was to be had there: since the seventeenth century, for example, 'The Mogul' had stood in Drury Lane, figuring in *The Momus and Vocal Visitor* of 1833 as 'Turkish Saloon (Cook's) Great Mogul', described in a guide for the would-be street-wise as 'the greatest link of the cockney between the music and the drama'; later it became the Middlesex Music Hall, but continued to be known to insiders as the 'Old Mo'.[19] In the surrounding streets were the rapidly multiplying pleasure resorts of the visitors and the London clerks, shop-workers and gents: taverns, singing clubs, 'Free and Easies', 'Cock and Hen Clubs' (the distinction being that in the latter women were admitted), Judge and Jury entertainments, where spoof cases of 'crim con' – adultery – were tried, and private theatres. These last catered to theatrical aspirants who had no access to a career on the professional stage, but sought to gain the experience they craved by paying for their roles in classic plays. The Minor in Catherine Street was the longest-established of them: opened in 1807 for conjuring shows, it was an upstairs room holding 160 spectators before a stage 14ft (4.3m) square.[20] In 1830–3 it was calling itself a acting school, though it had no official permission to exist at all, and was one focus of the protectionist anger of other branches of the profession. Oxberry's *Dramatic Biography* said it was 'more disorderly than a cockpit or a bull bait', (both of these were still legal in 1832 – baiting until 1835, cockfighting until 1849) and worse than these because 'females frequent it';[21] Thomas Dibdin lamented that there was a private theatre in every tenth street in London, doing 'incalculable mischief to public morals' and turning out cheap actors who were then employed, 'depriving the families of respectable and fairly-established regular practitioners' of bread.[22]

In effect, a new theatre district, the beginnings of the modern West End, was fighting its way into existence between the two older centres. The battle could be quite overt. Early in 1832 the provincial performer Benjamin Rayner arrived, fresh from a court triumph in which sympathetic magistrates had found a technical reason not to convict the management of illegal performance at the little Orange Theatre in Pimlico (behind a coffee house).[23] He moved into the West End, taking an old exhibition hall in the Strand, the riverside road that borders Covent Garden. Previously known as Burford's Panorama, the 'New Strand Subscription Theatre' was without a licence of any kind. He aimed for style and fashion, redecorating in gilt and crimson with a curtain that drew sideways like the one at the Olympic (see below); his first piece was a burlesque dubbed a 'local extravaganza' – code for a topical satire – about the 'march of intellect' in Parliament and on the stage, with much talk of 'a clear stage and no favour', and claptraps about Reform. However, his bills were torn down by hired hands and the papers bombarded with assertions that he had closed down in response to the patentees' threatening letters. By April 1832 he was out of business and in prison for debt. More conflict followed, but eventually this house became the Strand Theatre, a home of light musical comedy.[24]

By 1830 the Strand already had several fully licensed theatres. Regular confrontations took place between the proprietors of the patent houses and these aspirant venues, only a stone's-throw away, where a class of customer that Drury Lane and Covent Garden seemed to have lost was admitted to bright, modern and relatively inexpensive entertainments. The Lyceum, the Olympic and the Adelphi all enjoyed annual licences granted by the Lord Chamberlain (on behalf of the King) to perform 'burletta', music and dancing, and 'the entertainments of the stage'. Exactly what this allowed was always a subject of dispute, but it was generally agreed that it did not include Shakespeare or the rest of the repertoire of classic comedy and tragedy – the legitimate drama.[25] The bills reveal that patrons could expect distinctive, but interrelated, experiences at each of the new houses. The Lyceum was perhaps most obviously aspiring to rival the Theatres Royal, having been built by Samuel Arnold to serve as an English opera house, as part of his protracted campaign for a third patent theatre for the capital.[26] From 1830 to 1834 it was awaiting rebuilding after a major fire. The other two were not so simply related to the established culture.

The bills (see plate 3) of Madame Vestris's Olympic, newly and luxuriously refurbished in 1831, are an index of fashionable aspiration in a new mode. They ape those of the Haymarket, with similar typefaces and, superficially, a very similar programme of three or even four pieces a night. Closer inspection, however, reveals that here the fare is entirely comedy with lots of music, and while the little stage and intimate auditorium do not accommodate large-scale spectacle, the bills tell us who made the dresses, who painted the new act drop as well as the new scenery, and that the pieces are fashionably adapted from the French or jokingly derived from current publications and classical reading, with a delicate layer of innuendo: 'Prometheus' Work Shop, in *Body* colours, with *the Devil to Pay* for Peeping'. At the foot is the announcement that 'The performances are so arranged as to terminate as near Eleven as possible.' Reading intertheatrically, it seems that here is a modern take on the aristocratic tedium of the legitimate: a polished enterprise targeted at an *arriviste* audience of admirers of the fashionable world; lady-like luxury, light music, genteel farce and carefully packaged glamour drew in an audience of the idle rich together with those willing to pay to be in their company, who, however, wanted to be home before midnight so as to be at their counting-house desks early next morning.[27]

Of the three Strand houses, the Adelphi was most obviously catering to an audience that might otherwise be at a Theatre Royal, and was, indeed, familiar with the work there. The theatre sometimes put on the kind of serious new plays that critics wanted to see added to the national repertoire, thus competing directly with the patents.[28] But it embedded such work within a racy programme of modern attractions that in 1831 included a satirical spoof of Drury Lane's *Hyder Ali*, in which its popular stars played various animals. The leading comedian John Reeve (whose famous performances from previous seasons included a song called 'the quadrupeds') plays the lion and Fanny Fitzwilliam the tiger.

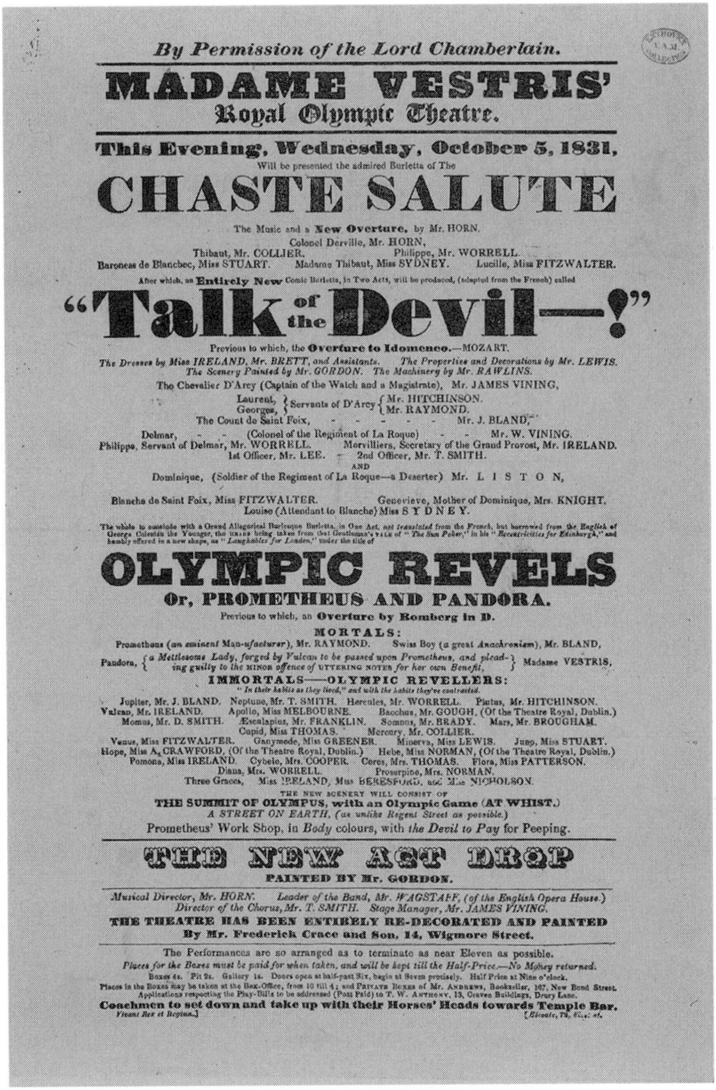

By Permission of the Lord Chamberlain.

MADAME VESTRIS'
Royal Olympic Theatre.

This Evening, Wednesday, October 5, 1831,
Will be presented the admired Burletta of The

CHASTE SALUTE

The Music and a New Overture, by Mr. HORN.
Colonel Derville, Mr. HORN,
Thibaut, Mr. COLLIER. Philippe, Mr. WORRELL.
Baroness de Blancbec, Miss STUART. Madame Thibaut, Miss SYDNEY. Lucille, Miss FITZWALTER.

After which, an Entirely New Comic Burletta, in Two Acts, will be produced, (adapted from the French) called

"Talk of the Devil—!"

Previous to which, the Overture to Idomeneo.—MOZART.
The Dresses by Miss IRELAND, Mr. BRETT, and Assistants. The Properties and Decorations by Mr. LEWIS. The Scenery Painted by Mr. GORDON. The Machinery by Mr. RAWLINS.

The Chevalier D'Arcy (Captain of the Watch and a Magistrate), Mr. JAMES VINING,
Laurent, Georges, } Servants of D'Arcy { Mr. HITCHINSON. Mr. RAYMOND.
The Count de Saint Foix, - - - - - - Mr. J. BLAND,
Delmar, - - (Colonel of the Regiment of La Roque) - - Mr. W. VINING.
Philippe, Servant of Delmar, Mr. WORRELL. Morvilliers, Secretary of the Grand Provost, Mr. IRELAND.
1st Officer, Mr. LEE. - 2nd Officer, Mr. T. SMITH.
AND
Dominique, (Soldier of the Regiment of La Roque—a Deserter) Mr. L I S T O N,

Blanche de Saint Foix, Miss FITZWALTER. Genevieve, Mother of Dominique, Mrs. KNIGHT.
Louise (Attendant to Blanche) Miss S Y D N E Y.

The whole to conclude with a Grand Allegorical Burlesque Burletta, in One Act, *not translated* from the *French*, but borrowed from the *English* of George Colman the Younger, the IDEA being taken from that Gentleman's TALE of "*The Sun Poker*," in his "*Eccentricities for Edinburgh*," and humbly offered in a new shape, as "*Laughables for London*," under the title of

OLYMPIC REVELS
Or, PROMETHEUS AND PANDORA.

Previous to which, an Overture by Romberg in D.

MORTALS:
Prometheus (*an eminent Man-ufacturer*), Mr. RAYMOND. Swiss Boy (*a great Anachronism*), Mr. BLAND,
Pandora, { *a Mettlesome Lady, forged by Vulcan to be passed upon Prometheus, and pleading guilty to the* MINOR *offence of* UTTERING NOTES *for her own Benefit,* } Madame VESTRIS,

IMMORTALS—OLYMPIC REVELLERS:
"In their habits as they lived," and with the habits they've contracted.

Jupiter, Mr. J. BLAND. Neptune, Mr. T. SMITH. Hercules, Mr. WORRELL. Plutus, Mr. HITCHINSON.
Vulcan, Mr. IRELAND. Apollo, Miss MELBOURNE. Bacchus, Mr. GOUGH, (Of the Theatre Royal, Dublin.)
Momus, Mr. D. SMITH. Æsculapius, Mr. FRANKLIN. Somnus, Mr. BRADY. Mars, Mr. BROUGHAM.
Cupid, Miss THOMAS. Mercury, Mr. COLLIER.
Venus, Miss FITZWALTER. Ganymede, Miss GREENER. Minerva, Miss LEWIS. Juno, Miss STUART.
Hope, Miss A. CRAWFORD, (Of the Theatre Royal, Dublin.) Hebe, Miss NORMAN, (Of the Theatre Royal, Dublin.)
Pomona, Miss IRELAND. Cybele, Mrs. COOPER. Ceres, Mrs. THOMAS. Flora, Miss PATTERSON.
Diana, Mrs. WORRELL. Proserpine, Mrs. NORMAN.
Three Graces, Miss IRELAND, Miss BERESFORD, and Miss NICHOLSON.

THE NEW SCENERY WILL CONSIST OF
THE SUMMIT OF OLYMPUS, with an Olympic Game (AT WHIST.)
A STREET ON EARTH, (as unlike Regent Street as possible.)
Prometheus' Work Shop, in *Body* colours, with *the Devil to Pay* for Peeping.

THE NEW ACT DROP
PAINTED BY Mr. GORDON.

Musical Director, Mr. HORN. Leader of the Band, Mr. WAGSTAFF, (of the English Opera House.) Director of the Chorus, Mr. T. SMITH. Stage Manager, Mr. JAMES VINING.

THE THEATRE HAS BEEN ENTIRELY RE-DECORATED AND PAINTED
By Mr. Frederick Crace and Son, 14, Wigmore Street.

The Performances are so arranged as to terminate as near Eleven as possible.
Places for the Boxes must be paid for when taken, and will be kept till the Half-Price.—No Money returned.
Boxes 4s. Pit 2s. Gallery 1s. Doors open at half-past Six, begin at Seven precisely. Half Price at Nine o'clock.
Places in the Boxes may be taken at the Box-Office, from 10 till 4; and PRIVATE BOXES of Mr. ANDREWS, Bookseller, 167, New Bond Street. Applications respecting the Play-Bills to be addressed (Post Paid) to T. W. ANTHONY, 13, Craven Buildings, Drury Lane.
Coachmen to set down and take up with their Horses' Heads towards Temple Bar.
Vivant Rex et Regina.]

3 Playbill for Royal Olympic Theatre, 5 October 1831

Their parody extends to the bills. Drury Lane's 'gorgeous spectacle'(see plate 1) promises 'Sadhusing . . . discovered sleeping on
a lion!' then in 'a terrific combat' with it; a magnificent 'diversion
of a tiger hunt', and finally Sadhu 'borne by twenty soldiers with
the conquered lion at his feet!!!' At the Adelphi, patrons were
offered 'one of the most Gorging spectacles ever produced!' and
it included 'Sadhusing on intimate terms with a lion', followed
by 'some idea' of a tiger hunt, and Hyder Ali on a sagacious
elephant, a close relation of one that appeared at the Adelphi
last season; it culminated in 'the overthrow of the bipeds by the
quadrupeds, and apotheosis of the present stage of the stage'.[29]
    We learn from such a bill that a high degree of knowingness
about the theatre world and its internal disputes could be expected of the Adelphi habitué. While the Haymarket expects
those in the know quietly to decode its announcements, this theatre would seem to foster a more self-conscious culture, actively
amused by the bill, as well as by the evening it announces. The
intertheatrical joke about what was going on at the patent houses
was shared by such frequenters of the theatres – who might well
have seen the lions, as well as enjoying their old favourite John
Reeve taking them off.

*Old entertainments, new theatres: the fairground
comes to town*

While the London cultural establishment was divided in grap-
pling with new challenges of the kind provided by commercialism
at the Olympic and satire at the Adelphi, they had no hesitation in
condemning, or simply disregarding, the cultural evolution that
was taking place in provision for the increasing population of
urban workers at every social level. The simplest response to this
was to regard it an issue of law and order. The oldest sites of entertainment in the capital, the London fairs, seemed fit only for suppression. From ancient times Bartholomew Fair and Southwark
Fair, later foundations such as May Fair beside Hyde Park, and an
outer ring of metropolitan resorts like Bow, Stepney, Fairlop Fair
in Epping Forest, Greenwich, Edmonton, Barnet and Mitcham
Fairs, and a series of similar seasonal events, had included entertainment amongst their marketing activities. In and around
London, indeed, such events had tended to become leisure

activities from an early period. In the closed season the actors from the Restoration and eighteenth-century Theatres Royal had set up their booths at the fairs, and competed with the menageries, rope-walkers and freakshows to attract all ranks of holidaymakers. But by the nineteenth century the fairs were beginning to be looked upon as disruptive: immoral and dangerous outbreaks of disorder, which allowed the lowest classes to invade or traverse areas of town now appropriated to business or to upper-class occupation.[30]

The fairground theatre was not going to disappear without resistance, however, just as its potential audiences hugely expanded. The travellers, and the class of hereditary entertainers who managed the fairs, were modernising their enterprises and spilling over into cellars, gaffs and opportunistic tents and converted buildings all over the East End and other working-class districts of the city. Venturesome newcomers with an eye to a developing business joined them; and they did not only cater for the poorest customers. Middle-class London was in a state of rapid expansion, and people began to think that it would be better for the new-built middle-class districts to have their own places of entertainment, to avoid the journey into Covent Garden and its concomitant annoyances. Many caterers were responsive to a new opportunity. Taverns were looked upon favourably by the magistrates when they applied for music and dancing licences if they seemed likely to have a genteel clientele.[31] Londoners' old pleasure haunts on the country fringes of town, like Sadler's Wells, were now surrounded by new suburban homes, and with an eye to a new audience their managements acquired new buildings and aspirations to theatrical distinction. During the 1831–2 season the Sadler's Wells company changed places with one from the new Royal Clarence Subscription Theatre down the road near King's Cross, and the Wells welcomed another of the new female managers, Fanny Fitzwilliam, whom the *Morning Chronicle* enthusiastically coupled with Vestris of the Olympic as saviours of the drama.[32] Pimlico and Chelsea, where Walton had met milkmaids by the river, were no longer rural, and Robert Cubitt the developer had already acquired a lease from the Duke of Westminster, but before the house building got under way old taverns and tea-rooms amidst the doomed market gardens sprang forth into theatrical venues: the King's Road, for example, boasted several, including the prosecuted Orange Theatre. Along the Marylebone New Road, the southern fringe of Regent's Park, more theatres sprang up, as they did in Paddington and Bayswater and off the Edgware Road – everywhere there might be an audience.[33]

In the City itself theatres began to be established to cater for the businessman and his family. Following, perhaps, the successful lead of Vestris just west of Temple Bar, Harriet Waylett (whom Catherine Oxberry dubbed 'Vestris in water-colours' and the gutter press called a drunken whore)[34] and her partner John Kemble Chapman set up the New City Theatre in Milton Street, late Grub Street, in April 1831. They and their friends were veterans of the patent wars, but some were more dextrous than others at defending themselves in the mêlée. With musician Alexander Lee and his associate Ann Tree, these two had previously set up at the Royalty in Tottenham Street, in 1829, and been cried up by the Radical press, especially the *Tatler*, as offering entertainments as good as those in a country Theatre Royal. This had proved too much provocation for the patentees, who laid information against them in June 1830 for playing without a licence, and drove them out.[35] Chapman's new venture in Milton Street, carefully set up to bring theatre comfortably to the doorsteps of the 'Citizens and Freemen of the City' – he was a City Freeman himself, he stressed[36] – did not save him when the old prosecutions caught up with him. By February 1832 he was in the King's Bench as a debtor. But such defeats could not suppress the growth of the new theatres: after Rayner's defeat at the Strand (see above, p. 49) Harriet Waylett rented that theatre from him and brought in Chapman, Lee and Tree to carry on. They mounted not only Lee's new pieces, but *The Beggar's Opera* and *The Barber of Seville*.

The West End theatres survive today, and some of the evanescent fringe venues for middle-class patrons have struggled into historical visibility; but those which catered for poorer audiences are less easily rediscovered. The greens and taverns of Tottenham Fields and Tottenham Court hosted shows about which we now know nothing. Bills do survive, however, from some large new theatres such as the Pavilion in Shoreditch, an old clothing factory reopened after fire at Easter 1831, and the Garrick in Leman Street, opened in January 1831. These were single-class venues, full of cheap seats and offering rich mixtures of music and melodrama, with ongoing success. After rebuilding in 1856 the Pavilion was said to seat more than five thousand people, with a stage only a little smaller than the largest in Europe, that at La Scala Milan.[37]

An instructive example of the new entrepreneurial spirit in the provision of entertainment is the Royal Albert Saloon and Standard Tavern and Tea Gardens in Shepherdess Walk, Shoreditch. There Hector Simpson began to give varied entertainments, his big success being a pantomimist called William Smith, who had learned his trade in Richardson's travelling theatre. Simpson rechristened him Paul Herring; he became a star in the minors as Bluebeard, and in 1831 was creator of the part of 'Drolinsko' in Astley's *Mazeppa* (see below, p. 61). The Royal Albert threw up a flimsy auditorium backing onto the road, in which two stages were built, facing into the pub one way and into the gardens the other, and gave shows that might include pantomime, singing, gymnastic feats, comic ballets (Herring's speciality) and full-blown melodrama. Harold Scott records that when the 1843 Act finally removed the brakes from their dramatic activities, the Albert's bills included one combining *Black-ey'd Susan* and *Venice Preserved*;[38] I have not discovered this phenomenon, but plate 4, the bill for 13 February 1843 (immediately before the Theatre Regulation Act, which was introduced in July of that year),[39] is typical of the opulent fare already on offer.

Here we have first the 'Grand Feast of Apollo', which is a concert of popular songs, the embryo of the music hall bill; then a spectacular Gothic melodrama, which offers 'gorgeous Scenery, extensive Machinery, superb Properties, Dresses and Appointments' displaying an

Extensive and magnificent subterranean grotto, the abode of the fairies, in which will be introduced a panorama on a peculiarly novel scale!! Representing the degrees of COLD and HEAT from the NORTH POLE to the EQUATOR. Grand Chorus of Fairies. Arrival of their Queen, her resolve to despatch the Imp on an embassy to the Castle to thwart the designs of the Demon Knight. At the Queen's summons the Ponderous Rocks break, and the IMP appears . . . Magnificent Garden of Hernswolf castle! . . . The borders of the Black Forest. Peter in Peril . . . Song, Peter, stand and deliver . . . The Goblins' dell at the foot of the Hartz mountains! Goblins at their gambols . . .

ROYAL ALBERT SALOON

SHEPHERDESS WALK, CITY ROAD.

First Night of the Grand Romantic Spectacle of Enchantment and Diablerie.

FIRST APPEARANCE IN THIS COUNTRY OF

HERR VON HARTZTAL, THE FIRE PHENOMENON!

Positively the Last Two Nights of the Pantomime.

MONDAY, FEB. 13th, 1843,
AND WEDNESDAY.

The Entertainments will commence with a Grand

FEAST OF APOLLO,

Supported by Messrs. T. Jones, Howell, Ismay, G. Herbert, E. F. Taylor, Llewellyn, Swinn, Scott, and Johnson; Mesdames Robinson, Julia Carr, Montgomery, Innell, Tunstall, Howell, &c.

After which, will be presented, an entirely new Romantic Melo-dramatic Spectacle (which has been some months in preparation) with gorgeous Scenery, extensive Machinery, superb Properties, Dresses, and Appointments, entitled THE

GOBLIN OF THE HARTZ MOUNTAINS

OR THE IMP OF THE HAUNTED CASTLE!

The Piece produced by Mr. F. EDE—the Scenery, by Mr. J. WRIGHT—Machinery, by Mr. ROWE—Properties, by Mr. ABEL—Dresses by Mr. SHOARD. The Choruses and Melo-dramatic Music composed and arranged by Mr. F. BOULLAND—The Overture, a MS. of the late H. Nicholson, Esq.

Baron Hernswolf .... Mr. J. P. HART.		Count Waldman .... Mr. ISMAY.
The * * * * or Dark Knight .... Mr. E. F. TAYLOR.		
Martin, (Steward of the Castle) .... Mr. JOHNSON.		Peter Block .... Mr. T. JONES.
The Imp of the Castle .... Mr. PAUL HERRING.		

Hans Klaus, Conrad, Bremo, } Robbers, { Mr. HOWELL. Mr. J. B. HILL. Mr. W. H. BENSON.   Givolpho, Schwartz, Britz, } Goblins, { Mr. G. HERBERT. Mr. BROUGHTON. Mr. NATHAN.

Christine, (Martin's Daughter) ..... Miss J. CARR.   Bridget ..... Mrs. HOWELL.
Clotilda (in love with the Unknown Knight) .... Mrs. ISMAY.
Queen of the Fairies ..... Miss ROBINSON.
Singing Fairies, Goblins, &c., Messrs. Scott, Swinn, Harper, Williams, Mesdames Montgomery, Tunstall, Hill, A. Cushnie, and a numerous train of Auxiliaries.

Synopsis of Scenery and Incidents.

EXTENSIVE AND MAGNIFICENT SUBTERRANEAN GROTTO,
THE ABODE OF THE FAIRIES,—in which will be introduced

A PANORAMA ON A PECULIARLY NOVEL SCALE!!
Representing the degrees of COLD and HEAT from the NORTH POLE to the EQUATOR.
Grand Chorus of Fairies.   Arrival of their Queen, her resolve to despatch the Imp on an embassy to the Castle to thwart the designs of the Demon Knight.
At the Queen's summons, *the Ponderous Rocks break, and the IMP appears.*
His antics, and departure to save the Lady and pluck her from the Demon's grasp.

VIEW NEAR THE CASTLE.
A Father's command, and a Daughter's disobedience.   "Ah me, the course of true love never did run smooth." *Song, Christine.*
Arrival of the love-lorn swain, Peter Block.   A tailor's courtship, a mysterious tale.   The Imp at his pranks.

Magnificent Garden of Hernswolf Castle!
Meeting of the lovers.   Fearful oath.   Supernatural warning. Clotilda swears to become the bride of the Dark Knight.

CHAMBER IN THE CASTLE.
The Imp's visit to Old Bridget, he takes his seat on the Fire.   Awful alarm.   Meeting of the Rival Knights.   The Challenge.
Sudden appearance of a Friend.   His Advice.

THE BORDERS OF THE BLACK FOREST.
Peter in Peril.   Song, Peter, stand and deliver.   The runny-nuisances of two Schoolfellows.

THE GOBLINS' DELL AT THE FOOT OF THE HARTZ MOUNTAINS!
Goblins at their gambols.   Chorus.   Dance of Fire Demons, Messrs. Nathan, Elliott, Henry and Arthur.   In this Scene will be introduced
THE FAR-FAMED FIRE FIEND,

HERR VON HARTZTAL
(FROM GERMANY,)
It's First Appearance in this Country, who will go through his *Surprising Performances.*
Hans Klaus in trouble.   His escape from the Goblins, and *fierce encounter with the Fiery Dragon!*

CHAMBER IN THE CASTLE.
The Imp a Fortune-teller.   Peter's ill luck.   Comic Dance by the Imp.   Robber's attack on the Castle.   Their overthrow.
ARRIVAL OF THE FAIRY QUEEN, AND IMPOSING TABLEAU.

[......blower, Printer,]

4 Playbill for Royal Albert Saloon and Standard Tavern and Tea Gardens, 13 February 1843

ACT 2---PICTURE GALLERY IN THE CASTLE.

The Animated Picture. Alarm of the Domestics. The Imp disguised as Old Bridget. Comic equivoque. Bridget's fourteen Children. Clotilda's perplexity. The Fairy Queen's Warning---" WED NOT THE STRANGER KNIGHT." The affection of Wassan. She signs the Nuptial Bond with her own Blood, "'Tis done! she is mine eternally."

VIEW NEAR COBLENTZ.

Hans Klaus turned Baron. Song, Hans. Peter in danger of being shot. "Oh this love, this love." Trio, Martin, Hans, and Peter.

GRAND ARENA WITH GALLERIES

PREPARED FOR A TOURNAMENT!

August Assembly of Barons, Lords, Knights, and Ladies. *New Ballet.* Principal Dancers, Mr. HOWARD LEWIS and Miss ANN CUSHNIE.
In this Scene will be exhibited the peculiar mode of

CHINESE WARFARE by the CELEBRATED HERR VON HARTZTAL!

Terrific Combats by Messrs. J. B. Hill, Broughton, Taylor, Shoard, Barton, and Benson.

Overwhelming prowess of the Dark Knight, who seizes and bears away the Lady Clotilda. He is pursued and overtaken by the Baron, whom, to secure his Bride, he slays. The Lady is surrounded by Goblins, and hurried away to the *Hall of Terrors.* The Count's vow to pursue and rescue her. The Fairy Queen proffers her assistance.

EXTERIOR OF CASTLE, GROUNDS, AND LAKE.

The Imp at work again, they pursue him, he jumps into a Gondola, and rows off, they follow him in another. He disappears with his barons, and re-appears at various parts of the Stream. At length he lands, and, by command of the Fairy Queen, agrees to conduct the Count to the *Hall of Terrors.*

A GLOOMY CAVERN.

Chorus of Goblins. Appearance of the Fire Fiend, who, with the Goblins, oppose the Imp and Count's progress with their brands of Fire. Their united efforts are vain. The Imp and Count gain an entrance into

THE HALL OF TERRORS!!!

THRONE AND BLACK BANNER OF THE DEMON KNIGHT.

Clotilda is discovered overwhelmed with the horrors which surround her. The Demon Knight casts off his disguise. The Enchanted Sword, which, once drawn, the spell is broken, and the Knight becomes the prey of the Evil One. The Count's courage after a terrific struggle. He obtains the Sword and draws it. The horrors which surround him disappear.

The Demon Knight with his partners in crime descend in Flames.

The scene changes to

THE FAIRY BOWERS.

The Queen, with her Fairies, arrive. They congratulate the Knight. The Lovers are united. *Grand Finale amidst*

Showers of Brilliant Coloured Liquid Fires!

PRODUCING THE MOST EXTRAORDINARY EFFECT EVER WITNESSED ON ANY STAGE.

To conclude with an entirely NEW PANTOMIME, written by Mr. W. ROGERS, *Comedian,* to be called the

CHINESE WAR!

Pantaloon......*Mr. A. ABEL.*   Harlequin......*Mr. HOWARD LEWIS.*
Clown........*Mr. PAUL HERRING.*   Columbine.........*Miss ANN CUSHNIE.*

TUESDAY and FRIDAY.

Grand Concert.   Feats Gymnastique.   Dancing.

To be followed by the Grand Romantic Spectacle of THE

IMP OF THE CASTLE,

A SAILOR'S LEGACY.

TO CONCLUDE WITH

BROTHER & SISTER.

THURSDAY and SATURDAY.

THE IMP OF THE CASTLE,

MY MASTER'S SECRET.

Thomas.....................*Mr. T. JONES.*

To conclude with, for the first time,

THE ADOPTED CHILD.

The Adopted Child............*Master E. F. HILL (his First Appearance in that Character.).*

Manager and Director   -   -   *Mr. T. JONES.*

Doors open at Half-past Five, performances commence at Six, and terminate at Eleven.

ADMISSION---SALOON, SIXPENCE.

Stalls, One Shilling, including a Refreshment Ticket.

Machinist, Mr. J. ROWE.   [HORNBLOWER, (late PARSONAGE,) Printer, 1½, Wilderness Row, Goswell Street.

By this stage the story is on hold and singing and dancing are being enjoyed; and here is interjected the headline fire-eating act of the new-engaged speciality performer Herr von Hartztal the 'far famed fire fiend'. The second act shifts scene entirely to a 'Grand Arena with Galleries', where are set some terrific combats and a New Ballet, and Herr von Hartztal exhibits 'the peculiar mode of Chinese warfare'. The denouement is the descent of the Demon Knight in flames, and his supersedure by the Fairy Queen in 'Showers of Brilliant Coloured Liquid Fires!' This over, the bill concludes with a new pantomime, complete with the traditional harlequinade, advertised as 'written by Mr. W. Rogers, comedian' – the audience presumably knew his work and could distinguish between the value of pantomimes by various hands. The forthcoming attractions listed at the end are summed up in gothic script as 'Grand Concert. Feats gymnastique. Dancing' before three plays a night are named. All this costs 6d when the doors open at 5.30, or 1s including a good seat and a drink.

This bill is typical of the offerings of the new theatres, and needs to be read so as to combat the prejudice of critics intent upon belittling the theatrical skills of the audience to whom it is addressed. Clearly it is much more of an advertisement, a puff for the wares on offer, than the Haymarket bill; and it lies outside the metatheatrcial sparring of the West End theatres. But it is still, in important ways, a document that is part of the evening's entertainments, and one which suggests a sophisticated reading, a knowledgeable response. For one thing its dense text supposes a high degree of literacy, and a willingness to read. As a souvenir of the evening, it could be enjoyed in retrospect, the reader reminded of the visual excitements of 'entirely new romantic melodramatic spectacle' *The Goblin of the Hartz Mountains*. But it is not only a souvenir; read beforehand, such descriptions, I think, have the effect of preconditioning the audience actually to see these things, in a display of painted scenery and a performance that might otherwise be inexplicable dumb show and noise: the synopsis makes the action clear and helps to *make* the settings magnificent. This is not unlike the function of Disneyland's saturation advertising, that makes smallish, ugly lumps of plastic into fairy castles, or the modern programme for a classic play in which we are given a compilation of images, quotations from critical and scholarly commentary, fragments of interviews, directorial statements, a foretaste of design and interpretation, to orient us to this particular *Twelfth Night*, or whatever it is: the programme puts the reader in the frame of mind to understand how we should respond to the performance.

During the performance – the running of the bill – a high degree of interpretative skill would be called upon not only to 'see' the scenery, but to cope with the flow of events through the evening.[40] The opening concert is performed by the same company as act in the play; so the audience had already greeted them, *in propria* (stage) *persona*, before they appeared as goblins, knights and robbers. Paul Herring, resident leading man, does not appear until he plays the Imp, and the visiting star's performances are set up and framed within the play – the fire-eating rather more integratedly than the Chinese fighting; their reception would no doubt be built into, and cut across, the dramatic structure. And then Herring reappeared as clown in the pantomime. Surrender to and withdrawal from dramatic illusion, admiration for the visual effects, and applause for the individual feats of skill would ebb and flow throughout the night, effortlessly deployed by an audience well educated in what they were witnessing.

Always on the margins: entertainment south of the river

The oldest of London's pleasure grounds was on the south bank of the Thames, away from the regulatory reach of Westminster and the City authorities. That district was no longer as thriving as it had been in the time of the Globe and the Tudor bear-baiting arenas, and had suffered demographic shifts that removed the fashionable audience in the same way as had happened in Covent Garden, but it still maintained places of entertainment. In keeping with the demographic shift downmarket, the most notorious place of entertainment in 1831–2 was the Rotunda in the Blackfriars Road, built in 1797 as the Surrey Institution, where Hazlitt and Coleridge had lectured. By the 1820s it was an unlicensed wine and concert rooms, putting on theatrical exhibitions to the annoyance of its neighbours.[41] In 1827 the nuisance was compounded by the building of a large circus in its back garden, and then in June 1830 the infidel–Radical publisher Thomas

Carlile rented the concert rooms and began to stage political meetings of the National Union of the Working Classes, interspersed with spectacular theatrical performances. No bills have survived to inform us about these, but what evidence there is suggests, once again, a culturally self-conscious audience, in this case one which was fully, indeed gleefully, aware of itself as dissenting from the dominant discourse. A thousand people, paying only 3d or 6d a head, crammed into a space built for five hundred to see a play celebrating 'John Swing'. The rick-burning food riots that raged across the countryside and frightened the property-holding classes were accompanied by threatening notes signed 'Captain Swing'. Even more subversive, immediately parodic of the sacred texts of the culture, were the Rotunda's rabble-rousing burlesques of divine service, staged by the Rev. Robert Taylor, in which the whole assembled throng would participate.[42]

This was new in the heady years of Reform; but also on the south bank were the oldest surviving London leisure institutions that we know of, and they were at the opposite end of the political spectrum. Vauxhall Gardens dated from the Restoration, and Astley's Amphitheatre was begun in 1770 as a riding school. These were both outgrowths of the open-air pastimes which the aristocracy traditionally shared with lower-class pleasure-seekers, founded upon riding, dancing, music, sex, food and drink, and the admiration of wonderful sights and sounds. They shared the liminal status of the Rotunda, but rather because their activities required relatively large open spaces and were a nuisance to their neighbours than for any overtly political reason. Vauxhall was in some trouble by 1832, having to contend with encroaching suburban housing whose inhabitants objected to the fireworks and the noise, and with the fact that public dancing had gone out of fashion for any but the lowest classes of women. It was providing theatre – operetta and musicals, but also massive spectacles, staging the Battle of Waterloo.[43] The more modern Astley's was thriving on similar offerings. The proprietors, the West family and the fabulously beautiful and athletic equestrian Andrew Ducrow, had been granted a new lease in 1831 and undertaken a grand redecoration of the old amphitheatre, a huge building which combined a circus ring and a large stage, standing at the southern end of Westminster Bridge (near to the last surviving horse pastures of the city). They had repainted the lobby and corridors with tableaux of classical wrestlers, covering the ceiling with the life story of the horse and the proscenium with Pegasus and Apollo, and filling the house with the glitter of mirrored walls and columns lit by hundreds of lustres and a revolving 'crystal expanding chandelier' with eighty moving gas-jets inside a pictorial transparency. A shrine to muscle, horseflesh and bad mythology, Astley's was a sort of Regency schoolboy's idea of heaven; few new thoughts ruffled its sweating self-contemplation, and for two decades more it was to enjoy the condescending fondness of commentators amused by its mute offerings and its vulgar innocence. In 1831 it first staged one of its most famous equestrian dramas, the house dramatist Milner's dramatisation of Byron's romance *Mazeppa*, which was an instant hit, reaching 231 performances by August 1832. Its high point was when the hero, clad only in fleshings, was lashed to the back of a 'wild horse' (the press found its savagery comically questionable) and galloped off pursued by cut-out wooden wolves and was attacked by a vulture (on a wire) before being rescued by loyal Cossacks and returning to burn down the fortress of his oppressors. Astley's was a treasured English eccentricity, a delight to simple minds in every rank of life.[44]

The tongue-in-cheek acceptance of Astley's blend of the physically actual with the preposterously factitious was an aspect of the cultural discourse of the day which can well be argued to have been understood and enjoyed differentially by the simple and the sophisticated participant. But the newer theatres of the south bank, forced to operate with circumspection under magistrate's burletta licences, were more conscious of their challenge to the status quo, and contributed their efforts both obliquely to the political ferment of the day and directly to the campaign against the theatre licensing laws. They had been the major sufferers from the persecution of the patentees: George Davidge of the Coburg said that he had 'been persecuted, and prosecuted, and tried, and convicted, and compelled to pay the penalties'[45] for many years by the patent theatres determined to squash competition. His theatre, a large, modern auditorium built in 1816 on the model of the Paris boulevard theatres, had certainly been repeatedly prosecuted whenever he tried to put on serious drama, especially when he engaged major tragic actors between their legitimate seasons. The bill (plate 5) for the 'third appearance of

Royal Coburg Theatre,

Under the Patronage of His Royal Highness Prince Leopold of Saxe Coburg.

THIRD APPEARANCE OF

Mr. BOOTH

127

Who was greeted with the most distinguished Marks of Approbation & Enthusiastic Applause by a crowded Audience.

☞The Public is most respectfully informed, that the Proprietors, Performers, & Artists of this Establishment have used every Exertion to produce the New Classical MELO-DRAMA, as was intended on *Monday last*, but from the multiplicity of the Scenery, Machinery, Dresses, Properties, &c. it has been found impracticable, until MONDAY, January 3d, 1820. The New Melo-Drama is founded on that interesting Trait of the Roman History, the Combat of the Horatii and Curiatii, and will be got up in a Style of Magnificence never yet attempted at a Minor Theatre.

THE PRINCIPAL CHARACTERS.

Mr. Booth.   Mr. Kemble.   Mr. Barrymore.   Mr. T. P. Cooke.   Mr. Stanley.   Mr. Gallot.
Mr. Bradley.   Mr. Auld.   Mr. Gibbon.   Mr. Higman.   Mr. Randall.   Mr. Harwood.
Mrs. Stanley.   Miss Smithson.   Miss Love.   And Miss Watson.

WEDNESDAY, Dec. 29th, 1819,—And During the Week,—At Half-past Six o'Clock precisely, be Presented, a Melo-Drama, in 3 Acts, founded on Cibber's compiled Tragedy, from Shakespeare, interspersed with Music by Mr. T. Hughes, Which will be Called,

KING
Richard the Third!

Or, The Battle of Bosworth Field!

King Henry, Mr. GALLOT.   Tressel, Mr. STANLEY.   Duke of Buckingham, Mr. BARRYMORE, Sen.
Duke of Norfolk, Mr. AULD.   Prince of Wales, Miss BODEN.   Duke of York, Miss C. BODEN.

Richard,   -   -   Duke of Gloster,   -   -   Mr. BOOTH.

Ratcliff, Mr. CARTLITCH.   Lord Stanley, Mr. HOWEL.   Catesby, Mr. BISHOP.   Lieutenant of the Tower, Mr. HOBBS.
Lord Mayor, Mr. CAINSLEY.   Tirrel, Forest and Dighton, (Assassins,) Messrs. EDSWORTH, COLLINGBOURNE and GEORGE.
Richmond, Mr. T. P. COOKE.

Queen, Mrs. STANLEY.   Lady Anne, Miss LOVE.   Duchess of York, Mrs. GALLOT.

In ACT II. will be introduced the
Assassination of the Prince of Wales and Duke of York.
By the Emisaries of Richard, to secure to himself the Crown of England.
In ACT III. will be Fought the Single Combat between Richard & the Earl of Richmond, at the Battle of
BOSWORTH FIELD,
And the DEFEAT of RICHARD the THIRD.

A COMIC SONG BY Mr. BRYANT.

To conclude with the highly Popular Serio Pantomime, with the Original Music, composed and Selected by Dr. Arnold, New Scenery, Dresses, Decorations, Characteristic Dances, &c. Called,

OBI
Or, Three Finger'd Jack!

Captain Orford, Mr. AULD, his Third Appearance at this Theatre.   Tuckey, his Servant, Miss BENNETT.
Quashee, Mr. COLLINGBOURNE.   Sam, Mr. BRADLEY.   Obi Woman, Mr. GEORGE.
And Three Finger'd Jack, Mr. T. P. COOKE.
First Overseer, Mr. GIBBON.   Second Overseer, Mr. RANDALL.   Planter, Mr. HOWEL.   Jonkanoo, Master ASBURY.
Rosa, Mrs. STANLEY.   Sam's Wife, Miss WEBSTER.   Quashee's Wife, Mrs. BRADLEY.   Negro Children, Masters BLACK & BROWN.

NEW SCENERY.
Plantation in the Island of Jamaica.—Apartment in Planter's House.—Obi Woman's Cave.—Picturesque View.—Montego Bay. View of Kingston.—Planter's House.
JONKANOO BALL, WITH A CHARACTERISTIC DANCE,
By Monsieur and Madame Le CLERCQ.
AND A COMIC DANCE by MASTER ASBURY.
Interior of Slave's Hut.—Entrance to Jack's Cave.—Subterranean Passage.—Inside of Jack's Cave.—Mount Lebanus, with
Combat and Death of Jack.—Procession.—Grand Finale.
Director of the Scenic Department, Mr. SERRES.   Stage Manager, Mr. T. P. COOKE.

Boxes 4s.   Upper Circle 3s.   Pit 2s.   Gal. 1s.   Doors open at Half-past 5, to commence at Half-past 6.   Second Price Half-past 8.
Private Boxes have been made & may be had Nightly. Places cannot possibly be kept later than Half-past Seven o'Clock.
✦Places to be taken of Mr. RORAUER, (late of the Surrey Theatre,) at the New Box Office in the Grand Marine Saloon of the Theatre, & for the Accommodation of the Nobility & Gentry at the West End of the Town, at Mr. FENTUM'S Music Warehouse, No. 78, Strand, at Mr. GILLMAN'S Boot and Shoe Warehouse, London Street, Greenwich, and at No. 182, Piccadilly, opposite Burlington House.
‡‡ For the Accommodation of numerous Visitors from Greenwich, Deptford, &c. a Coach will be at this Theatre a Quarter before Eleven, At which time the Performances terminate.   [ROMNEY, Printer, Lambeth.]

5 Playbill for Coburg Theatre, 29 December 1819

Mr Booth' was part of this campaign. It flags as forthcoming but unfortunately delayed by its very ambitiousness a 'New Classical Melodrama' based on the story of the Horatii and the Curatii, 'in a Style of Magnificence never yet attempted in a Minor Theatre', before announcing that today, Wednesday Dec. 29 1819, Booth will star in *King Richard the Third!* and, after a comic song by Mr Bryant, T. P. Cooke will appear in the Serio Pantomime *Obi or, Three Finger'd Jack!*

This bill suggests to me the possibility of a complex intertheatrical response to the evening's entertainments. The main characters in the two pieces have in common the ambiguity, repulsion/attraction, of the powerful stage ogre: classical and verbal in Shakespeare's Richard, and originally mute and still primarily physical in *Obi*, where the bill stresses scenery, dancing and a procession; both plays include the combat and the death. Seeing both on the same night would be an enrichment of each; they gloss each other, especially when one considers the audience reaction to the two stars: the visiting Booth, from the antagonistic upper-class world north of the river, which was likely to punish him and his patrons for this appearance, and T. P. Cooke – ex-sailor, leading member of the resident company whose reputation was made south of the river – a local boy made good. The audience would be held throughout the bill, not expected to wander off, as at the Haymarket; they would have taken part in a complex event, in which their reactions and the expectations and loyalties with which they came were a significant part. Davidge was prosecuted for putting it on.

The state of the law that forbade Booth to appear was so manifestly absurd by the 1830s that Edmund Kean, in his round of farewell performances, appeared at the Coburg in June 1831, and in Spring 1832 Harriet Smithson took a benefit there that was actually attended by the Lord Chamberlain; both of them, of course, played the 'legitimate' repertoire. Apart from such appearances, the Coburg was bold enough in the 1831–2 season to offer amongst its 'proper' minor theatre material a play called *Reform!* in March, and another about *Gypsey Jack the Buonaparte of Humble Life*; a bill was even issued, apparently by the theatre, for Fielding's old play *Tom Thumb* with 'all sorts of political allusions' and personal references to the great and the good.[46]

The other south bank minor, the Surrey, had had its most defiant days under Robert Elliston's first lesseeship, 1809–14. He was back at the theatre from 1827 to his death in 1831; at this point the house specialised in libertarian modern drama such as *Virginius* and *William Tell*, and Elliston himself was still appearing defiantly in the standard repertoire – he put on *Othello* or *A New Way to Pay Old Debts* whenever it suited him, and one of his signature roles was Dr Pangloss in *The Heir at Law*. A Surrey bill for 13 August 1830 (plate 6) suggests how the juxtaposition of pieces may have modified the political valencies of some plays. Jerrold's *Black-ey'd Susan*, the pro-Navy money-spinner which almost accidentally lifted Elliston out of financial crisis, appears here in the ebullience of its early runs – 13 August 1830 was its 199th time. But Jerrold was a member of the Radical intelligentsia, and his plays were often read as very controversial during the Reform years[47]. The response to the happy ending of *Black-ey'd Susan* was surely greatly qualified by its being played on the same bill as Jerrold's much grimmer play *The Press-gang*, about the evils of flogging, in which the rescue of the Jack Tar hero by the discovery that he is a sprig of the nobility is patently ironic; and T. P. Cooke plays the sailor hero in each piece. The interplay of patriotic and ironic sentiment is further highlighted by the play between, a 'Local Bagatelle' about an election – the Reform crisis election had just taken place – which has characters called Justice Peculate and Lawyer Pettifog. This was soon to be replaced by 'Vive la Liberté!', a dramatisation of the French revolution of 1830, at this point less than three weeks past. There were also introduced songs on the bill that must have crystallised the excited and conflicting state of popular feeling. On 13 August the pro-monarchist 'The king and the jackets of blue', was sung by Cooke himself, and 'Hurrah for the King and the Navy' sung by Miss Somerville. On 19 August, however, these were joined by a 'local' (i.e. topical) song with very different sentiments, an attack upon the hated practice of impressment, 'The press!! pressing!! and press-gangs!!!' sung by Mr Vale; but this did not last until Cooke's last night, 21 August. Thus the bills were tweaked and modulated, leading and responding to audience reaction, shaped by theatrical circumstances and the wider world.

SURREY THEATRE.

UNDER THE DIRECTION OF MR. ELLISTON.

LAST WEEK BUT ONE OF Mr. T. P. COOKE.

This Evening, FRIDAY, AUGUST 13th, 1830,

Will be presented (33rd time) an entirely original Nautico-Domestic Drama, in Three Acts, called The

PRESS-GANG:

OR, ARCHIBALD OF THE WRECK.

Archibald of the Wreck, Mr. OSBALDISTON,
Bullion, Mr. ALMAR, Slingsby, Mr. HONOR, Turnstile, Mr. VALE.

Arthur Bryght, (the Press'd Man) Mr. T. P. COOKE.

With a HORNPIPE, and an entirely NEW SONG, (composed by Mr. BLEWITT) entitled

"THE KING and the JACKETS OF BLUE!"

Tommy Wren, Mr. ROGERS, Orchard, Mr. GOUGH, Yawley, Mr. HOBBS, Captain Fenton, Mr. HICKS,
Lieutenant, Mr. BANNISTER, Parmor, Mr. RANSFORD, Scrape & Scratch, (Rival Fiddlers) Mr. MONK & Mr. ASBURY,
Lucy Dove, Miss SCOTT, Pansy, Mrs. VALE.

The Last Scene will exhibit, upon an extensive scale, a view of the

LARBOARD QUARTER OF H. M. S. THE TRIDENT,

With the appalling Preparations for the PUNISHMENT OF THE PRESS'D MAN THROUGH THE FLEET,

THE SHIP'S LAUNCH

alongside, prior to its commencement, attended by Guard-Boats, &c. &c.—Impressive and interesting Denouement.

In the course of the Evening an entirely new Song, composed by Mr. Blewitt, entitled

"HURRAH FOR THE KING AND THE NAVY!"

By Miss SOMERVILLE. (in Character.)

To which will be added, (for the Sixth Time) a new Local Bagatelle in one Act, (by the Author of SHAKSPEARE's FESTIVAL,) called

Electioneering!

Or, VILLAGE POLITICIANS.

Jack Nobody, (a Village Foundling,) Mr. HONOR, Justice Peculate, (Candidate for Rottenborough,) Mr. MONK,
Lawyer Pettifog, (Candidate for Rottenborough,) Mr. DIBDIN PITT, Butts, (Landlord of the Royal William Public House,) Mr. ALMAR,
Jasy, (a political Barber in the Whig interest, protector of Jack Nobody,) Mr. VALE, with a new Comic Song called
"ALL THE WORLD'S ELECTIONEERING."
Mend'em, (a Reforming Cobbler,) Mr. GOUGH, Stitchthose, (a Patriotic Tailor,) Mr. ROGERS,
Warrant, (Agent to Justice Peculate,) Mr. WEBB, Parwig, (Clerk and Emissary to Lawyer Pettifog,) Mr. ASBURY,
Andrew, (Servant to Justice Peculate,) Mr. LEE, John, Mr. BANNISTER, High Bailiff, Mr. HICKS.—Voters, Villagers, &c.
Susan, (Daughter of Butts, beloved by Jack Nobody,) Miss SOMERVILLE, with an entirely new Song composed by Mr. Blewitt, entitled
"HAIL ROYAL ADELAIDE!"

The Piece to conclude

With a Representation of the Election for Rottenborough, Hustings, Orations, &c.

CHAIRING OF THE SUCCESSFUL MEMBER.

To conclude with, (199th Time) the very popular Nautical Drama, entitled

BLACK-EY'D SUSAN;

Or, ALL IN THE DOWNS.

The Overture and Music composed, and selected from Dibdin's favorite Songs, by Mr. BLEWITT.
Admiral, Mr. GOUGH, Captain Crosstree, Mr. HONOR, Degerure, Mr. DIBDIN PITT,
Gnatbra'n, Mr. VALE, Lieutenant Pike, Mr. HICKS, Raker, Mr. RANSFORD, Hatchet, Mr. ALMAR,
Jacob Twig, Mr. ROGERS, Blue Peter, (with the original Ballad of "Black-Ey'd Susan,") Mr. BENSON,

William, (with a Parody on "BOUND 'PRENTICE TO A WATERMAN,") Mr. T. P. COOKE,

Black-Ey'd Susan, Miss SCOTT, Dolly Mayflower, Mrs. VALE.

A DOUBLE HORNPIPE, by Mr. T. P. COOKE and Miss BARNETT.

On Saturday, (34th time) The PRESS-GANG; or, Archibald of the Wreck—Archibald of the Wreck, Mr. Osbaldiston, Arthur Bryght, Mr. T. P. Cooke,
after which THE FLYING DUTCHMAN—Peppercoal, Mr. Dibdin Pitt, Von Bummel, Mr. Vale, Toby Varnish, Mr. C. HILL,
(from the Theatre Royal, Bath,) his first Appearance on this Stage. Lestelle, Miss Somerville. To conclude with (first time) an entirely
new and original Drama, (by the Author of "The Brigand,"—" Montalto," &c. &c.) entitled

"VIVE LA LIBERTE!"

Or the French Revolution of 1830.

Embracing an Historical Outline of Truly Memorable Events of

THE THREE DAYS, (July 27th, 28th, and 29th.)

Boxes 4s. Pit 2s. Gal. 1s. Doors open at SIX, Performances commence at a HALF-PAST SIX. Stage Manager, Mr. OSBALDISTON.
Children under 12, Half-Price. S.G. Fairbrother, Printer, Bow Street, Covent Garden.

6 Playbill for Surrey Theatre, 13 August 1830

Conclusion

These final examples of bills from the vilified 'transpontine' houses, which exhibit the complex, subtle and active intertheatricality of performance as it flowed through the political discourses of the Reform years, do something, I hope, to substantiate my contention that a fuller and a better way of reading theatre history may be found. The years leading up to 1832 in London theatre are full of vitality and contestation, and reading them across the whole canvas from the fairs to the patent houses, avoiding literary logocentricity in our judgements of what matters in the performance culture, reveals the roots of the weakness in the binary Modernist version of theatre history, and then suggests new ways to read the story since that time.

4 Theatre history and Reform

Reform and the illegitimate theatres, 1831–2

Having set the scene in chapter 3 for the on- and off-stage dramas of the Reform crisis, I now turn to consider, side by side, the text and context of the Reform years in the London theatre. On 22 September 1831 the veteran political writer Leigh Hunt visited the Theatre Royal, Haymarket, and was thrilled to hear the audience hiss Edmund Kean for uttering the patriotic claptraps in *The Surrender of Calais*.[1] On his way home he heard the Marseillaise played in the London streets. Like many Radicals, Hunt thought – hoped – that the nation was at last on the brink of democratic revolution. In 1813, in his twenties, he had been jailed for criticising the Prince Regent, and since then had watched and waited for decades while England responded to revolutions in Europe by ever-greater repression coupled with self-satisfied assertion that this was the oldest and best democracy in the world. But in 1830 a relatively bloodless second revolution in Paris brought the Duc de Orléans and bourgeois officialdom to power, and the corresponding classes in Britain began to grow uneasy and even emulous. A series of failed harvests and manufacturing crises had also brought the nation's poor to a highly volatile condition, with riot and starvation beginning, and from the Continent news of further revolutions made Britain, for a short but heady time, feel itself to be on the brink of participation in the universal wave of democratic change. The hegemonic reaction was the Radical movement for parliamentary Reform, which recruited the distressed and discontented poor to feel they had common cause with the newly empowered but still disenfranchised middling classes, whose base was neither in the land nor the aristocracy, but in manufacturing and mercantile interests.

Three bills setting forth Reform of the parliamentary franchise in England, Scotland and Ireland were made to seem the remedy for all ills; and their exciting progress towards enactment, replete with triumphs, set-backs, aristocratic villains and heroic rescues, provided London with high drama in the press and on the streets throughout 1831 and into 1832. The delirious public excitement on the night Hunt recorded was over the passing of the Second Reform Bill through its first reading in the House of Commons the day before.

The whole cultural life of the nation was involved in the Reform debates, and that discourse reveals the complexity and depth of the hegemonic negotiations that were needed to bring the newly enfranchised groups real power and influence. London theatre partook of the tensions and conflicts that were boiling over into political action elsewhere; it is not therefore surprising that the forces of Reform appropriated the discontents of the working people in the entertainment world, just as they did the energies of rebellion in the wider public sphere.[2] The Reform Acts of 1832 offered a solution to popular unrest, a focus and an apparent solution for needs and ambitions which might otherwise have overwhelmed the existing structures of power; but they drew upon that new political energy and the fears it generated to admit only a small percentage, the propertied and upwardly mobile middling sort, to participation in power. The crystallisation of oppositional class consciousness, manifest in the Chartist agitation of the 1840s, followed upon the discovery of this betrayal. At the subordinate level of representation, in the theatre, Radical intellectuals appropriated the frustration and anger of people oppressed by the entrenched self-interest of the ruling classes, and turned their demand for freedom of expression and of work in the arts and the entertainment trade into a redefinition of rights, values and cultural capital that favoured an intellectual elite. Profound divisions along pseudo-class lines became engrained in British entertainment. The leader of this breathtakingly clever move was Edward Bulwer Lytton.

Edward Lytton Bulwer (as he called himself at the time) was returned by the old franchise in the crisis election of April 1831 to a House of Commons on the brink of radical Reform. He was a new politician, but he had trained himself to perform well in debates; his dandified appearance and his weak voice made more

impression on his hearers than his powerful intelligence, but he
was determined to overcome all obstacles to a glittering career in
the House. He was already prominent as a fashionable novelist.[3]
Of ancient but not particularly high birth, he was not a party man,
but he was at this time sure that personal and national advancement would be achieved through the cause of Radicalism, which
was indeed the cause of those like himself, outside the power
bases of either old Toryism in the country or the grand Whig
aristocratic circles. He advocated Reform not only of the House
of Commons but of all the systems of government and administration: he wanted to see new Poor Laws, universal education and
the abolition of the 'Taxes upon Knowledge' – the stamp duty on
paper that made cheap publication of serious news and political
views impossible – with the ultimate aim of avoiding revolution
on the bloody continental model by recruiting more layers of
Britain's heavily stratified society to the side of a new order.[4] Of
this new order he and his kind, the liberal intelligentsia, would be
the philosophers and leading lights. Accordingly, like many other
educated gentlemen of a liberal turn with a literate, articulate vision of a new future in power, he made himself a champion for
those he condescendingly called the 'sturdy middle classes' with
their 'warm and hearty attachment to the security of property'.[5]

In the spring of 1832, having been advised to wait to bring forward the issue of Stamp Duty until a fresh sitting of Parliament,[6]
Bulwer happily discovered a new cause, a further plank for his
platform, in the shape of reform of the stage. Here was a clear
case of 'Old Corruption', an area of the public sphere in which
an outmoded system allowed the dregs of aristocratic privilege
allied with venial cynicism and ignorant sensuality to gull the
purchasing public and to debar the moral and intelligent middle classes from control. It is but justice to note that the need
to modernise the theatre was not a new idea for Bulwer: it is
included in notes he made in 1824, when he was nineteen, for a
'History of the British Public', one of his earliest pieces of theorising and polemical writing;[7] but now public agitation about the
theatre licensing system suddenly presented him with a golden
opportunity to make his mark. Accordingly on 31 May 1832 he
successfully moved for the appointment of a Select Committee
to look into the legislative situation governing theatrical performance, and was made its chairman.[8]

As he wrote in the *New Monthly Magazine*, a Radical periodical of which he was soon to become editor, the cause of the stage was not unimportant in the politics of Reform:

In a literary age, acknowledged to abound with writers endowed with a true poetical spirit, the decline, or rather the extinction of the English Drama seems a paradox as curious as it is lamentable . . . Nor let it be said that Parliament is too much occupied to attend to what some persons may choose to denominate trifles: to relieve injustice, to remove oppression, ought at no time to be considered as a trifle. It was during the busiest period of the Revolution, that the French legislature could find leisure to protect the interests of a favourite branch of their national literature. And, after all, is the Drama a trifle? – has it not exercised a mighty influence on the thoughts, the feelings, and the morals of the nation? – perhaps not the less powerful because somewhat unsuspected.[9]

Consciousness of the need to capture the media, the public organs of communication, for the expression of the interests of the new order and as a means to negotiate a new hegemonic consensus is even clearer in the less polished expressions of Mr Hunt who seconded Bulwer's petition for a repeal of the dramatic laws on 22 May:

According to the present system, there is a complete monopoly of talent, or what may very properly be called a monopoly of tongues: and when it is considered that in consequence of that monopoly immense sums are given to performers, and the public are charged a high price for visiting the large theatres, it is high time that the system which has led to this monopoly should be done away with.[10]

A 'monopoly of tongues' that empowered a suspect group of outsiders, prevented free trade, and exercised a covert influence upon the thoughts and feelings of the nation was clearly in need of intervention.

Protest and public meetings

Action in theatre circles for some reform of the ancient systems under which they laboured had been on the cards since the beginning of the season, back in September 1831, when Leigh Hunt had been so excited by the triumphant crowds. Political excitement pervaded every public place. Throughout the Reform debates actual attendance at the theatres was low, while more important business summoned Londoners onto the streets, but when they did go to the play they responded violently to every political allusion.[11] On 8 October the Second Reform Bill was rejected by the House of Lords, sparking off countrywide rioting and marching and petitioning all over London. The feeling was that the King would not allow the Bill to be lost – so in the theatres people shouted their loyalty, to reinforce his reforming intentions. On 12 October the prima donna at Covent Garden, Mary Inverarity, was forced by the gallery to sing 'God Save the King', twice, in the midst of the opera. On 17 October the song was demanded at Drury Lane, while at Covent Garden that night Fanny Kemble played Belvidera in *Venice Preserved*, and was startled by the way the audience read the tragedy of political betrayal to refer to the current crisis.[12] On 20 October Parliament was prorogued; it returned on 6 December to vote the Bill a second reading, and to adjourn until the new year. London felt the people had won. Over Christmas the pantomimes, conventionally the site of topical reference, celebrated the triumph of Reform, and the theatre jokes about Shakespeare and Henri Martin's lions were coupled with criticism of the House of Lords and advocacy of the Bill, which were met with 'tremendous rounds of applause from the gods'.[13]

At this point managements, as opposed to players and audiences, finally made the connection between the state of the theatre and the state of the nation, and seized the moment to make their own points. On 19 December the solicitors Messrs Lowdham, Parke and Freeth, acting for the committee of proprietors of Drury Lane and for the acting proprietors of Covent Garden, sent a letter of warning to Benjamin Rayner at the New Strand Subscription Theatre, citing the recent judgement against Chapman, and asserting the illegality of putting on plays outside the Theatres Royal. Rayner reacted in the spirit of the times, and called a public meeting of managers and actors on Christmas Eve. An excited crowd turned up, and when Davidge urged practical measures they made him treasurer and began to collect subscriptions; Thomas Serle, an actor–dramatist working with him at the Coburg, was to head a committee drawing up a petition to Parliament.[14]

He brought the document to the next meeting on 3 January at the Freemasons' Tavern. Radical speeches were heard, the most extreme from Eugene Macarthy, a shadowy figure in the theatre world credited at this point as being 'of the Dublin Theatre'. He denounced the great theatres, 'converted into harems for rival Sultanas and theatrical Bashaws' and demanded the revocation of the patents, thundering 'displace but one stone from the temple of corruption, and all the reptiles who infest it cry out in alarm'. He was greeted by loud cheers, but the more pragmatic Davidge and Serle reminded the meeting that this would be a matter for the King, and they could only approach Parliament; Macarthy magnanimously agreed to print his speech rather than insisting they adopt it here. Excited theatre men put their names to the petition and subscribed their money to the fund; benefit nights were pledged by Sadler's Wells, the Pavilion, the Coburg, the Queen's, the Surrey and the little Orange Theatre, whose manager, fresh from his triumph in court, was cheered when he spoke up in this high company. Even the keeper of the crown jewels in the Tower of London promised a day's takings. It was remarked that management from two of the minors – the Olympic and the Adelphi, the nearest to the centre of power – were not present, and dark suggestions were made that they had been bought off; but actors from these houses spoke up for the workforce, and George Raymond and John Reeve led their colleagues in putting their money into the fund. Writers and other theatre artists were present to subscribe: Douglas Jerrold, whose hit *Black-ey'd Susan* was still making money at the Surrey and whose *Rent Day* was running at Drury Lane; the elderly Cumberland; the editor of the *Monthly Magazine* and Robert Cruikshank the stage portraitist put in their guinea each, and provincial managers sent in theirs. A man called Lewis – perhaps the Lewis who was manager of a tiny new theatre, the Pavilion in Portman Market – had collected thirty shillings penny by penny from very lowly sources, and handed it over to Davidge. Many actors signed and paid, and a rallying cry asking 'Englishmen! Lovers of the Drama!' to add their signatures at any of the illegitimate theatres was inserted in the *Morning Chronicle* of 25 January.[15]

The next meeting on 24 February was at the City of London Tavern, perhaps the most important political meeting-place in town; and not only the venue had shifted. It is clear from the reports that the theatre protest had suddenly been taken up by the politicians. Rayner was no longer present – he had opened

at the Strand on 26 January and immediately received a notice
to cease performing from the Lord Chamberlain's office, and he
may not have wished to offer such a public challenge by coming
to the meeting that the patentees would feel obliged to respond by
means of informers and process servers. But Davidge and Serle
were also less in evidence now; the chair was taken by Bulwer
Lytton, MP for St Ives, author of the newly published sensation in
the world of the novel, *Eugene Aram*. He and his friends, including
the MP Colonel Evans, were welcomed by the meeting as able
to 'rally all the forces of public opinion' to the cause, but in fact
they brought with them a new agenda, whose imposition caused
some friction.

Bulwer began the proceedings with a clever speech blending
self-aggrandisments about 'what we have done, and what we are
doing, in greater matters', popular phrases about liberty and
enlightenment and his personal version of the history of the
Drama, centred upon the 'literature of that great nation which
gave Congreve to comedy, and Shakespeare to the world'. He
wished, he said, that 'the Proprietors of the Minor Theatres . . .
will cheerfully co-operate with the Dramatic Poet in obtaining
that reward – that compensation – that inducement, which the
law denies him now'. He left it to a sidekick, the assistant editor of
the *New Monthly Magazine* Samuel Carter Hall, to give a name to
this Dramatic Poet. Hall was to become the model for Dickens's
Pecksniff,[16] so one may imagine the unction with which he informed the professional audience that Bulwer himself might have
been a dramatist and composed *Eugene Aram* as a tragedy if the
stage had been 'in a condition in which genius of a high order
could find its proper place'. Moncrieff, with barely contained annoyance that may have had something to do with the fact that his
own dramatisation of *Eugene Aram* had already been successfully
staged at the Surrey and even attended by the Duke of Sussex
(a pro-Reform peer), assured Bulwer and his supporters that the
minor theatres had no shortage of authors or dearth of dramatic
talent. But others were beguiled by the great men in their midst.
Macarthy, now representing himself as a mere member of the
public, was effusive about Bulwer's powers; and while Serle was
defensive about his drafting of the petition to avoid clouding the
issue with 'extraneous matters' such as dramatic copyright, he
put down Moncrieff's suggestion that the minor theatres had no

need of Shakespeares old or new, and at the end of the meeting a Mr Smith saw to it that the copyright issue was added to those resolved upon.[17]

Serle's identification of his own best interests might have been behind his stand at the next great meeting for the cause. It did not take place until 22 March, after the Lord Chamberlain had made a visit to the Coburg for Harriet Smithson's benefit. In the midst of rumours but without direct intervention, Rayner had continued with a full dramatic programme at the New Strand, and now he felt sufficiently well supported to host the meeting in his theatre. It was very well attended, and the platform party included four Radical MPs headed by Thomas Slingsby Duncombe. Bulwer and the Radical leader Sir Francis Burdett, who had agreed to take the chair, were detained in the House, working on support for the Reform Bill in that evening's debate; Duncombe, an exquisite whose immediate connection to the stage was that he was one of Vestris's string of lovers, and who was to be vice-chair of the eventual Select Committee, was apparently dispensable from the House of Commons meeting; he took the chair at the Strand. Other Radicals spoke, including the famous advocate of the working classes, Francis Place. An interesting range of Radical positions were voiced, mostly by lawyers: Charles Wilkins 'of the Temple' was very witty and erudite from an upper box; Mahon, also a lawyer, was entrusted with a motion to read out, and told the assembly in Latin that wild beast shows corrupted the populace of ancient Rome, and denounced the King as 'a sensual despot'. Eventually the ultra-Radical lawyer Edmonds tried to speak; the *Morning Chronicle* dubs him 'of Rotunda notoriety', and suggests he was not listened to. The speeches that are reported show an impassioned negotiation going on between extreme and ameliorist political positions. But before they were allowed their say Serle, standing in for Bulwer, had launched and set the tone of the occasion, taking his cue, now, from above. His speech is about the decline of the drama 'whose decline is generally the sign of the decline of the talent, industry, and intellect of the nation', and begins with 'the shortest possible historical view of the British stage' to demonstrate that Shakespeare is the model of free trade in theatricals on which their case should be based. He was greeted with 'loud applause' and stood down on the line 'those who contributed to the amusement of the public, should not be allowed to remain the only slaves' to 'loud and long-continued cheers'. Serle was to become one of the circle patronised by Bulwer, working as writer and stage-manager with Macready to recapture the national stage for the middle-class voice. Colonel Jones spoke next and continued as best he could the literary, historicist discourse set up, beginning with the observation that 'The Drama had always been a distinguished feature in history. The Greeks and Romans gave encouragement to it' and so too does France; it behoved Englishmen to do the same. After that a disappointed dramatist rejected by management at a minor was hissed, and then the meeting grew ever more Radical and self-congratulatory; the cause had become a national one, and its representative was the dramatic poet. It remained to be seen who, besides Shakespeare, would come forward to fill that role.[18] Meanwhile the new season in the theatres began, Rayner confining himself to hornpipe-dancing and fireworks, but Tottenham Street defiantly opting for *Jane Shore* and *A School For Scandal*; and the petitions for freedom and a copyright act were sent to the House of Commons.

Bulwer Lytton and the House of Commons

When Parliament returned on 7 May 1832, it was to a sensational new turn in the drama of Reform. The Lords Committee attacked the Bill, Prime Minister Grey requested that the King create new peers to pass it, and, when he demurred, resigned. The next public meeting of the citizens of Westminster chaired by Sir Francis Burdett was a response to this crisis in what had seemed an inevitable progress towards freedom. No alternative prime minster could be found, however, and on 15 May Grey was asked to resume his position. The theatres were very thinly attended during this astonishing series of real-life events; a report in the *Morning Chronicle* of 15 May pointed up the substitution of Parliament for the theatre by metaphorically casting all the Members in roles from the legitimate repertory. On 17 May King William told the House of Lords to drop their opposition to the Bill, and the crisis was over. Drury Lane announced for that night a bill that included the 'republican' opera *Masaniello* and Macready in *Alfred*, a new historical drama of obvious relevance to the rhetoric of the rights and liberties of Englishmen and the rejection of 'the Norman yoke' – the dominance of an imported aristocracy. It was generally thought that the King's vacillation at this crisis was caused by the aristocratic anti-Reform attitudes of Queen Adelaide, and the theatres had an upsurge of misogyny, condemning petticoat influence. On 11 June at the Surrey, for example, *Andreas Hofer*, a republican drama, included 'a round lecture upon the mischievous tendency of female interference in matters of government' which the audience was 'by no means backward' in applying.[19]

As soon as a semblance of normal business resumed in the House of Commons, the theatrical petitions were presented. Bulwer offered that of the 'noblemen, gentlemen, traders and others of London' on 22 May. He was supported by a petition from Westminster presented by Sir Francis Burdett, one from Clerkenwell presented by Hume, from Lambeth by W. Brougham, and from the City by Alderman Waithmann. Counter-petitions from the patentees were also presented.[20] On 31 May Bulwer moved for a Select Committee. His speech spelt out his concern in the matter quite clearly: he wished firstly to 'inquir[e] into the State of the Laws affecting Dramatic Literature', and only secondly to consider 'the performance of the Drama'. He went on to set out the issues with which the Committee should concern itself. The law forbidding unregulated theatrical performance had been instituted in the first place, he said, not so much to suppress indecent performances as for the sake of protecting the drama. But the 'march of intellect' – a Reformist phrase of which he was fond – had already done away with all indecency on stage, and the patent monopolies had by no means promoted great writing over the last fifteen years – else 'where are the immortal tragedies, where are the chaste and brilliant comedies?' he demanded, to supporting cheers. The main point launched he turned to more practical matters, and stressed the need for theatres to be smaller but more numerous and widespread, because of the inconvenience of the area of Covent Garden for middle-class Londoners who lived elsewhere, and the damage done to dramatic writing by the size of the two great theatres, fit for nothing but spectacle. He quoted Sir Walter Scott's opinion that the more theatres the public were prepared to support the more chance there was of excellence in playwriting manifesting itself; and in his peroration returned to what was for him the most exciting prospect: the protection of dramatic copyright.[21]

The manifest tendency of Bulwer's speech is to touch on popular issues in support of his concern for the future writers of great plays. He presented this concern as to do with trade, in that proper markets lead to due payments, and to workmanship being encouraged by proper reward. Much more importantly an abstraction or spiritualisation of the notion of the rights of property allowed him to suggest the high moral and spiritual status of the artist, his right to eminence through his unique qualities of genius. He thus strove to constitute a new idea of social worth, including the writer within the idea of the gentleman, placing a high value on expertise and industry, and suggesting that their proper reward is wealth and station. Charles Wetherell, one of the leading opponents of Reform, attacked this novel claim to importance through expertise and progress through market forces as essentially a vulgar attack upon the prerogatives of the Crown, expressing supercilious amazement at the notion that the encouragement of *more* of anything – whether plays, theatres or audiences – could possibly mean they would be improved. Most of those who supported Bulwer made a simple connection to the main issues of the day, the promotion of free trade and the abolition of privilege. Others were more interested in the issue of public morality, which he had handled somewhat dismissively as safely left in the hands of dramatic authors. But this was a particularly important moment of shifting ground in the construction of social identities and therefore of moral definitions and of sexualities, and the theatres were far more deeply implicated in that discourse than Bulwer here allowed. His reassuring conviction that the intellectual spirit of the age would prevent indecency on stage was certainly not shared by the representatives of the Church, from the Bishop of London down to the gentleman in charge of the Whitechapel Road Sunday School, who had all publicly pronounced that the theatre was fatally corrupting. In the meetings of the minor managements, considered above, the only invocation of sexual morality was in connection with the habits and demands of the high-born patrons of actresses, singers and dancers; for this emphasis on the perils of the performer's lot Bulwer had substituted a concern for the self-expression of the author; but exchanges in the House show that there denunciation of sexual laxity at the theatres had little to do with words on a page, or even delivered from a stage. John Campbell, the future Lord Chancellor, used Wetherall's reactionary remarks as another opportunity (amongst many) to discredit the anti-Reformers by personal attack. The *Morning Chronicle* reported his speech thus:

The law was violated night after night. Every person felt the necessity of such amusements. Even the Honourable and Learned Member for Boroughbridge, as soon as he had recovered from his extraordinary fatigues on behalf of the Reform Bill [a laugh], feeling the necessity of some relaxation, would probably go to the Olympic [a laugh]; he would go to Madame Vestris in order to recruit himself [much laughter]; and as he was sure that Hon. and Learned Member would never sanction anything which ought to be put down by law, he anticipated that they would have even his vote. There was much objection to the great theatres, also, on the score of immorality. It was impossible to take a modest woman there, without the danger that something might occur [laughter]. Scenes took place, night after night, at our theatres, which were never exhibited at the theatres of Paris, Naples, or any other city on the Continent [hear!] It was essential that the law should be reconsidered, and that public morals should be efficiently protected.[22]

There is an uneasy movement here from suggestive jokes at the expense of the unfashionable and elderly Wetherall, the effect of which depends upon the knowing and sympathetic response of the Members to ideas about Vestris and her theatre as a sexual icon, to righteous denunciation of prostitution in the lobbies of the Theatres Royal. The transition is difficult, so that the laughter recorded here appears to be at the expense of the 'modest woman', but by the end of the next sentence the House has caught up, and moved from sophisticated sniggers to righteous denunciation of unEnglish immorality – though whether this is on stage or off is by now entirely obscure. This issue around the consumption/involvement of women in the theatre, and the morality of the performance space, was to prove a persistent undertone in the ensuing negotiations.

Bulwer got his Select Committee, and set its agenda: the introduction of copyright and the removal of censorship of plays, to make the stage safe for writers; the disestablishment of the patents, and the licensing of more Metropolitan theatres permitted to stage plays of all kinds, so as to create more, smaller stages, with fewer opportunities for lavish spectacle to outweigh serious drama; and better regulation and management to render the auditoria safer places to which to bring middle-class families – to listen to serious drama. Here indeed was theatrical Reform. In the event, two parliamentary Bills were formulated in the following year to put in place the reforms he urged, but only one of them, that establishing Dramatic Copyright, passed into law; the changes to the licensing of theatre spaces had to wait another ten years, until 1843. In the decade that followed his 1832 bridgehead the ideological and material battles of the quarter-century for control of theatre space continued and came to a head.[23] Most of their ways and means were canvassed at the hearings of the Select Committee; arguably the aspect of their work that had the longest-lasting effects in British Theatre was the capturing of the definition of theatre and theatre history for the cause of Bulwer's vision of the stage.

The Select Committee and the definition
of theatre history

The Select Committee Appointed to Inquire into the Laws Affecting Dramatic Literature was concerned to establish 'the state of the laws affecting the interests and exhibition of the Drama'.[24] This formulation is based on the main concerns voiced in the petitions laid before Parliament, about the licensing system and the suppression of competition; but it does not fully represent the agenda that Lytton and his Committee pursued. That their real interest was in the reformation of London theatre to admit of their own voices is quite clear from their lines of questioning: they return again and again to the issue of the size of the patent theatres – auditoria where, they fear, serious drama of an intimate modern kind could not be properly heard; to the remuneration of all concerned, especially the excessive charges of the Lord Chamberlain's office that discourage new plays, and the difficulties authors have in obtaining a professional level of remuneration; to the cultivation of good taste – for serious plays and realistic acting – in the new audiences across the metropolis; and to the control of the prestigious patent houses by the aristocratic patrons and rentiers, which prevents experimentation with new dramatic forms, and the mounting of appropriate productions of the national dramatic heritage to which new dramatists will eventually contribute their own masterpieces.

The Committee hearings began, however, by addressing the legal issues, and used that inquiry to establish one of its most powerful weapons for appropriating the theatre: the deployment of history. It asked its first witnesses about their understanding of the tangled skein of theatrical legislation stretching back to Charles II's Patent of 1660, which granted to Davenant and Killigrew the right to establish theatrical companies in London. This historical inquiry was not simply pragmatic. A wider and more significant history was sought, as a means of understanding the present situation but also, more significantly, in order to project an ideal state of affairs to which such a story might tend, towards which it might, indeed, be directed by the Committee. Nineteenth-century European thought has as one important foundation a passion for history, which 'becomes both an epistemological and an ontological principle, the determining condition of life and therefore of all knowledge'.[25] Hegel's *Philosophy of History* appeared in 1830–1, Comte began to publish *Cours de la Philosophie Positive* in 1830, and these texts are the culminating expression of a profound shift, identified by Hayden White, away from the pessimism and irony of Enlightenment rationalist thought towards 'the enthusiasm for historical studies which was characteristic' of the early nineteenth century and established its 'self-confident tone'. This shift led to 'sustained debate over historical theory and . . . the consistent production of massive narrative accounts of past cultures and societies'.[26] On the micro-level of the London stage such a movement was also afoot; and the Committee, chaired by the Radicals Bulwer Lytton and Thomas Duncombe, was deeply interested not only in establishing and appropriating the story of the British theatre to date but also in the ways in which it might now approach the telos embodied by their cause, the cause of Reform: they wished to submit the theatre, as an important part of the new, modern cultural life, to 'the fair experiment of Public support'.[27] For this purpose, they would uncover and retell the history.

The witnesses they called in the first two days of their inquiry, 13 and 15 June 1832, were four: Thomas Baucott Mash, Esq., Comptroller of the Lord Chamberlain's Office and thus the representative of the current legal authority over the theatre;

Mr James Winston, 'connected for several years with various theatres', the stage-manager at the Haymarket 'for 15 or 16 years
and at Drury Lane seven' (S.C.Q. 189);[28] Mr John Payne Collier,
who 'officiated once as licenser' 'in August and September last'
(S.C.Q. 242 and 3) and Mr William Dunn, treasurer and secretary to the committee of management at Drury Lane. Mash's
evidence, chiefly about the established practice of licensing plays,
the periods of theatre opening, the patents themselves, and the
fees paid to his office, is recorded in eight and a half pages of the
Report. Winston was not summoned as a historian, and having
no access to the documentation from which other witnesses
quoted, he was not asked nor able to answer larger historical
questions. His responses are about his opinion on the extent of
the rights and responsibilities of the Lord Chamberlain's Office,
and occupy only two and a half pages; William Dunn's cover four
pages. Both these witnesses, particularly Dunn, were expected to
know about the law as it had actually affected their work, and they
answered with working definitions and instances from their experience. But the evidence on 13 June of John Payne Collier, the
least qualified witness in terms of practical involvement with the
London stage, occupies over sixteen pages of the Report, and he
returned again to speak on 18 June. His real qualification as a
witness is not recorded in the Minutes of evidence: he appeared
before the Committee as the author of *The History of English
Dramatic Poetry to the Time of Shakespeare; and Annals of the Stage
to the Restoration*, which was published by the important house
of John Murray in 1831. The three volumes were dedicated to
the Lord Chamberlain, the Duke of Devonshire, who had given
Collier a present of £100 for this honour and for his guidance
and advice, and entrusted him with the care and augmentation
of his dramatic library. Collier had been examiner of plays for
barely a couple of months only because Devonshire had failed to
persuade the incumbent office-holder, George Colman, to stand
down to make way for his valued protégé.[29]

   The Committee was interested, as was everybody in 1832, in
making history, and perhaps, therefore, in employing historians
to help it with this task. Their greater interest in Collier, as opposed to the various interested parties in the disputed arena of
modern theatre, is indicative of where they placed their emphasis
in their advisory and legislative duties. Collier was at this time

'at the height of his fame as a literary historian'.[30] His authoritative history of the stage is modestly called 'annals', but it is not in any way a development of the earlier theatre historiographical tradition. The volumes comprise one of the compendious cultural surveys that were the result of the historiographical self-confidence of his age. Collier begins with a clearly ideological statement, opening the very specific theory of teleological development which the three volumes are intended to amplify and prove:

No country of Europe, since the revival of letters, has been able to produce any notice of theatrical performance of so early a date as England* . . .

*The plays of Roswitha, a nun of Gandersheim, in Lower Saxony, who wrote at the close of the tenth century, and which are mentioned in a note by the Editor of the last edition of Warton's Hist. Eng. Poet.; ii 68, were not represented.

The scholarly exposition of the superiority of England is launched, and continues into nice questions of Warton's interpretation of Stow's translation from William Fitzstephen; and the footnote's assertion – for it is no more – that Hroswitha's work, the work of a Catholic female living in Lower Saxony, *does not count* is buried under the weight of Latin quoted on the first page.[31]

Collier's *History*, like his evidence to the Committee, is conspicuously and insistently documentary in its derivation and underpinnings. A country must be 'able to produce' a 'notice' in order to claim an earlier theatre than that of Great Britain. His work had been on the acquisition, rediscovery and interpretation of such 'notices'. Unlike the other witnesses, called to give an account of themselves and their proceedings, in some cases in an adversarial atmosphere of some hostility and under cross-examination, Collier was able to come briefed and therefore prepared with answers.[32] When he returned on 18 June it was at his own request, because he had given two answers in the last session that he wished to correct: 'the largest theatre in the time of Shakespeare' was not '45 feet [13.7 m] square within', as he had suggested from memory, but 55 feet (16.8 m) square; and having looked at papers which he said 'I have in my hands' – he had purchased the huge Larpent collection of plays and other documents, for his own use[33] – he was now in a position to tell the committee the exact sums that Mr Larpent had received as examiner of plays in the years 1820–4 (S.C.Q. 549, 550). Larpent's profits were germane to the Committee's deliberations, and in a less direct way the size of theatres in Shakespeare's time was also relevant information; but the difference between 45 and 55 feet (13.7 and 16.8 m) square is important only as proof of the authenticity, reliability and precision of Collier's knowledge and expertise. The importance of such authentication in the historiographic tradition to which Collier belongs is evident on every page of his *History*; it was so important, indeed, that Collier was later discovered to have altered, forged and fabricated documents where none could be found to substantiate his (even more important) arguments.

John Payne Collier and the invocation of Shakespeare

In putting their faith in the history of John Payne Collier rather than of Winston, whom they did at least see, or of the Rev. John Genest, of whom they had probably never heard, the Committee were following their own agenda in seeking confirmation of their opinions about the decline of the drama and its roots in the corruption of the modern stage. The history they required had been summarised at the meeting held in 'Mr Rayner's Theatre in the Strand' – the meeting at which the parliamentarians took over the movement, described above. Serle's statement of the cause began with

the shortest possible historical view of the British Stage. I shall show you that, in the time of Shakespeare, when the population and extent of London was scarcely one-fifth of what it is at present, there were seventeen theatres, each possessing equal rights . . . By this open competition both actors and authors realized fortunes . . . our glorious Shakespeare retired at comparatively an early age to his native town to enjoy . . . the comforts and happiness with which his merits had been rewarded . . . Thus stood the stage in its high and palmy state . . . Upon the restoration of Charles it was thought necessary to raise the drama from its ashes, to collect its scattered materials, which had been thrown all over England . . . from the exercise of a most arbitrary power, patents were created for services which I need not name. Thus those monopolies commenced, and they have proceeded in a manner worthy of their origin; they began in infamy and ended in treachery [loud applause].

So Shakespeare was a free-trader, and retired rich; the patent houses are founded upon corrupt practices – abolish the patents and seventeen theatres will again enrich the actors and, especially, the dramatists of today. Lytton, in introducing the petitions, had made a similar point to the House of Commons, but for that audience he did not need to disguise the distinction, the opposition that was crucially important for him, between the profits of the theatres and those of writer:

If Shakespeare himself were now living – if Shakespeare himself were to publish a volume of plays, they might be acted every night all over the kingdom – they might bring thousands to actors, and ten thousands to managers – and Shakespeare himself, the producer of all, might be starving in a garret.[34]

By this date Shakespeare had already become 'the centre of English literary culture', indeed 'the paradigmatic figure of literary authority';[35] and this is the position he occupied in Bulwer's argument, and in Collier's account of the stage. In Shakespearean scholarship too there was a contentious eighteenth-century tradition which is relevant to the politics of theatre history in the nineteenth century. Unsurprisingly, this genealogy is not, like that of the tribal scribes, unknown to modern scholarship; it is the subject not only of continuous development, but also of much recent scrutiny and debate. Here, indeed, is the history of the theatre as told by the victors in the battle for the stage.

Collier's *History* begins with the early history of the British stage, in much more detail than the paragraphs from Dodsley borrowed by the scribal volumes, and proceeds with 'annals' throughout the first volume, only reaching the accession of Charles I; the annals end in volume 2 with Davenant's *Siege of Rhodes*. He then embarks upon 'the history of Dramatic Poetry' in which for over 625 pages he considers literary developments; after which, at the end of volume 3, he appends 'an account of the old theatres of London'. The plays are clearly the most important matter, but they are bolstered by his scholarly exposition of theatre history in two forms – neither of which, however, is mere anecdote. Confining his annals to the period before 1600

has great advantages. He avoids engagement with the received
text of the hacks and tribal scribes who have already constructed
the more recent period. His work is squarely centred upon the
plays of Shakespeare, rather than the modern stage. He does
enter into debate, but not with prompters and minor actors –
rather, with the leading scholars of the previous generation:
'[w]hen I commenced my researches, nearly twenty years ago,
I was discouraged on all hands by those who imagined that Malone, Steevens, Reed, and Chalmers had exhausted the subject'
(preface, vii). His claim to supersede these august authorities –
gentlemen, members of the Royal Society, editors of Shakespeare published by the dynastic house of Tonson – is that of the
modern documentary historian: he has, he says, 'found many
valuable original documents' in the State Paper Department,
the Privy Council Office, the Chapter-House Westminster –
all sources hitherto neglected – and even in the British Library,
where no one had looked carefully enough.

The scholarly tradition Collier invokes centres upon Shakespeare. This is not the place for a protracted exposition of the central position in anglophone culture occupied by Shakespeare, nor
of the twentieth-century disputes within Shakespearean scholarship; but the eighteenth-century roots of the Shakespeare phenomenon are bound up with the establishment of modern theatre history as a whole. The connection begins with Alexander
Pope's edition of the plays in 1711. Until this expensive book
appeared the surviving Shakespearean texts were no more than
part of the raw materials available for playhouse use and adaptation, along with the work of other old stage writers. Pope laid
claim to Shakespeare as an author, and established a text of his
work by wholesale excisions and extensive emendation, fitting
the plays into the polite and gentlemanly diction of modern poetry. In his introductory matter he constructed the poet himself
to fit this conception. His life of Shakespeare made him appear as
a natural, untutored genius, and all the material in the published
work that did not fit the mould was attributed to the trashy, vulgar or sophisticated interpolations of the actors. The assertion
of Pope and the gentlemanly tradition of editors that followed
him was that to understand his work aright, and to fit it for the
public cultural domain, one needed simply a refined taste free
of all low, interested professionalism, whether of the stage or

the pen. This opening salvo provoked responses from the two groups who felt themselves attacked: a pamphlet response defending the actors, from 'a strolling player', and a defence of professional expertise from Lewis Theobald, who was both a writer for the theatre and a professional scholar. He dedicated his *Shakespeare Restored*, published in 1726, to the theatre entrepreneur John Rich, with whom he had worked on pantomimes and harlequinades.

Successive editors handed down as their *textus receptus* both the texts of the plays, with more emendations to suit their personal taste, and the anecdotal history of Shakespeare's personal life, beginning with his conviction for poaching deer, that set him up as a wild child of nature and so justified their correcting hands. War between these gentleman editors, relying on taste alone, and the professional scholars not published by Tonson, who resorted to bibliography and philology to substantiate their corrections to the texts, continued for many decades, but the opposition between sublime poetry and the low players became a binary accepted by both sides, pitting Shakespeare against 'harlequin' – the low spectacle of the stage. The ultimate stage professional David Garrick, however, recaptured the idea of the Bard by a brilliant manoeuvre. Throughout his career he identified himself with Shakespeare in the public mind, using the notion of the sublime poet to help him project an image of himself as a member of the upper gentry, full of domestic virtue, as distant as possible from the notion of the dissolute and disreputable player. He reclaimed Shakespeare *for* the stage – or at least for himself as an actor – by making the stage the home of Shakespeare, and Shakespeare the mirror of mercantile domesticity. The ironic dimension of his publicity stunts like the Shakespeare Jubilee was, of course, that they were pure manifestations of 'harlequin', stage spectacles that did not necessarily include the actual dramas of their iconic hero at all, and certainly did little to free them of theatrical adaptation and interpolation, at which Garrick was a master.[36]

With the end of the eighteenth century and the ensuing cultural upheavals, appropriations of Shakespeare became ever more complex and urgent. The 'astonishing circumstance' of revolution in France made a British national bard, exemplifying British cultural superiority, a major discursive weapon, whatever side of the debate about democracy one took. Both radicals and reactionaries, however, built their claims to the Bard on an exclusion of the claim of the stage. The Shakespeareanism of Romantic poets and critics is pervasive and powerful, and was a major strand in their construction of a British identity under pressure from the new ideologies; famously, Lamb, Hazlitt and Coleridge constructed Shakespeare as a dramatist most deeply enjoyed as one enjoyed modern poetry – in private reading, in the closet. In 1790 Edward Malone, the inheritor of the gentlemanly tradition of editing, made a major break from its practices, in the interests of 'authenticity' – a revolutionary virtue, but one which could be turned to the support of British culture. His principles not only became the foundation of modern editorial beliefs but also established the dogmas of scholarly theatre history. In his work 'the authentic text pre-empted the received text; actual usage in Shakespeare's time superseded standards of correctness contemporary with the editor'; and, crucially for theatre history, 'factual accounts discredited traditional anecdotes' in the telling of Shakespeare's story.[37] He included a 'historical account of the English stage' in his volumes, and added to it considerably in successive editions, always building on Steevens and contemporary Shakespearean debates, but also substantiating his additions to the factual account from the stores of documents that came into his hands. His attitude to the theatre is explicit, and marks no change from that of his predecessors. His interest in the practices of the Elizabethan stage includes the understanding that it was customary to revise the plays of others: this enables him in reviewing *Titus Andronicus* and *Pericles* to free Shakespeare of the 'miserable trash' foisted upon him in the playhouse. In his history of the stage he notes

the entertainment in the middle of the reign of Elizabeth was diversified, and the populace diverted, by vaulting, tumbling, slight of hand, and morrice-dancing; and in the time of Shakespeare, by the extemporaneous buffoonery of the Clown, whenever he chose to solicit the attention of the audience; by singing and dancing between the acts, and either a song or the metrical jig . . . at the end of the piece; a mixture not more heterogeneous than that with which we are now daily presented, a tragedy and a farce.

Heterogeneity and long bills are calculated for the amusement of 'gaping spectators'. He greets the advent of Shakespeare as the moment when 'the great luminary of the dramatick world blazed out' to extinguish the 'contemptible and few' works that went before, and become 'the boast and admiration of his countrymen'.[38]

This is the work to which Collier turns as the illustrious foundation for his own highly authentic, better-documented, more rigorous account. It is a theatre history at the service of the dramatist's text, rejecting the *textus receptus* of theatre lore along with that of the plays. Understanding the problem it was convened to solve as 'the Decline of the Drama', it was to Collier that the Select Committee turned to help them appropriate the stage for the purposes of Reform, free trade and the voice of the new middle-class intelligentsia. The history he gave them is a history that is, at its very basis, hostile to its own subject: the traffic of the stage.

Conclusions: Bulwer Lytton's victory and the establishment of Modernist binary theatre history

The Committee therefore had, as the foundation to its deliberations, a history explicitly committed to criteria of authenticity and textual purity, that valued the multiplication of intimate small stages as serving the needs of new groups of educated people and therefore provoking the genius of new writers, based upon their pseudo-Shakespearean ideal of a writer's theatre in which women neither wrote nor performed, and where popular entertainment was the enemy of the verbal perfection of the text and could be blamed for the lamentable gaps between literary perfection and the adulterated scripts of performance. It interrogated managers, investors, performers, dramatists, functionaries of the Lord Chamberlain and volunteering members of the public – all men – and asked them all leading questions revolving round the same few issues that arose from this perspective. These were variously articulated depending, in the main, upon the expected position of each man they addressed. Witnesses who benefited from the current arrangements were subjected to hostile interrogations about those aspects of the present system which ran counter to ideas of free trade, such as the emoluments of the investors in the patent houses and of the examiner of plays, and the abused privileges of the legitimate managements. The Committee repeatedly wondered how vested financial interests should be satisfied, and what claims were strong enough to stand in the way of progress, linking this with questions about public morals, fair and unfair competition, the market in entertainment and how it was to be satisfied and encouraged to improve. Ambiguous, illogical and unfair custom and practice was repeatedly exposed; the objective in questioning often seems to have been to provoke an appeal to precedent and tradition, and then to reveal how self-interested and indefensible such precedents were. On the other hand, witnesses who might be supposed to have progressive ideas and whose self-interest would lie in change were invited to describe the bad effects of the present system, its failure to support morality and political decency on stage and in the theatre buildings and districts, and to agree that change was essential for the encouragement of 'good' new plays and the education of public taste for them through reform of licensing. The Committee was particularly pertinacious in trying to get professionals to condemn the large size of the patent theatres, and to endorse their own reading of its significance – that large theatres encouraged spectacular melodrama, rant and poor acting, and vitiated public taste, and that if the minor theatres were permitted to stage good plays, then cheaper prices, intimate dramas and less expense in smaller spaces would revive the popularity of theatre-going and enable the stage to contribute to public education. They were not well supported in this – minor actors were sceptical about a widespread taste for straight Shakespeare south of the river, and those who appeared under the patent managements were understandably unwilling to profess themselves unable to act effectively in the cavernous spaces of Drury Lane or Covent Garden.

But the committee was not to be put off. It painted a picture of decline and decay, in which the provincial nurseries of talent had disappeared, able writers had deserted to other, less restricted and better-paid forms, audiences in the minor theatres had no taste or education and the patent houses had no audiences, and sexual immorality, illegal sleight of hand and selfish complacency dominated management. Its conclusions began with the statement that the decline, both of the 'Literature of the Stage' and 'the taste of the public for Theatrical Performances', was 'generally conceded'. Its proposals were intended to address the remediable causes of this decline, which it identified as 'the uncertain administration of the Laws, the slender encouragement afforded to Literary Talent to devote its labours to the Stage, and the want of better legal regulation as regards the number and distribution of Theatres'. Lytton's agenda was proven, agreed and executed: his Committee recommended Parliament to deliver the theatre from the hands of contending vested interests, the rival financial claims of old and new managers, investors and professionals, into the control of 'fair competition' and, especially, of dramatic authors, who were to be relieved of 'indefensible hardship and injustice' by providing them with 'a greater variety of Theatres at which to present, or for which to adapt, their Plays, and a greater security in the profits derived from their success'.[39] Of the two Bills brought in to effect this rescue, that in favour of Dramatic Copyright was passed, but soon rendered ineffective; that on the Regulation of the Theatres was defeated in the Lords by the vested interests it sought to dispossess, and Lytton's theatrical supporters spent the next ten years working to achieve the end of the Radical appropriation of the stage without its help; when it was passed, in 1843, they were well on their way to victory.

From this point onwards, therefore, the theatre was increasingly appropriated to the middle-class voice in Britain, and the received theatre history was written to suit that project. The binaries discussed at the beginning of this introduction were established: it was understood that Shakespeare, and writers for the theatre who followed his literary banner, were ill-served by harlequin – the actors and the managers. Other histories were defeated or discredited. Winston did not publish his work, Genest was ignored; anecdote, inherited wisdom, professional interest in the box office – all the material and emotional heritage of the stage – was viewed merely as the context which helped (or more often hindered) the realisation of the written dramatic text. As I hope to suggest, other histories survived and survive, but their status has been suspect throughout the Modernist period.

The case studies that follow will therefore be a self-conscious attempt to read nineteenth-century theatre history in post-Modern ways, while calling upon pre-Modern techniques. I want to explore how far the kinds of history valued by theatre professionals in the past and still, in some cases, important to them today, can offer us a different academic understanding of the development of entertainment in Britain. The first study takes up the importance of anecdote in personal and professional histories, and seeks a particularly theatrical dimension of such storytelling in the art of mimicry. The second turns to the discursive management of the binary between art and entertainment, the setting up of an idea of 'the popular' with which to control and incorporate the ancient people's theatres of the market and the fair. The final study challenges received academic history with genealogy, taken in its literal sense as the histories of families. This is an unfashionable 'history from below' which is, I argue, especially significant to theatre professionals. It is moreover an approach that offers some purchase on the otherwise hidden histories of women in nineteenth-century theatre.

Part II

Case studies

5   Anecdote and mimicry as history

Introduction: reading biographies

In this study I want to consider what alternative possibilities there are for accessing and retelling the history of the period from 1790 to 1832 in the British theatre, and to begin upon such an alternative account. The printed materials I revisit in this chapter are works of memoir, biography and anecdote, the descendants of the eighteenth-century scribal compilations discussed in chapter 2. They have often been trawled for 'factual' information that can be extracted and corroborated from other documentary sources, in the approved manner that makes them into evidence that can be trusted;[1] but they have not often been read for what their writers or their subjects seem to stress, or what their contemporary readership might have understood of theatre history from them. They are in the tradition of a kind of popular publication that is still created in large quantities and unwillingly used, but never completely trusted, by academic theatre historians. Jocular, nostalgic or admiring memoirs about and by performers, TV series about 'Heroes of Comedy' or the 'Best of British' entertainers (both titles that were made and screened in Britain in the late 1990s), gossip in fanzines and behind-the-scenes features in listings magazines tend not to be regarded by historians[2] as the authentic histories of the profession, but rather as publicity material and media hype that forms a distorting background noise to real research. In the early nineteenth century there was already an eager readership for a range of published books and papers containing information, good stories about the theatre, or private details about individuals great and small.

Such works appeared at several levels of respectability, in publishing terms. The rapid increase in ephemeral publication included a succession of theatrical journals which appeared monthly (*The Monthly Mirror*, *The Theatrical Inquisitor*) or more often, up to five or six times a week (*Theatrical Gazette*) as penny or twopenny single folded sheets. Some offered the latest listings and reviews for performances at the London theatres together with anecdotes old or new that filled the bottom of a column;[3] others, like the series called *Oxberry's Dramatic Biography and Histrionic Anecdotes*[4] placed a memoir or biography of a performer past or present on their front pages and filled out a single printer's sheet (folding down to sixteen sides of print, in small octavo) with brief comments and items of theatre gossip. Catherine Oxberry was the 'proprietor' of this successful series. She claims[5] to be compiling and editing materials left by her actor husband on his untimely death, and says she can write more frankly than he could have done, inhibited as he was by friendship with the subjects of his reports; she also enlisted the help of other journalists and writers around the theatres, eventually marrying one of them, Leman Thomas Rede, and continuing to publish the paper with his aid.[6] The first number, 1 January 1825, sets the pattern for them all: it features a portrait and an eight-page life of Edmund Kean, full of tart asides and critical personal remarks apparently drawn from intimate acquaintance. This is followed by a note about the multiple authorship of *The Beggar's Opera*, a short but heated and knowing diatribe about current theatrical misman-agement, an 'exact copy of an play bill in Garrick's time', and a series of more or less funny and/or risqué puns and ripostes, ascribed to theatrical luminaries from Tate Wilkinson to the Margravine of Anspach. To judge from the length of *Oxberry*'s run and the unauthorised continuation that it generated, this was a successful format.

At the other extreme in the hierarchy of publication were the weighty biographies of leading players, which appeared in in-creasing numbers, often from prolific publishers like Colburn and Bentley. James Boaden, a gothic dramatist of the turn of the century who had then moved to journalism and the editorship of a weekly newspaper, *The Oracle*, chose to embody his history of the stage from Garrick 'to the present period' in the lives of John Kemble, Sarah Siddons and Dorothy Jordan, published in 1825, 1827 and 1831, and added in that year an edition of Garrick's personal letters. He was confident about the importance to be attached both to his subjects and to his own memories with which he interlarded their stories: his lavishly published biographies are pompously dedicated to the King, claim Colley Cibber as their model and predecessor, refer repeatedly to Capell, Steevens and the other editors and scholars of Shakespeare; and at every turn he presents himself ('one like myself, so intimately acquainted with . . . the whole family of Kemble')[7] and his personal qualifications as observer, friend and biographer centre stage. Boaden sets himself up as an important writer, for serious readers in their leisure hours; he self-consciously offers the last word on his '*not uninteresting*' subject for Royal patronage and approval.[8]

Theatrical autobiography: whose story?

Theatre people themselves sought to shape their own lives and relate them to the history of their calling in published autobiographies. But most of these are mediated to us through one or more intervening layers: few early nineteenth-century performers left written accounts unproblematically recording their own careers and asserting their position in public life. Thomas Dibdin, born into the theatre, a writer, manager, pantomime-arranger and actor, who is credited with hundreds of plays and thousands of songs, and so may be trusted to have written his own *Reminiscences*, published them with Colburn in 1827. He is the exception, and his picture of the theatre of his day from the point of view of the creative entrepreneur with deep roots in the theatre world is relatively easy to accept at face value. Fanny Kemble, on the other hand, from a much more exalted family within the theatre world, also wrote a great deal, having ambitions as an author from a very young age, but she used her hoarded letters and diaries to compose a careful picture of herself in her early years which she did not publish until 1878. Her *Record of a Girlhood* is the story of a girl caught up, more or less against her will, in the Regency theatre; and this construction is seen through more than forty years of Victoria's reign.[9] Some writers around the theatres engaged in the self-conscious processing and exhibiting of their own lives: the prolific dramatist Frederick Reynolds, for example, published his *Life and Times* with Colburn in 1826 and then in 1831 turned them into a cheap novel called *A Playwright's Adventures*.

But most early nineteenth-century performers did not have the confidence to publish their own lives, even if they did write something down. Instead, others wrote for/about them. Theodore Hook, for example, an indolent but extremely able gentleman who wrote for the stage to finance a fast London life-style, had the self-confidence to ghost the extensive memoirs of the singer Michael Kelly and was supposedly the chosen biographer of Elliston, but died before he got round to that task.[10] His racy novels often fictionalise adventures that he shared with his friends from the theatre. In his work the interlocking of enacted and related fictions on and off the stage and in print formed a web of self-creation and display. The leading comedian Charles Mathews was one of his playmates, and remained a close friend until Hook picked up 'some traditional accounts' of strolling players and worked them into a story which Mathews conceived as an insult to himself and his *esprit de corps* with all other actors, however lowly. His offence lasted for two years, and was not mended, according to Charles's wife Anne Mathews, until Hook wrote assuring the actor that he had not meant to insult 'any man in your sphere or station'.[11] The sensitivity of the actor shows up the social divide between the writer, who is a gentleman amusing himself in mixed company, and the paid performer who is at any moment liable to find himself not the coadjutant but merely the instrument of that amusement. In his letters home, Charles often records invitations to the social occasions of the great – but also notes that he was usually required to 'tumble' for his dinner. Many actors hated to be 'lionised' by society hostesses, and some – Kean is the obvious example – refused to go into the society that they felt only wanted them as playthings, inviting them into their houses but maintaining an invisible class barrier around the performer even as they satisfied their curiosity about him. The situation was, of course, far worse for women.

Charles Mathews began to write down his own life story just before he died in 1835, and his wife Anne incorporated his account into her long book, *Memoirs of Charles Mathews, Comedian* which Bentley published in 1838–9. There are several layers of interest in this creation: Mathews is constructed for the reader by his wife, who incorporates his brief written work and many letters but also draws upon stories he told her, anecdotes of incidents that made up both his private life and his performances;

she simultaneously tells her own story as a performer and participant in the world he created; and then, in 1860, Edmund Yates, Victorian journalist and the son of Fred Yates, of one of Mathews's collaborators, and a famous actress, Elizabeth Brunton, produced a heavily abridged edition of Anne Mathews's work.[12] What he chooses to include and exclude is a suggestive guide to the reconstruction and incorporation of the history and of performers, male and female, by the next generation in the theatre. Thus the medium of print is subject to all sorts of interventions and mediations; its witness to its own times and its transmission of the history of the stage must be read as part of the hegemonic process even where autobiography might seem to offer direct revelation of actions and contemporary opinion.

Performance as autobiography

Possibly the most suggestive 'published' form of autobiography and anecdote that we may scrutinise for its contribution to theatre history is the performance. If we are prepared to attend seriously to non-documentary evidence, attitudes to the function and the history of the theatre might be extrapolated from every staged play and, especially, revival; but they are perhaps most self-consciously and obviously present in the solo performance that dramatises the contemporary moment. Acting out of various personae off stage, for a variety of purposes, was turned into a paying proposition on stage in the one-man show. From Samuel Foote inviting the mid-eighteenth-century public to take a dish of tea with him at his unlicensed theatre to actors appearing on TV chat-shows to discuss their own careers and those of their contemporaries, performers have offered their satirical embodiments of the society around them and commented by their virtuoso personal skills upon the nature of stage entertainment and its traditions, laws and hierarchies. In the early nineteenth century such self-referential virtuoso exhibitions occupied a politically important place in the cultural negotiations for possession of the stage, and several solo performers acted out their version of the current political situation in their profession, and their understanding of its history and their own place within it. Such solo entertainments were frequent and popular. Superficially concerned mainly with commentary on topical issues and fashions, many also suggest the performers' construction of history. The one-man shows of the most celebrated solo performer of the period, Charles Mathews, should be read alongside his biography; his extraordinary talents as a mimic were the basis of his professional success and are imbricated in his private life as Anne Mathews records it.

Such virtuoso displays were sometimes read with considerable hostility by critics who objected to actors' self-advertisement and self-importance; the ideological sensitivity of such self-presentation is clearly indicated in the excessive responses of journalists who apparently felt that the behaviour of actors on stage was part of a wider crisis in cultural self-assertion, in which the performance of identities to which the professor was not entitled was undermining the distinctions of caste and class:

Actors have an idea that they are the greatest people in the world, and that every one must feel a curiousity regarding their private history. We believe that lawyer's clerks, linen-draper's apprentices, and other fashionable frequenters of the saloons at half-price, feel themselves highly honoured by the acquaintance of actors, and have a most *gentlemanly* taste for prying into their concerns, *extra* their profession. But exclusive of these horribly insignificant creatures who are content to forego meals or any thing for the sake of sporting a clean collar for a few hours in the evening when they walk, (the gods of the saloon,) in all the consequence that three and sixpence (the half-price) can purchase; exclusive we say of these disgusting people, no body cares where this actor was born, or where that performer gets drunk after the fatigue of his evening's exertion. *Quoad* the stage, players are well enough, but off they are for the most part dull and dissipated, so that a private acquaintance with them is very seldom agreeable. We do not include all actors in this censure; we only speak of them as a body, which of course contains many decent men, though none who are calculated to *shine* in private society. Our objection is to the airs they assume, because they are *lionized* in low company, and are adulated by such wretched and presuming *riff raff* as stroll, in fine cloths (often bought by plunder from their masters tills) up and down the saloons of the two large theatres.[13]

Here the desire to put the actor in his place as a tradesman coincides with the urgent task of placing all tradesmen at a distance from true gentility, a task undermined by the mendacious social performance. It is perhaps especially significant that the performance that provoked the attack quoted above was by a woman. Fanny Kelly's *Dramatic Recollections* was a three-hour solo show mounted in London and the provinces from 1833. Frances Maria Kelly was niece and pupil of Michael Kelly and a comic actress as highly regarded as her brother-in-law Mathews;[14] she ventured into solo performance, partly as a political gesture, at a crucial moment in her career.

Theories of autobiography: 'We retell their tales so that they are the told and not the tellers'

The question remains of how I propose to read these materials, the self-representations and anecdotal exchanges of the times, if I choose to reject the straightforward historical method of combing through them for factual statements which may be checked against other sources and established as 'true'. Since the 1980s a body of theorising around the idea of the autobiography has been developed in the area of women's studies, with the intention of developing a more complex understanding of the women of the past whose stories have been marginalised or hidden from history.[15] It is from one of these writers, Jane Marcus, that the warning at the head of this section is drawn. She is troubled by

the sense that the study of female subjectivity in narratives of self reduces author and text to the object. Our voices assign the writers to categories and design the trajectory of their return to the realm of the read. Our compositions, to paraphrase Gertrude Stein, are their explanations. We retell their tales so that they are the told and not the tellers.[16]

To avoid such an appropriation I would propose to read this auto/biographical material as far as possible in its own terms, accepting the picture it paints as the intended activity of its authors, male as well as female. They are intent upon projecting an image of the world in which they are actors, those who do, not objects; they deflect us from themselves even as they describe who they are. Importantly this implies an acceptance of a feminist understanding of personal story-telling. The masculinist assumption is that men choose to publish their life stories when and because they have a sense of their own autonomy and difference, and their unique importance in the public life of their day. The most pervasive characteristic of *female* autobiography, on the other hand, is argued to be self-definition in relation to significant others; so that, rather than a sense of individual autonomy, a sense of identification, interdependence and community is key in the development of women's identity and therefore also central in their stories of themselves.[17] This insight resonates with Sarah Siddons's statement as she began her brief and apparently unrevealing autobiography:

I begin by professing that the retrospect of my Domestick life, sadly presenting little but Sickness, Sorrow, and death Is too painful to my feelings to dwell upon, too sacred and dellicate for communication. Remenicences of a less private nature would associate me with persons too August too noble, and too illustrious, for me to presume to mingle them with the private details of so inconsiderable so humble a person as myself; so that nothing remains, except meer commonplace-matter, and events already partly known. When I am laid low however, even this imperfect Narrative may perhaps have some interest for those few friends who may yet survive, to remember me and my appropriate qualities.[18]

She feels herself too unhappily bounded by her female, family role to describe herself as a private individual, and too unimportant to describe the role she had in public life, despite that fact that she admits she had such a role; her 'appropriate qualities' are therefore almost impossible to reveal. I would suggest that this problem about claiming an individual and unique identity may extend to other actors, male as well as female, in the period I am discussing and perhaps beyond. The actor George Raymond excuses his life of Elliston by saying that like Adolphus's life of John Bannister, and the Mathews, Dibdin and Reynolds lives, it is of the 'inferior standard' of biography: books whose objective is 'only amusement' so that they must be not 'a record of the man alone' but must also recount events 'characteristic of the station in which he moved'.[19] The stories that these theatre people tell around their own biographies are not an assertion of their own particular importance in the world, so much as an attempt to construct a group identity, in which their individuality is seated. Thus the recounting of anecdotes, which are the building blocks of theatrical memoir and biography, may be understood not simply as the vehicle of more or less dubious or provable facts, but as a process of identity-formation that extends beyond individuals to the group or community to which they belong.

The uses of anecdote

Anecdotes, I would argue, are chiefly important as a control of social resources through the making of myth and legend. The anecdote is not the same as 'a story' because it claims to be true, about real people; it occupies the same functional space as fiction, in that it is intended to entertain, but its instructive dimension is more overt. It purports to reveal the truths of the society, but not necessarily directly: its inner truth, its truth to some ineffable 'essence', rather than to proven facts, is what matters most – hence its mythmaking dimension. Jonathan Bate makes this point in relation to the biographical stories about Shakespeare that he examines: 'the *representative anecdote*, like the horoscope, is precisely a form of which the purpose is to distil someone's characteristic disposition, their "genius". The point of the anecdote is not its factual but its representative truth.' Other biographers tend to gesture towards this idea but nevertheless back away from its force, still seeking objective verification before they will admit the significance of stories about their subjects: see the simultaneous acknowledgement of theatrical stories and exclusion of them from its own scholarship in the preface to the modern *Biographical Dictionary* of eighteenth-century performers.[20]

Theatrical anecdotes told by their subject tend to be both self-exposing and self-protecting, in that while they may reveal weakness or personal faults, they simultaneously ward off criticism by making that weakness into an amusing story to disarm the listener, and fulfil the contract between the entertainer and the audience. If they concern other performers, they give the teller a chance to impersonate that performer, and so display a talent to amuse, and also to appropriate the cleverness or skill of that other entertainer. By impersonating another performer, past or present, actors claim for themselves familiarity, a knowledge that implies membership of a group, a community, and they also protect and ingratiate themselves with the audience. If they do it in private, with other actors, they show they belong and have credentials in their knowledge of stories about and mannerisms of famous members of the fraternity; if they do impersonations in public they are valued and applauded because they are able to admit the listeners to an inner circle of those who know something of the lives of the famous.

If in the early nineteenth century theatre itself and the social world to which it had belonged was undergoing a crisis of confidence, which to external eyes was construed as 'the Decline of the Drama', performed autobiography offers a different perception of the problem, through the energetic self-explanation and community-construction of its participants. Rather than assuming that of all the autonomous individuals whom Kant observes performing themselves in the social world,[21] actors would be the most self-confident, the most adept at personating a public identity that was a performed assertion of individuality, I take the prevalence of anecdotal autobiography and the assumption of multiple identities on stage and off by, for example, Charles Mathews, to be an attempt to understand and deal with insecurities of individual role and group identity. Mathews based a career on solo performance but could not bear to be looked at off the stage; his auto/biography, whether written out by himself or his wife, centres upon the collection of pictures of great actors and the *im*personation of them and of other people. For such an actor auto/biographical writing and especially performance is not the revelation, but the construction, of identity. To understand the theatrical anecdote, and its most characteristic publication in the solo performance, I therefore reach for theorising about collective memory, the formation and perpetuation of group identities, and the formation of the individual within that.

Theories of storytelling: the uses of history

'Collective memory' is a concept crystallised in modern historiographical writing by Maurice Halbwachs, a member of the editorial board of *Annales* when it was first set up, who brought to their historiography a voice from sociology. He was critical of the group for focusing upon description rather than explanation; the notion of collective memory is a contribution, therefore, to an understanding of history as an active force in shaping society. He defined it as 'that totality of traditions pertaining to a body of functionaries . . . there are at last as many collective memories as there are functions, and . . . each one of these memories is formed within each of these groups of functionaries, through the simple play of professional activity', adding, '[a]t the basis of a social function one always finds a set of traditions'.[22] For him the past is a social construction, shaped by the concerns of the present, within the human group – the family or the collectivity of work. Building on this, Jerome Bruner and Carol Fleisher Feldman set up an experiment in which they demonstrated, by the interrogation of three New York theatre companies, that groups constitute themselves by telling stories about themselves, and that not only do the stories of individuals constitute the group's identity, but at the same time the group's identity also constitutes the identities of its members. They conclude from their analysis of the language and narratives of their three groups that '[e]vents are shaped for narrative purposes with a view toward meaning and signification, not toward the end of somehow "preserving" the facts themselves'.[23] In this analysis, the selection of events in the shared experience of groups for telling and retelling is clearly a function not of their external importance, nor even of their verifiable truth, but of their importance in the self-understanding and in the marking of time and boundaries by the group. This is developed by Paul Connerton. He maintains that 'the production of more or less *informally* told narrative histories turns out to be a basic activity for characterisation of human actions. It is a feature of all communal memory' and is not the same as the formal history.[24] These informal histories shape the past for us, and may not coincide at all closely with 'objective' fact, or with the emphases of the formal account: he cites the report by the oral historian Primo Levi of a village in which the memory of World War I was of far less importance than tales of the War of the Brigands in 1865, even though every family had had a member involved in the later conflict. He also stresses that such images of the past 'commonly serve to legitimate a present social order' and are inherently conservative; and that they are 'conveyed and sustained by (more or less ritual) performances'.[25]

Joseph Roach picks up this point, asserting 'the interdependence of performance and collective memory' as he explores theatre as one of the 'many devices for supporting the transmission of a complex and nuanced body of practice and belief without writing'.[26] His next move is to ritual and 'restored behaviour' as the root of theatre, but my interest remains with the enactment of remembered stories and individualities within the history-making act of the performance, whether public and paid for by an audience or intimate and a matter of the actor's paying for or claiming group membership.[27] The actor telling stories about theatrical moments and imitating colleagues and predecessors is making the shared culture of the community. A group of dentists or teachers might do the same thing, though without the possible dimension of public performance; but the skill of the telling, and especially of the imitation, sets the theatrical anecdote apart. I will also argue, below, that the act of retelling and imitation is especially significant for the theatre, a kind of history that is perceived as a possible continuity in an evanescent tradition.

Acting it out: the performance of anecdote and theories of performance

There is a distinction between the private solidarity generated by the exchange of anecdotes and the public impact of theatrical presentation. A mimic enacting characters, either recognisable other individuals or types in a story, is claiming, and playing with, identities in a way that has social implications more powerful and more potentially alarming than might attach to conversation, or to a printed story. Hence the elision made by the hostile critic quoted above between the actor telling stories about her career and the obnoxious pretensions of the clerk in the audience who apes the dress and behaviour of a gentleman, mimicries which have superficially only a tenuous relationship. As an audience responding to such a performance on stage, we are intrigued by the simultaneous presence before our eyes of two people, the mimic and the subject; we are impressed by the clever observation, selection and reproduction of characteristic traits – a cleverness in which we share, via our recognition of the subject performed; and we are also perhaps disturbed or excited by the 'uncanny' likeness that seems against nature, transforming one individual into another of quite different size or voice or jizz: our comfortable sense of the unique fixity of individuality is challenged and upset. But on a social level, mimicry is a threat to our own sense of ourselves and our dignity – people rarely like to see themselves 'taken off' – and, more importantly, to the confidence with which we recognise not only other individuals but classes of individuals by their manner and appearance, and so make the stream of decisions and recognitions upon which our positioning of ourselves in society depends. The mimic may be a loose cannon in a social situation, and one of the deep roots of the opprobrium which fuels the anti-theatrical prejudice is here, in moral disapproval and fear of false appearances and deceit about who we are.

The professional community has developed an elaborate and now complex and multiple defence against this accusation, designed to ward off fear and superstitious loathing provoked by the theft of the self and by the social deception perpetrated by the diabolical cleverness of the imitator. The first step in explaining representation differently is the assertion of a distinction between two kinds of 'acting'. The Horatian tag, 'Si vis me flere, dolendum est primum ipsi tibi [if a actor is to move me, he must first be moved himself by the feeling he exhibits]' was the basis of eighteenth-century theorising about acting; whatever distinctions were made between classicist and Romantic ideas of how this was achieved, there was a general repudiation of the mere imitation or aping of externals of appearance, a denial that this was the art of acting at all.[28] In the twentieth century such theorising has only intensified, and it is as if the art of the mimic is unmentionable in the same breath as serious acting skills, is, indeed, something about which the real actor is likely to be secretive and even ashamed in non-acting company. It may be, as I hope to show, that here is another consequence of the binary thinking that crystallised in the early nineteenth-century appropriation of the theatre: as audiences, we distinguish completely and without a moment's hesitation between serious acting and the entertainer's skills of a mimic like Rory Bremner or Alistair McGowan. Those modern actors who 'find' a character from its externals – the shoes or the funny voice – are not quite the thing; it may be clever, but is it art? When actors (usually having achieved a secure eminence) reject this defensive constriction of their art, their rejection is felt to be subversive or uncomfortable. An example is the distinction, quoted in Anthony Holden's biography of Lord Olivier, that John Gielgud made between himself and Laurence Olivier: 'Olivier . . . is a great impersonator. I am always myself.' Sir Peter Hall concurred, and made the distinction a matter of judgement: 'Acting is not imitation but revelation of the inner self. This is not what Larry does or sets out to do. He is a performer.'[29] There is a world of damnation in that use of the word 'performer'. Holden's opening statement is that his subject has 'a curious personal anonymity' and has succeeded 'entirely by donning disguises' because he can 'assume any shape or appearance he pleases'. With a slight sense of scandal, he illustrates this with an anecdote of Olivier playing a joke upon a group of tourists at the Chichester Festival Theatre where he was rehearsing for Othello: he slipped away and came back as 'a drunk and disruptive West Indian stagehand', and thoroughly embarrassed everybody.[30]

Anthony Hopkins is another modern actor who plays with identity by mimicry, challenging and disrupting the 'artistic' situation of a rehearsal or a film set by the assumption of vulgar comic characters. In the 'Heroes of Comedy' TV documentary celebrating the entertainer Tommy Cooper,[31] Hopkins asserts his admiration for Cooper's down-to-earth laughter-making ability by telling anecdotes of his own life, in which he claims that he interjected imitations of Cooper's horse-laugh or his catchphrase into rehearsals of *Uncle Vanya* and the Merchant Ivory film, *The Remains of the Day*. The mimicry here is challenging artistic pretension with vulgar fun, and also, crucially, testing the other performers, and especially the directors, of high art to recognise the reference to a more 'real' but less polite form of entertainment. If they do not know that this is Tommy Cooper, and not an incomprehensible gaffe, Hopkins implies, they are further from the centre of the profession and its heart than he. And he tells this story to a TV audience of millions, setting himself up for approval as a man of the people, and so making another twist in the assertion of superior authenticity, while challenging the defensive artistic construct of the feeling, serious actor.

Charles Mathews, comedian . . .

'"an imitating rascal; a tall, cut-down, taking-off scoundrel!"'

As soon as he went to school Charles Mathews, the only survivor of twelve children born to a 'serious' Calvinist bookseller and his consumptive wife, realised that he could amuse others by 'that irresistible impulse I had to echo, like a mocking-bird, every sound I heard'. This 'nearly proved fatal' when he innocently sought the approval of the subject of his first human imitation, an itinerant eel-seller in the Strand, who battered him severely; and his story is punctuated with the assaults, both physical and verbal, of others who resented his 'sinister operations' upon their personalities. An actor called Lee Sugg haunted Mathews most of his life, after resenting his impersonation to the extent of knocking him down with an iron bar.[32] Occasionally in later life he himself apparently deployed the accomplishment as a threat, as when he wrote to an American preacher who had denounced his show asking that he should preach again on the subject, so that Mathews could come and get up an imitation.[33] He hated to hear his art decried as 'mimicry', as theatre critics regularly did, even as they made an exception in their reviews for his own performances. His wife quotes a review from *Blackwood's* that she says 'agrees perfectly . . . with my husband's feelings' in this respect, which calls him 'the very best actor on the English stage' because he is 'more plastic' than Kean or Dowton in his physical powers, which are 'more under the command of his will, and his intellectual resources more various, and more immediately available to him . . . It is idle and invidious to attempt to distinguish this kind of acting from any other, by calling it *mimicry*. Who thinks of calling Wilkie's pictures as mimicry?'[34] [original emphasis]

The accomplishment was an asset in the greenroom, and the imitation of other actors was a means whereby he ingratiated himself with managers. His letters home from his first engagement in Cork show him almost starved to death by Daly's parsimony, but eagerly learning the mannerisms of all his fellow actors, startling them by imitating them in role on stage, and being asked to perform his impersonations at the manager's benefit. Engaged at York, his first London break came when Colman, the manager at the Haymarket, came to see him and hired him in a letter that ends 'P.S. – Don't take off Suett again till we meet.'[35] Even his colleagues were always more eager for imitations of other people than of themselves, and the belligerent quotation in the heading of this section is from an offended performer, Hurst.[36] This is a common feature of impersonation between actors: Proctor reports of Kean that he too gave precise imitations of other performers to amuse his friends, with the inevitable result that Incledon the singer was vastly amused until he was taken off himself, and then left the house in offence.[37] When he came to years of discretion Mathews tried hard not to 'do' people to their faces, so that Braham once hid under the table at a dinner party as the

only way to see what Mathews made of him.[38] But of course people loved to see impersonations of their friends and colleagues.
Such community glue sometimes seeped out into public in potentially dangerous ways. There is a story about an early actress,
Catherine Corey, being persuaded by Lady Castlemaine into
taking off one of the Duchess's rivals on stage at Drury Lane,
being arrested, freed and asked to repeat the performance in private for the amusement of the king.[39] A very similar tale has it
that Mathews introduced an impersonation of Lord Chief Justice
Ellenborough in the character of Flexible, the judge in Kenney's
comedy *Love, Law and Physic*. On the second night 'the pit was
dense with gentlemen only'[40] – presumably gentlemen of the
law – and he was so alarmed that he cut the imitation, placat-
ing their demands with a series of lightning sketches of actors.
There is a long history of on-stage mimicry as a weapon in political and theatrical dispute, as Mathews was no doubt aware when
he denied anything smacking of 'personalities'.

However he liked reviews that took his skill as a testament to
his artistic control, Mathews practised it compulsively. When he
gave his evidence to the 1832 committee he claimed that he was
quite unable to tell them John Kemble's opinion without adopt-
ing his voice and manner, and accordingly regaled the solemn
committee with a lightning sketch. (S.C.Q. 3022)[41] This may
have been a political move; but it was typical of his lack of cau-
tion. In describing his young manhood Anne Mathews often includes stories of his irrepressible impulse to imitate or to create
characters in everyday life, and escapades in which he and as-
sociates like Theodore Hook bewildered turnpike keepers, river
bailiffs or staid citizens in their own houses by impersonating
outrageous, obstreperous or insane individuals. He invented an
alter ego called 'Mr Pennyman', a well-dressed and respectable
gentleman but very eccentric and demanding, with whom he
pestered his personal friends and 'caused the theatre to be a scene
of general confusion and misrule' to the point where the porter
at the Theatre Royal Liverpool threw him bodily out of the stage
door, knocking him out, and at Drury Lane during his second
season they called in a doctor to certify this intrusive individual
who was ruining rehearsals.[42] Anne Mathews seems proud of
this accomplishment, but Yates cuts all reference to Pennyman
from his edition, and trims most of the other off-stage adventures

of this kind: perhaps he felt the dignity of the acting profession was undercut by such overflowings. When Anne feels the need to apologise for her husband, she offers the interesting excuse that 'these offsprings of an excitement' are 'so essential a part of an actor's life' and

> I think it fair to urge, that at the period these scenes took place he had no other opportunity of exercising his inherent and irrepressible powers of representation! In his profession there had been no scope for their display: he performed only in the regular routine of plays and farces. The drama's laws, then rigid, forbade any mode by which his unique talents could possibly be exhibited; and his spirits were so exuberant, that it seemed a necessity rather than a choice that they should find egress . . . The extravagant acts he practised were, in fact, like so many safety-valves[43]

On the face of it this is an odd claim; but Mathews's career does reveal a tension between the talent that brought him into the the-atre and the opportunities he found to exercise it there. By the time he gave his evidence to the Select Committee in 1832 he was there as the joint manager of a minor theatre, the Adelphi, which he sustained in a healthy financial condition partly by his own solo performances; he repudiated in his evidence any desire ever to stage or to appear in the legitimate drama again. (S.C.Q. 3076). But this was the end of a long journey. He spent years in the provinces waiting for other comedians – Emery, Suett – to relinquish legitimate roles that managers deemed appropriate for him, but which they would not take from their previous posses-sors. Anne records his frustration that men who might have writ-ten new plays for him – Hook, in particular – did not do so, with the result that he lacked opportunities to create legitimate roles. As he developed the solo show for which he eventually became celebrated, he made a point of only presenting it in the provinces, while awaiting the opportunity to appear in the legitimate reper-toire in the London Theatres Royal. When he finally presented the first *At Home* at a London minor theatre, the English Opera House, in 1818 he began with an apology for 'appearing be-fore you in this novel way' which hinged upon losing 'the first wish of my heart' which was to appear at the winter theatres in 'legitimate comedy.' He blamed the managers and also the press for thrusting him into the role of mimic, and indeed Hazlitt's review of his 1820 performance, for example, starts by putting him firmly in his place.[44]

He was certainly right in thinking that the actor as mimic was socially suspect, at a time when the profession was striving to achieve and maintain gentry status. James Boaden, describing John Philip Kemble and establishing his eminence and gentility, repudiates on his behalf anything like 'social mimicry' and claims that he was therefore the more acceptable in polite society; he draws a line between Kemble and other actors, however eminent, in this respect. Henderson 'poured himself out in the most ludicrous delineations of life', and in previous generations Kitty Clive amused her country neighbours with 'mimicry' and 'broad humour' and even Garrick, who had discovered his own acting talent through imitating actors he saw, and had always to be entertaining in whatever company.[45] But Kemble would have thought this 'abuse of talent' beneath him, and 'put on the actor only with the dress of the *theatre* and was contented in society with such distinction as the scholar and the gentleman could acquire'. He concludes 'the powers of Kemble and Mathews cannot combine together'.[46] Clearly the social hazard was well known to Mathews himself, and the idea that his name could not be spoken in the same breath as that of his dramatic idol[47] would hurt him; so he was deeply concerned about leaving the legitimate stage for 'illegitimate' celebrity, and making himself an even greater social pariah by imitating people on the London stage. Anne records instances in which invitations to polite gatherings and to sittings of the courts include half-joking warnings against taking off the host.

Mathews also worried about the construction of his solo shows without the support of a text or a writer. Horatio Smith earned a disproportionate gratitude from him by writing one of the early shows, which consisted of anecdotes embedding imitations that Mathews had already worked up, but which he felt he could not string together in an effective order on his own. But whatever the difficulties and psychological barriers in originating materials and finding London venues and managements that did not put him beyond the pale, financial pressure moved him steadily into the entertainer's role. Eventually the conflict was resolved for him by a serious coach accident, in which he sustained a hip injury that he was able to convince himself disabled him as a light comedian. Whether or not bodily perfection was really a requisite of legitimate success, he had found his excuse to concentrate upon the illegitimate form he had developed, and shelve the anxiety over status and hierarchy that had so far held him to the role of 'comedian'. He became an entertainer.

His place within the profession and its tradition was perhaps all the more precious to him because of this. The solo shows were fed by imitations of public men and worked-up impressions of national types and comic observations – he had a discriminating eye for the absurdities of the developing range of middle-class self-presentation, and could present many variations upon the ordinary Englishman as well as the inevitable Scotch fishwives, Irish coachees and Frenchmen with fractured English. But they also always contained some element of theatrical self-reference. He would include impressions of actors, however brief: Crabb Robinson remarked on his saying 'Good night' in the unmistakable manner of a string of other actors, for example;[48] and the one invariable structural element of the show was its closing sequence called his 'monopolylogue,' which was a farcical playlet in which the main joke was his quick-change impersonation of each of five or six characters. This was an old theatre form, the 'protean' entertainment, an example of which, *The Actor of All Work*, had been written for Mathews by Colman for his Haymarket season in 1817. It served to tie his new inventions to a tradition of performance. More than this, most versions of his ever-evolving show contained a song or two about the entertainment world; he did dialogues between various characters about the state of London theatre; and sometimes found a place for more elaborate theatrical impersonations. He wrote to a friend in 1827:

I should like you to see my last piece; a sort of copy of my Gallery. The whole stage is occupied with pictures; and, considering it is only scene-painting after all, most skilfully done indeed, by Roberts. I relate anecdotes of many of the principal actors, as I am reminded of them in the scene, and animate five whole lengths – Kemble, Cooke, King, Incledon, and Suett.[49]

The gallery he mentions here was his hobby and obsession, and an indicator of the importance he placed upon the theatrical tradition and his place within it. Despite the sneers of more scholarly historians and collectors such as Collier he was very proud of having gathered together a considerable body of theatrical portraiture and memorabilia. In 1835 the collection took four days to auction, stretching to 124 lots of pictures, besides the books, playbills, a 'very interesting and extensive collection of all the various portraits and prints' of Garrick, with 'every thing that could in any way throw light on his glorious career'; and memorabilia that included Garrick's two wigs for King Lear, Kemble's Coriolanus sandals and two snuff boxes belonging to Tate Wilkinson.[50] His sometimes ruinously expensive houses had to include a large space for his gallery to be exhibited. Anne Mathews describes the pleasure he took in showing 'intelligent' visitors round, which characteristically manifested itself in an 'imitation of the snuffling, monotonous, Dog-berry-like exhibiters, at Greenwich Hospital, and other show places'.[51]

The 1827 Gallery monopolylogue was described as follows:[52]

His gallery, he says, he has collected for the purpose of catching inspiration from the mimic semblances of the mighty masters of his art, an art declared by Colley Cibber and Garrick, whose words he quotes, to perish with the artist; this Mr Mathews denies, he says, imitation, which has grown into disrepute of late days from having been made the instrument of personality, can perpetuate both the art and the artist; we all know he continues how much, even the commonest portrait of our beloved Shakespeare would fetch. Now, he says, had imitation been encouraged, we might at this moment have had his living semblance, with all his peculiarities and manner, before us. I knew Tate Wilkinson, who knew Garrick; Garrick knew Betterton; Betterton knew Booth; Booth knew Davenant, who was Shakespeare's godson; Davenant knew Ben Jonson, and Ben Jonson was Shakespeare's friend. Now had they possessed the power of handing down imitation from each other, I might this evening have put Shakespeare before you. Ah, (he continues), if any stretch of fancy could animate these gifted shades . . . but that, says he, is impossible." [sic – there was no opening quote mark] After giving an imitation of John Palmer's plausible manner in wheedling an audience; vindicating the character of Cooke from the charge of habitual drunkenness; and reading an eulogy on Dickey Suett, from Charles Lamb's Elia Essays, Mr Mathews goes to sleep. Five whole length portraits of Suett, in Dickey Glossop; Kemble, in Penruddock; Incledon, as the Sailor in the Storm; Cooke, as Sir Pertinax M'Sycophant, and King, as Sir Peter Teazle, then become successively animated . . . Kemble presents an imitation of Garrick, in the opening soliloquy of Richard the Third; and relates a curious anecdote of Joe Millar . . . King presents an animated

picture of the old school of acting; and the monopolylogue ends with
Mr Mathews awaking.

The inspirational qualities for Mathews of the portraits of the
leaders of the profession is mentioned by Anne; and it seems to
have been a genuine conviction not only of Mathews but of other
actors at the time that the essence of performance could be passed
on, in a kind of living history, by serious mimicry, that preserved
the art of theatre. Campbell records that Tate Wilkinson was
'one of the most extraordinary mimics that ever lived' and could
render 'all the best actors and actresses' he had known in his long
life, except Susannah Cibber. Anne Mathews confirms this, and
naively assures her readers of the likeness of his imitations:

He . . . imitated some of the old actors and actresses, Garrick
(from which, I believe, Mr Mathews took his imitation,) and others of his day, for he was a incomparable mimic, and his representations carried with them the same convictions of their truth that
we feel when a fine portrait of a person we have never seen assures us (we do not know why,) of its faithful resemblance to the
original. Like such paintings, Mr Wilkinson's imitations of persons
of the old school, satisfied the observer that they must be perfect
likenesses.[53]

B. W. Proctor, as a prologue to the lachrymose climax to his
life of Kean, records that on his deathbed 'he would still turn
back to the stage, and show his son how Garrick and Barry had
acted Lear. (Sir George Beaumont had formerly explained their
manner of playing to him.)'[54]
    These performers, then, recognised mimicry as their special
tool of collective identity, a way of invoking sympathy and claiming to belong, as well as passing on a vital tradition written
only on the body. It is not about texts or roles, but the actors'
possession of his inheritance, which is the sum of his predecessor's unique talents, their beauties, essence: Mathews's flight of
fancy about how his audience might have known Shakespeare is
about Shakespeare himself, as an actor or simply a bodily presence, rather than about his plays. Among the imitations that he
does do is Kemble, not only as himself in a modern role, but as
Garrick playing a Shakespearean part. This is their special form
of history – a history in performance.

Fanny Kelly and woman's heritage of speech

> I have thought that a Woman ought not to be debarred her established privilege of utterance – her heritage of speech – and therefore under your favor will I –
> 'A round unvarnished tale deliver
> Even from my Girlish Days'   Fanny Kelly

Fanny Kelly did not share Mathews's special talent and compulsion to be a mimic. Indeed, when she did appear alone in her *Dramatic Recollections* at the little upstart Strand Theatre in 1833 she explicitly repudiated any ambition to 'tread the path our Mathews erst hath done / He who outstrips the pencil and the pen, / In sketching out the characters of Men!' She will not imitate, she says, but merely offer 'little narratives', 'trifles by experience won' (fol. 121).[55] The full text of her attempt 'to be the Mrs Solus of the Stage' was licensed, and so we may see that she did in fact do impersonations of characters and of individuals; the disclaimers are to turn away anger at her 'hazard and daring', which make her 'almost fear' she possesses 'the spirit of the amazon' (fol. 123). She was a born member of the profession, and in a long and successful career before she made this solo venture she had won much critical attention and audience affection in comedy, especially in maid-servant and other lower-class roles. She was not a beauty, though Charles Lamb, in whose circle she was an intimate, proposed to her and sighed for her 'divine plain face'[56] but she was widely regarded as a clever and adorable actress. She was unusual in that she apparently had neither lovers nor husbands, and accumulated a modest fortune over decades of independent and outspoken negotiation of the stormy professional waters between the patent managements and Samuel Arnold, for whom she starred in many summer seasons at the English Opera House while still appearing at Drury Lane in the winters. The 1832 convulsion in theatre politics brought her career to a crisis. She had no engagement; everything was changing around her; and at the age of forty-three she set out to fulfil her ambition to set up a school and educate girls for the stage. Her savings and the solo show were to finance her venture into managing and, eventually, building a theatre for this purpose.

Critics other than the insecure gentleman quoted above were inclined to be pleased and tolerant: Crabb Robinson 'had a pleasant few hours in the Strand' despite the fact that 'She looked old and almost plain, and her singing was unpleasant.'[57] His main interest was in who had written her material, which he found very amusing. His guesses were Lamb and Reynolds, with Hood contributing songs. The licensing copy is in a single notebook but in several hands, and the material is very uneven. The songs and some sketches – of, for example, a Dublin coachman – are standard and rather crude farce material, and could be by any theatre writer, while others, such as the character of Sally her servant, are versions of her existing stage roles; the more interesting materials, however, seem unlikely to be anything but her own, in some cases perhaps worked into place by a friend, as Smith did for Mathews. The best remembered character, billed as 'Mrs Parthian: obliviscent Reminiscences', is a theatre historian. Her jokes are the ones Crabb Robinson likes best – she confounds Horatio Smith with Adam Smith and Dodd the actor with Dodd the hanged forger, says Thomas Dibdin wrote *The Cardinal*, and is sure the elder Kean is nothing like Garrick, though she 'never was present when Mr David acted', nor when Fanny did, though she understands she is 'in Mrs Barry's and Miss Young's line'. At her second appearance she reads out the catalogue of her 'Gallery of Shakespearean Curiosities' 'got together at a comparatively small expense' by her nephew, who managed her finances 'for the purpose' (the purpose of lining his own pockets, we collect). It includes choice items such as Hamlet's own sword, 'A Picture Frame (very old) understood to have contained until quite lately a copy of an Original Picture of Shakespeare' and 'One of the Sixpences taken off the entrance to the Pit of Covent Garden Theatre in consequence of the memorable O.P. riots' (fol. 201–2).[58] While antiquarianism generally is a butt of decades of theatrical humour, it seems particularly rich that Fanny Kelly should target those learned outsiders who pretend to expertise in the history of the stage, with Shakespeareana as their object of especial worship.

The most interesting parts of the show – the best written and most vivid, as well as the most useful for my purposes – are the sections in which Kelly tells the stories of her own stage career. It is apparent from a 1935 biography of her that she kept a journal, then still extant, and that these sections of the show were transcribed from her writings there.[59] She talks about her childhood as a chorister at Drury Lane, about her catastrophes and triumphs on the road in small provincial venues, and her recent experience as a teacher of acting which has led her to try to set up her school; every anecdote is full of point and feeling as well, often, as self-deprecating wit and humour. Crabb Robinson did not wholly like to be told the human details of stage life in this way, and preferred the comic scenes to 'the sentimental'; but it is in the latter that she makes most clear what stage history and tradition mean for her.

An alternative history?

The professional community and its traditions

If then we interrogate these performances, and use the story-telling and autobiography of other performers as corroboration of what we might find there, what picture of the theatre over their lifetime do we see, and what part in their perception of their own times is played by their conception of theatre and its history?

If, as I suggest, we read mimicry as history in use within the actors' professional community, the construction of a tradition and a hierarchy is already clear from the examples I have given. Its touchstone, hero and fountain is David Garrick. It is not simply the text of the play, but Garrick's performance of King Lear that carries meaning for subsequent generations, so that Edmund Kean seeks on his deathbed to pass it on to his son. The conservative propensity of such oral traditions is stressed by Halbwachs and Connerton, and it might be seen as central to this form of communal memory; but Mathews's elaborate syntheses – he imitates Kemble imitating Garrick playing Richard III – suggest that there is in these recuperations of past performance an intention to build upon memory, an appeal to organic growth rather than simply to stasis. Turning to anecdotes about past performance, we may find belief in the transmission and synthesis of previous interpretations as the way to excellence. Stories of continuity begin with the flesh-and-blood bridges across the Commonwealth period – Hart was Shakespeare's great-nephew, he trained Nell Gwynne[60] – but such mythmaking is given substance by practical measures, such as Michael Kelly's study of the role of Macheath in John Gay's The Beggar's Opera in 1789. He says he 'took all the pains I could, and no young man ever had greater pains taken with him. Mr Linley remembered Beard and Vernon; John Kemble, Digges; they gave me imitations of these Macheaths: there was also then in London, the celebrated Irish Macheath, and worthy man, old Wildar . . .'[61] This actorly belief in a living tradition survives into the present: Lord Olivier begins his history of acting with the transmission to us of 'the Shakespearean mantle' via Burbage, Garrick, Kean and Irving, and 'the little cogs in between', a chain of contact, of training, which he proceeds to detail.[62]

But it is also noticeable that oft-told stories sometimes concern the triumphant overturning of traditional performance practice. The invisible ghost in J. P. Kemble's *Macbeth*, Sarah Siddons's rejection of a candlestick for Lady Macbeth's sleepwalking, are told and retold as markers of change, of the coming of new inspiration. The anecdote is also extensively used to record the role of individuals in shaping and perpetuating tradition, with stories in which they often comically or by contrast embody significant values and attitudes. Transgressive figures are used to explore the professional conflict between inspiration and discipline: Cooke's drunkenness, Sheridan's procrastination, form the centre of many tales. Actors are not the only subjects. Certain managers are constructed by a stream of anecdotes as pillars of the performance community, bearers of a comically old-fashioned but valuable and authenticating set of attitudes and knowledge of the trade. Thomas Dibdin does this with his stories of Sarah Baker, the creator of the Kent circuit where many London performers served their training; the most widely used exemplar is Tate Wilkinson, to whose loveable oddities Anne Mathews gives a whole chapter, which Yates cuts completely. Both these are striking examples of people whose theatrical roots are deep and whose sympathies are wide. Baker is elegant of carriage and foul-mouthed, the child of a rope-dancer, a good businesswoman who built a successful circuit without any book education at all, while Mathews's Wilkinson stories include his admiration of Shakespeare which is only surpassed by his garish taste for glittery clothes and stage finery. The reason they are so beloved is that they both have a clear notion of what is good acting, and also of what is required of management in order to foster it. It is very significant that these are the past generation of country managers, just as Garrick was the acme of the metropolitan star, and the senior Kembles are gone: there is a sense of passing and of impending disaster, of 'the world we have lost'. In his 1801 *History* Charles Dibdin the elder gives the most extreme expression to this deeply conservative position, with his long peroration about why he will, at the end of four successive paragraphs, 'drop the curtain at the death of Garrick'. His version of the decline of the drama is that '[e]xtraneous interest may ruin the theatre':

whenever the proprietors of theatres, are neither actors nor authors, and are no further connected with the interest of the concern than relates to the emolument it produces, without being responsible for its general fame, the exertions of authors and actors will infallibly be disregarded and the theatre by receiving all its advantage from gewgaws and spectacle will sink from its reputation, its consequence, and its honour.[63]

This view is traditional even in 1801, in that it is the form that complaints about mismanagement of the theatre had taken ever since the days of Christopher Rich. It might be put down to Dibdin's old age and sense of his own supersedure; but in 1831, when the Radicals were anticipating a brave new world, it is striking that the theatre people still focused upon a utopian past.

The 1830s and the crisis of management and employment on the stage

Both versions of history in 1831 share the perception that a point of crisis has arrived. In this story it is not, however, 'the Decline of the Drama' that defines the falling-off:

[l]et not . . .any of our Readers imagine, that the preference given to . . . trashy exhibitions arises from a dearth of genius in the present age of writers to produce the Legitimate Drama: the reverse is the fact, as there never was an era in which talent for Dramatic Composition of every description was more exuberant; but what avails it, if the Managers shut their doors against the Votaries of Melpomene and Thalia . . .[64]

According to such polemics, what has to be renegotiated is the *governance and management* of the stage, not for the sake of admitting new writers but in order to restore the commercial organisation of theatrical entertainment and to ensure the setting up of new mechanisms that will protect the servants of tragedy

and comedy and give them back their status and social definition. Thomas Dibdin's *Reminiscences* are entirely concerned with
locating himself within a tradition of writing, acting and management that is rooted in the previous century – Garrick was
his godfather, he was led on stage as Cupid to Sarah Siddons's
Venus at the age of four – and that he sees himself as having
developed by his own talent and hard work, only to find himself progressively edged out by pretension and money while the
London theatres go to rack and ruin.[65] The fury of Catherine
Oxberry at 'the basis of modern theatrical policy' is typical: she
asserts the failure of London managements to hire the right people or to pay them the right salaries, as if all expertise in this had
somehow evaporated.[66]

Both Mathews and Kelly found their careers shaped by the
actors' situation in London and provincial theatre management.
Anne prints a very revealing letter from George Colman in which
he responds to Mathews's request for a higher salary if he is to
re-engage at the Haymarket in the next season, warning him that
while he may be able to ask high fees now, he should bear in
mind that he will need the support of the theatre by and by,
when audiences tire of him, and should moderate his demands
accordingly.[67] Such paternalism meant that a wearisome wait for
dead men's roles had also long been a feature of the old company system. By the mid-eighteenth century the patent company
organisation had developed into a cartel where, in theory, the
major theatres did not poach each other's players, performers
belonged to the house, and in return for some security were
expected to accept their annual engagements on terms to suit
the Theatres Royal. By the end of the century the patent managements sought to justify their suppression of challengers by
arguing that tight control, with pegged salaries and the absence
of competition, led to the training and induction of new players into best practice, the concentration of talent in the national
theatres, and security for every player in a life-time's employment, according to his abilities. New managements, articulately
led by Samuel Arnold, contended that this system had manifestly
broken down into unfair practices on all sides: patentees trying
to stop the minors by punishing actors who engaged there, and
performers seeking higher salaries in a competitive market to the
detriment of strong ensembles, the loss of continuity of training

and security for lesser players and the confusion of managerial budgeting.

Many of the writers of biography express this dilemma for the actor in terms suggestive of the wider shifts in working patterns that affected Britain at the time. This was the generation of Luddism and Peterloo, of Combination Acts and of the making of class consciousness. Reform was demanded by rick-burning; and employment practice in the theatre was not exempt from change and dispute. Boaden talks about a difference having developed between country theatres and the new ways of the metropolis. In the provinces theatre is still dependent upon patronage and is accordingly servile to the great men of the district, while in London the situation is becoming modernised, a state of affairs in which the actor 'took his talent, as everything else is taken, to an open market, where the demand for the supply would always produce its exact value'.[68] We might see in this the emergence of a socio-economic structure built upon property rights and market relations instead of customary rights and paternalist obligations, but such a development was uneven and differentiated in many contradictory ways.

One of the most striking kinds of anecdote, told by and about a series of performers, is that in which the actor or actor–manager stands up to a member of the audience who is treating the theatre with disrespect, either by talking and laughing in a box as if in a private room, to the interruption of the play, or by attempting to take possession off-stage of an attractive actress. The assumption in both cases is about status: that 'the drama's patrons' are literally entitled to regard the performers as their property, at best their servants who can be ignored at will, at worst their purchased possessions to be used at their pleasure. The heroic tale of the actor who stops the play because someone is talking, withholding the service for which he has been hired, or steps between the actress and the crowd of officers and gentlemen who feel she is their perquisite, is told of Thomas Sheridan the Dublin manager, of John Philip Kemble, of Sarah Siddons, of Fanny Kelly – of the elite of the profession. It is no doubt founded in actual incidents, but its force is symbolic. There is real fear of the consequences of such an act of defiance, and real pride in the actor who has succeeded in it – a sense that a difference has been made.

The trope can, however, be read in two ways. On the one hand, it relates, as Boaden expresses it, to the Radical agenda, the rhetoric that denounces the privileges of aristocratic patrons, and seeks to establish 'free trade'; on the other hand the performers seem more concerned to reclaim for themselves a position which is nostalgically linked backwards, to a utopian period when players were the 'servants' of aristocracy, rather than of an ignorant and ill-bred set of people whose only qualification for domineering is their money. This is the implication of Fanny Kelly's delicately precise statement of her own social position:

actors brought up in the London theatres ought gratefully to appreciate and not presume upon their superior advantages . . . For my own part I dare assert that I have ever tried to evince that I feel a grateful pride in my graduate, moderate and I hope I may add permanent claim to favor from the London Public, consistently rejecting every temptation to gratify my vanity or better my fortune at the sacrifice of my respectability as one of his Majesty's Servants. (fol. 143)

The demand for a return to proper treatment, a situation in which social contracts are fully understood, applies both before and behind the curtain. In the stories the ideal theatre management relates *fairly* to the actors; this means not curtailing traditional perquisites such as a proper supply of candles just as much as conducting open auditions and paying salaries on the nail. In fact the performing community shares the Radical desire for a new relationship; but it is not simply under the banner of 'free trade'. Rather the modernising impulse for them is in the direction of a new professionalism.

The performer asserts the right to expect management to operate by professional standards, the standards of skill and talent, in which possession of the appropriate knowledge marks off group members from outsiders. The desire is to re-establish professional judgement according to group perception of degrees of expertise. This standard is often thought of as that of the great professional David Garrick, and indeed Garrick has recently been shown to have worked to get the actor accepted in new social category of 'the professional'.[69] The definition of such a relation to the mercantile and commercial world was being forged in his lifetime, and is the basis of the aspirations of both Fanny Kelly and Charles Mathews.

Stories about the definition of what is professional behaviour are an important focus of anecdote, and the bottom line is the ability to deliver, in person, in front of an audience. Thus Fanny

Kelly illustrates the straits to which country managements are sometimes reduced by describing her own 'transgressions' in desperate circumstances. The first story is about arriving to find that she is announced to sing 'Hope told a flattering tale' 'in character', because the doctor's lady likes the song and the manager has noticed that often songs are sung in character: he suggests that maybe she could carry an anchor on with her. 'Certainly I shall do nothing so ridiculous' she says, but finds that in any case the band have not turned up, having gone to play at a wedding – all except the drummer, who says he can play it on the flageolet – but only in D, not in the proper key of G. Eventually she makes up an extempore song about her disappointed hope of having a band, with which, she says, she 'quite astonished £2.17.0 worth of people' (fols. 144, 145). Here we have the dependence of country theatres upon patronage, and the failure of poor management to recognise the expertise of the performer or, indeed, the status of the performance event, as well as the professional triumph of the real trouper over adverse circumstances – and her wry assessment of the importance of the whole thing in terms of the minute takings.

Charles Mathews, likewise, was clearly struggling to achieve self-definition as a professional, and the history of his career then becomes important in those terms to ensuing theatrical generations. The working-out of an acute problem over relating self-image and status – individual and communal identity – to the management of work and income is very clear in Anne Mathews's memoir and its significant emendation by Edmund Yates. In his letters home Mathews always describes his successes, as Fanny Kelly does above, in the professional entertainer's terms: the amount of money he makes. Yates says in his introduction to his edition that he has not cut anything written by Mathews himself, but in fact he regularly removes as much as possible of this evidence of a mercenary, ungentlemanly interest in financial success as a measure of the artist. In terms of professionalism, however, the most important story in Anne Mathews's account, and the only one which made waves in the theatrical community of the 1840s when it was published, is about her husband's failure to deal with commercial exploitation of his own talents. By 1818 he was acutely aware that he could make more money alone in the provinces, at this time performing Colman's one-man 'protean' entertainment *The Actor of All Work*, than the managers were prepared to give him for legitimate performance in town.[70] As she tells it, his dissatisfaction with the winter managements came to a head; he 'panted for freedom, fancied it was now offered to him, and heedlessly rushed into tenfold captivity'.[71] The offer came from Samuel Arnold: he suggested the one-man show, and produced a contract whereby Mathews performed such an entertainment in London under Arnold's management for seven years, and in return received £1,000 p.a. and an annuity for life. Dazzled, she says, and never having had a head for business, he sold himself into slavery with Arnold – and she knew nothing of it, until Arnold came round to her drawing-room and suggested that someone in her position in life should not be burning so many wax candles. Mathews proceeded to collaborate with his new manager until the one-man show was created, and a great success; then his eyes were opened, and on 'the very verge of phrenzy' he took to his bed in a delirium that quite unfitted him to perform – until the contract was cancelled. Arnold deeply resented this account of the matter, and published a rebuttal that accuses Anne Mathews of delusions and monomania, and makes repeated mention of lying and unchastity; but he confirms that he and Mathews had made such a contract, in the hope of achieving a new professional relationship within the management situation that Mathews was finding held him back; but Mathews panicked, whether at the novelty of his situation or its implications in terms of alienating his talent and his own body. Hence the melodramatic response to his wage slavery, which was, however, perfectly efficacious as an assertion of his inalienable possession of his talents – his status as a professional.[72] If Mathews would not get out of bed, Arnold could not take the product he had bought.

Access to the profession: the actor's training

The induction of new people to an occupation is one of the ways in which its status is marked as being 'a profession', and the nineteenth-century stage had great difficulty in meeting the requirements, not least because it included women practitioners, who could never be said to be gentlemen, and were often admitted from anywhere in society, being qualified only by their good looks. The discrepancy between a professional estimation of the abilities of a performer and what the management thought audiences were prepared to pay for was a constant annoyance. The abuse of managerial power to audition and hire, and the appropriation of the articled pupil's potentially huge earnings were both central issues.[73] Women were especially vulnerable. Conceiving, therefore, of the idea of running a theatre school, Fanny Kelly brought herself into direct confrontation with the patent managements, not only by running an unlicensed theatre, but by challenging their control of access to the profession. Her show includes sketches of her dealings with stage aspirants – ladies who are reduced by the disasters of middle-class life to attempting to make a living for themselves or through their daughters, but who not only have no understanding that skills are needed for a stage career, but also despise those who successfully undertake one. Kelly makes these rather bitter and barbed impersonations amusing, but in her presentation of the stage as it used to be, and of her own understanding of and devotion to her calling, she expresses a passionate commitment to a utopian past where no such insults would be offered to an orderly, important profession.

She uses her memories of the theatre of her youth to suggest a heroic mythology: she is making her own myth, by way of asserting control of social resources. She was a child actor, but not a child prodigy, she says, and tells the story of John Philip Kemble's recruiting of her in due form. She was already about Drury Lane, where her uncle worked, and

at 7 years of age it appeared to my excessive though infantine ambition that to be great in any way needed only *a beginning* – in this spirit – I nightly took my station behind the scenes of Drury Lane Theatre in what is called the first Entrance to the Stage – and in rash defiance of an awful Board placed immediately near to the forbidden spot threatening the Penalty of *Half* a Guinea (to me at that time an impossible sum) to all intruders – There stood I devouring, through the hinge crevice of the Stage Door, the Ghost's first Scene in Hamlet – when John Kemble coming softly behind me and passing his hand gently down my face – thus – and, a little less gently, up again – said to me – 'Upon my word – You're a fine little fellow I wonder who made you a Grenadier?' Conscience-struck at my detected intrusion I made no effort to reply but stood in mute and trembling terror of my fate – 'And what's your little name?' 'Fanny Sir – Mr Kelly's Niece' – 'What, Mick Kelly's Niece?' – 'yes, Sir,' – 'Aye, Marry! And what can Mick's Niece do I wonder?'

'Sir!' – 'Can you read?' – 'Yes, Sir,' – 'And write?' – 'No, Sir,' – 'Do you think you can learn a little part?' – 'Oh, yes, Sir – I know ever so many' – 'What may they be Mick's Niece?' – 'Rolla Sir' – 'Eh! – Why that's my part' – 'And Cora' – 'Why that's Mrs Jordan's!' – 'And the Castle Spectre' – 'What the Ghost?' – 'Yes Sir – and Jobson and Nell in the Devil to pay' – 'What Jobson and Nell – well said Mick's Niece! Well, now run away out of this place as fast as your legs can carry you before Old Thompson takes your Nose off – and at the End of the play, if you'll come to my Room Mrs Banks shall measure you for a pair of Black Satin Breeches' –

My fortune was made – I do know that there were 127 stairs from the Stage to the Tailors Room but how my little legs – which actually trembled under me – ever found their way to the top of them I cannot now pretend to say – but oh – unspeakable happiness – the dress was put in hand – and the character of the Duke of York in Richard the Third written out for and presented to – *Miss Kelly to be learned immediately* – and accordingly in due course I made my first appearance on any stage in that Character with what my kind patron was pleased to pronounce 'unprecedented success!' – Let me be pardoned if I exult a little in the fact that John Kemble – the great – the inimitable – John Kemble – was the first to praise me – the first to urge me on to exertion – the first also to reward me – I believe there was not a member of the Profession – from the highest to the most subordinate – from the oldest to the youngest – who did not look up to John Kemble with profound respect – In some instances – especially amongst the Junior and inferior members with a sentiment approaching to awe – this sentiment was excited as well by his commanding talent as by the dignity of his nature and of his bearing . . .

She goes to see him next day and is called a good little girl and told some of these days she'll be an actress. His wife has given her a pin cushion which she shows him but he says

Aye, aye, I know all about that – but Mrs Kemble has nothing to do with my actors – so, here – take this crown piece which just fits the top of it, and keep them both for my sake (fol. 131–3)

Again the question of proper payment is the climax of the tale: she is to be an actor, and earn her own real wages – not pin money. That is built up to by her evocation of the rules of the theatre, which she defies in order to become an artist: her childish presumption, which is also her qualification as a performer, as Kemble recognises; her glad acceptance of the tasks he imposes, the 127 steps and the part to be learnt; and her formal qualification as a member of the profession, when John Philip

Kemble calls her a success. Theatre is a matter of discipline and due reward. But it is also a matter of feeling, as she understood from Sarah Siddons and Dorothy Jordan. She tells tales of both of them as grand ladies of the stage and awe-inspiring artists. She frames her Siddons story as her contribution to a debate between 'some celebrated poets of this age' who were

> warmly engaged in endeavouring to establish a Theory of their own – that *acting* in itself was so artificial as to preclude any Performer even the most celebrated from feeling the passion of a Character or Scene during the acting . . .
>
> I ventured to reply to this sweeping – groundless – assertion – which coming from the memory of one who spoke from experience did something I verily believe towards crushing the cold Theory –
>
> I told them that when I was a Child I stood up in Curls and White Silk Hose – straight yet trembling – the Prince Arthur to the Queen Constance of Mrs Siddons I stood awe-struck in her grasp as though the clutch of an Eagle was upon me – Her energy was appalling – It seems to strain me now! – but when she leant over me – lapsed in love – lost in majestic yet passionate sorrow – the dilated light of those large deep dark eyes fell on me like a Sad Glory and charmed me to the spot – then – then I felt that she was indeed Queen Constance and when her Grand forehead was torn from my little Shoulder – the small white collar on my neck was wetted through and through with her *tears*. (fol. 138–9)

Her Jordan story is framed as an evocation of the magic of backstage:

> In Old Drury Lane Theatre – I mean the sire of the present house – I first saw and as a very youngster was on the same boards with Mrs Jordan –
>
> Oh! how well do I recollect those hopeful happy days – those Nights to me – nights of perfect enchantment – the mornings of Rehearsal – the Evenings of performance – never came too often – for I saw Spirits of the drama – Nay, the like of whom I shall never see again! –
>
> There I was at the Stage Door punctual as time and I never crossed its dim threshold and threaded its dingy passage without a pleasure which I can hardly account for – I fear I was born for the Stage – when I went to Rehearsal at 11 – the smell of the one miserable lamp – feebly attempting to be a light – the growing-cold scent of Oil and Orange Peel and Sawdust as the dusty passage was trod – the magnitude of the gloom when the stage was gained were all delightful and even inspiriting to me – and oh! – then down – dimly – grouped in the front – between the Ounce of Daylight from the gallery and the darkness of the Stage I could glimpse the figures of those who to my young mind had attained

the height of human glory and happiness . . . I sigh'd as I looked on that sunny face – and wished – and wished that I too could have been *an Actress*. (fol. 171–2)

These pieces of writing are striking in their loving care – they are minutely amended and improved in the licenser's copy, in pencil, as if she was still writing them up when it was prepared. Her enactment of her personal history, set in the frame of Drury Lane and its famous past mistresses, is clearly an important assertion for her not only of who she is and where she is coming from, but of the values she wishes to rescue, preserve and pass on in her rebellion against what the patent system has become.

I hope it is clear by this point that the history of the theatre invoked by the mimics and memoirists is not the polarised vision of Bulwer Lytton and his followers; the Drama is not set up in opposition to the traffic of the stage. The solution to current problems is not that power should be taken from managements and actors, and handed over to authors, but that a proper understanding of how all parts contribute to the whole, and how skill, talent, work, history and tradition all contribute to successful theatre should be reinstated. One particularly rich stream of anecdotes illustrates the actors' hierarchic but inclusive vision. These are the stories of 'claiming kin' – incidents in which the great ones of the stage find themselves called upon to acknowledge their indissoluble connection to those at the very bottom of the pile. The stories are told as jokes, but they are none the less offered as true, and as containing a salutary lesson. Mathews, in the years of his early success, went on country jaunts with Hook and his other rakish friends, and they always visited the theatre if one was open. When Hook, drunk and hilarious, made fun of the performance, Mathews crept away and hid in an upper box because 'it would have been painful to him to have his humbler brethren of the sock and buskin suppose that he had come with a party "to flout at their solemnities".[74] Fanny Kelly claims to have hurt the feelings of a Punch and Judy man by sending him away from her window while she was studying a role: he said '"It's all over with the *Draymer* if we don't encourage *one another*"' (fol. 190). She also impersonates a Mrs Drake, who has sent for free admissions to a theatre performance on the strength of her own proprietorship of a wild beast show. Discovering whom she has admitted, she makes a political point of it:

And have I, thought I, been making Ducks and Drakes of the Drama –
and admitting the D[rake]s' claim to the honor of fraternity – I was a
little mortified – but I solaced myself with the reflection that so long
as the contents of each department of the profession kept to their own
Caravan – the Lions and the *Boas* of the two branches would not be
confounded on one common stage – Mrs Siddons would not jostle with
a Bengal Tiger – nor a Kemble star it against a Kangaroo – Little did I
think that the spirit of a Drake would sway the destinies of a Drury . . .
(fol. 191)

However misplaced the menagerie has become, and however
presumptuous the puppeteer, she allows the Drakes their own
caravan.

The development of the classic version of this anecdote shows
the way in which such stories respond to their cultural function. It
is told twice (at least) about David Garrick visiting Bartholomew
Fair. In the version offered in *The Every-Day Book* in 1826 by
the Radical writer Hone, supposedly told by 'an ancient barber
of Drury-lane', Garrick and his wife went to Shuter's booth in
the fair, but found themselves rudely pushed about in the crowd;
the Drury Lane bill-sticker Palmer was taking the money, but on
being appealed to for protection said he could not help his master
in this situation, where, he said, few people knew the great man.
When this is retold by Daniels in *Merrie England in the Olden
Time*, 1842, a significant book in the construction of a Victorian
version of ancient popular culture (see chapter 6) the story has
changed completely: the Garricks are 'marshalled' to the fair by
the bill-sticker, and the cashier 'recognising the fine expressive
features and far-beaming eye of Roscius, with a patronising look
and bow, refused the proffered fee, politely remarking, "Sir, we
never take money from *one another*!"'[75] Thus the subordination
of the popular within the professional hierarchy is accomplished.
In this form, of the recognition of the great actor, the story is
also passed on to refer to Edmund Kean outside Richardson's
booth and several other leading actors. It becomes a tale in which
the grandee, who rather assumes that he will *not* be recognised
by the humble folk, and attempts to enter a booth by paying
at the door, is made ashamed at his presumption of difference,
reminded of his brotherhood by a showman, at the poorer man's
expense. Anne Mathews's book of extra anecdotes contains this
version, with her husband meekly accepting the free admission

offered him by a fairground theatrical who refused his money 'with some dignity, though with great mildness', saying '"No! – *no, Mr Matthus! Ve never* takes from *von another!* . . . I'm werry appy, *Mr Matthus, Sir,* to see you in my the*a*tur!"'[76]

Conclusion

The difference of view between these anecdotal enforcements of a particular construction of the profession and its history, on the one hand, and the rhetoric of the Radicals about 'the Decline of the Drama', on the other, is not perhaps immediately obvious. The performers, like the writers, are seeking to establish themselves and their status in a new social hierarchy, and appeal to history to do it. The classic stage of Drury Lane is Fanny Kelly's touchstone of excellence, and it should be peopled with a dramatic company rather than with lions, of human or feline varieties; Mathews complains of management malpractice and a lack of good new vehicles for his talents, and demands his rights as a leading comedian. But they do not draw a hard line between themselves and the rest, or claim that the theatre is there solely to embody their personal inspiration. Their vision is of subordination and precedence, but not of a battle or a balance sheet. The entertainment world is a pyramid: the security of the pinnacle of excellence depends on there being a properly built and graduated pile below it.

By this appeal to the practices of actors in performance, on stage and off, in the recounting of stories and the mimicry of other actors, I am suggesting two things. The historiographical point is that we should give serious consideration to the ways in which history is continuously and developmentally used within the theatrical profession, rather than taking volumes of biography and autobiography, memoirs, anecdotes and enacted reminiscences as raw material for academic histories which require external verification in order for them to acquire meaning. There is, I would suggest, a world of historical meaning in what they say about themselves, whether or not we have tangible proof of its truth. This does not mean, of course, that such statements are to be accepted simply at face value; rather that the testing and probing to which we should subject them should always be aimed at understanding who said what and why, within the context of their own perception of their world. My second objective in this study has been to adopt such an approach to the idea of 'the Decline of the Drama' in the 1830s, and to suggest an alternative history to the one written by the victors in the battle for control of the voices of the stage. I cannot, of course, suggest what would have happened if the analysis offered by Charles Mathews and Fanny Kelly had become the accepted story; but I am sure that the ensuing development of theatre in Britain would have been very different.

6   Theatre history and the discourse of the popular

Introduction

In this study I want to consider the discourse that crystallised the binary division between art and entertainment, considering how the reforms of the 1830s used the notion of inferior, popular performance in their vision of the theatrical world. The two cases I take, Bartholomew Fair and the *Tom and Jerry* plays, differ in what they show to be the results of this effort. The Fair, according to all official records, was completely suppressed in the flesh, and took on a useful existence in the imaginary of the middle classes, where it came to be part of the trope of 'Merry England', a popular cultural event whose quaint antiquity, comfortably in the past, could be contrasted with the debasement of modern popular entertainment. The *Tom and Jerry* plays, on the other hand, were irrepressibly of the present, and while they themselves came and eventually went, the kind of urban entertainment they presaged grew and throve, and had, after the 1843 Act, to be contained in the music halls. I suggest, at the end of this study, what is lost to theatre history and indeed to the development of English drama by the strict segregation between that vigorous theatrical lifespring and nineteenth-century Drama.

In attempting my first revisionist reading of nineteenth-century theatre history, I was able to revisit copious first-hand materials: the many thousands of words written by Anne Mathews, Fanny Kelly, Theodore Hook and others involved in performance in the period, and the millions more collected or composed by industrious historians of the time to carry their own views of the past and present. Moving beyond the attempt to understand the early nineteenth-century construction of the field of theatre and its past and future, to approach instead what was conceived as its Other, entertainment beyond and outside the hegemonic realm of the theatres, one is immediately in a different discursive situation. There is very little unquestionably first-hand evidence; it is indeed the nature of the Other of culture that it is mute, inexpressive, unrecorded, passed on, if it is passed on, by oral and traditional transmission rather than by written, rational communication. The burgeoning print culture of the nineteenth century includes enormous amounts of material published to amuse those with basic levels of literacy – broadsides, penny bloods, serial novels, cheap caricature, theatre and fashion prints and so forth – and also copious and usually aggressively hostile commentary upon that cheap culture, and attempts to replace it with moral and improving works; but doubt is cast upon these materials, as we may read them now, by twentieth-century strictures as to their functions and intentions.

The discourse of the popular

Since the 1960s the field of 'popular culture' has been under intense and partisan scrutiny and in the hands of competitive theorisation, with the result that one can no longer say that any printed or oral account of the pastimes of past times is self-evidently an authentic record, or represents meanings anticipated, shared or accepted by the sharers in the performance it describes or critiques. A complete, convincingly nuanced reading of surviving printed materials that were part of the entertainment culture of the nineteenth century is difficult, perhaps impossible, to achieve from where we stand; any account we give of performance or practice based on contemporary commentary is almost bound to be a reading against the commentators' grain, and cannot rely upon its sources to include what matters most to us. Moreover, one of the most striking aspects of 'the discourse of the popular' as it has developed in academic writing is that it is overtly as much political as literary, as much concerned with social, and especially class definition, as with aesthetics; and over none of these terms is there a consensus amongst recent theorists of the popular. Set on foot by more or less Marxist literary critics following George Lucacs and Raymond Williams, the twentieth-century academic study of popular culture started out as an assertion of the importance of studying the arts and entertainments of the majority, a study which began with the rejection both of industrially produced leisure activities imposed upon the masses and of elite cultural artefacts and institutions as the measure of aesthetic value and pleasure, in favour of something conceived of as by, for and about the people: folk art, traditional culture. The field predictably fissured into debates about the relative authenticity of texts and the credentials of their producers and consumers. Materials and practices generated by peasant or industrial communities for their own use, marketed by capitalists, used by the masses, transmitted in oral tradition, printed, sung, danced, declaimed, pirated, parodied, subverted or reported all became ammunition in a battle between various liberal and leftist theories. Post-Modernism's denial of the master narrative, and its assertion that there is no longer high or low in the bricolage of simulacra, does not go very far in enabling us to deal with the experience of difference, empowerment or its reverse in modern culture; and for me it has little explanatory power when attempting to understand past structures of feeling. The bottom line in cultural studies is a dispute about power: we disagree about how, or how far, cultural activity changes the political and social situation of those who take part in it. Is carnival ameliorative, constitutive or subversive of the social order which it inverts? What is the use of cultural capital? If popular culture, as well as elite art, is not merely part of a superstructure wholly determined by an economic base, how is this manifest in action?[1]

Such questions, *mutatis mutandis*, were also being asked during the politicised cultural and class formations of the early nineteenth century. I would argue, indeed, that the roots of our debate strike into the performances and writings denigrated by nineteenth-century commentators in their assertion of the need to restore the Drama to pre-eminence in the national culture, and their construction of certain forms of spectacle and language as the abjected Other of high art. In this study, therefore, I hope to consider some of the reprobated or appropriated sites and materials of performance in nineteenth-century London, alongside the printed texts they used, where any exist, and the commentaries upon them by interested parties who wished to construct them as utopian, character-forming and patriotic, or on the other hand as dangerous, immoral and low. As in the mid-twentieth-century debate, here too the commentators tend to be consciously politicised. The Tory minority are nostalgic but hearty, interpellating the poor man as True-born English, the salt of the earth, and describing a utopian world of rural or quasi-rural festival and fun in which gentlemen rub shoulders with their tenants and servants in a saturnalia of physical amusements which all tend to the condition of the battle or the game, the race or the hunt. Appreciation of this masculine world of excitement glosses over the suffering of the unfortunate animal and human losers, and focuses on good fellowship and national prowess. These books and shows found a large audience, and presumably one that included many classes, and overlapped with that for the popular publications that are castigated by the anti-barbarian majority of writers.

This majority, on the other hand, is once again liberal and even radical, all in some degree of the left, setting themselves up as champions of the people, interpellated now as sensible and sensitive, compassionate, desirous of education and eager to work; and asserting the universal right to decent and appropriate culture and amusements. These commentators are not interested in alliance with the aristocratic classes, but in forming a new power bloc with those below themselves in the social scale, raised up to an appreciation and acceptance of their own values. They were working on at least two fronts: attempting to monopolise the cultural media for their own voices, and therefore to deprecate sexuality, cruelty, spectacle and irrational pleasures, they attacked the current manifestations of 'low' art; at the same time, however, there was advantage to them in appropriating certain of the values of popular pleasure to their construction of a national identity, as long as the people's activity could be clearly articulated to middle-class moral and social concerns. The amusements of the people were thus reconstructed: their history, and their present role, were carefully described to appropriate them to a middle-class system of values, while actively suppressing their potential for resistance, or even difference and independence.

A basic trope in this discourse is the note of nostalgia and regret that the study of popular culture shares with theatre studies. The bewailing of the theatrical event as always-already lost has a certain material logic – every individual live performance that has ended truly *is* gone, and cannot be recreated or fully enjoyed again. In the case of 'authentic' popular art, however, the conviction that it belongs to the past, that the researcher has always just missed the moment of its true manifestation, and is living in a time of its decay and corruption, is much more ideologically charged. Florence Hardy, in her rather wistful record of the stories told to her by her famous husband about the young life she had not shared with him, recounts a harvest home that he attended at nine or ten years of age. A child of the upper-servant, professional class, he went in the low company of a 'strapping' 'young woman of the village' in the hope of seeing a lady whom he adored, and found himself stranded amidst rude strangers, whom he dared not speak to, until three o'clock in the morning. After this consciousness-forming, class-bound ordeal he never attended another such rustic celebration, but the memory of 'the young women in their light gowns sitting on a bench against the wall in the barn, and leaning against each other' as they sang the ancient ballad called 'The Outlandish Knight' stayed with him vividly, and he somehow knew, at least in hindsight, that this was a privileged moment of witness. He was present at a death: 'the railway having been extended to Dorchester just then . . . the orally transmitted ditties of centuries [were] slain at a stroke by the London comic songs that were introduced'[2] and 'The Outlandish Knight' was sung no more. How he knew this, since he never went again, is not recorded. The elegiac evocation of rural life in his novels clearly owes much to the sexual and emotional patterning of such a memory – elements of this scene, indeed, occur in several of his stories; and Hardy was by no means the only Victorian to carry into a more rational and disciplined time such charged memories of childhood or young-manhood. Thackeray, Dickens and many less famous writers[3] repeatedly recall moments of dubious enchantment in streets, barns, fairground booths or low singing-rooms, in the company of their social inferiors. Such cherished experiences invested popular pastimes dead and gone with worth and significance that distinguished them completely from the crude performances of current popular culture. The same, of course, can somehow be said by successive generations since: the foundational book of British twentieth-century cultural studies, Richard Hoggart's *The Uses of Literacy*,[4] is a powerful instance. But the 1820s and 30s were arguably the site of the initial, or at least the most explicit and intense, negotiation of this now-familiar paradox.

My authority for the discourse of the popular is Morag Shiach, who traces the development of the concept 'popular culture' from an eighteenth-century point of origin. Her argument is that 'the very recognition of certain cultural forms as "popular" is already bound up in a set of cultural and social discourses'. Her aim is to demonstrate a range of positions of 'the popular' within cultural discourse; it is variously conceived as 'a guarantee of social stability and unity, or as a dangerous threat to society' until the mid-twentieth century, when analyses begin which 'look to "the popular" as a site of opposition, of resistance'. She 'aims to demonstrate that assertions about culture, about national identity, about poetic value or popular taste are part of the process by which historical and political developments are negotiated and made sense of'. The debates she dissects and the artefacts on which they (often very selectively and partially) focus reveal contested spaces, which may be read as the sphere of the marginalised and oppressed, the dangerous edges of experience from which the young and vulnerable need protection, the site of cultural authenticity and naturalness, or as a breeding-ground of corruption that threatens the national language, literature and identity. In the early nineteenth century, she suggests, 'the shift from feudal, hierarchical relations to the more complex and diffuse power relations which characterize capitalism' were thus negotiated. 'The conflict between "the country" and "the city" was a crucial part of this struggle,' she adds.[5]

Nineteenth-century theorists of the popular

The ideological conflict over entertainment can be very clearly seen to contribute to these debates, and to be both a process of marginalisation and suppression of certain forms, practices and possible meanings, and also an appropriation of the wide and powerful appeal of popular performance. An overview of British writings about popular entertainment might begin in the antiquarian and local-history obsessions of the eighteenth century, with Strutt's *Glig-Gamena Angel-Deod, or the Sports and Pastimes of the People of England*, 1801,[6] whose thrust is anthropological, and concerned with the extrapolation of a national character. It is not long, however, before this interest is linked to the battle for the literary appropriation of the stage, and specifically

to Shakespeare. In discussing the turn to Shakespearean theatre history (above, chapter 4) I cited Edward Malone's condemnation of heterogeneous entertainment that included dancing alongside Shakespeare in the past, and, in his own time, a
tragedy and a farce on the same bill. Antiquarians like Francis
Douce took Malone's attempts to purge Shakespeare of the interpolations of 'harlequin' as permission to scrutinise past popular performance. Douce's *Illustrations of Shakespeare* are focused
upon 'the clowns and fools', popular tales, and 'the English
Morris Dance'. He asserts the necessity, for this serious purpose, of 'reading books too mean to be formally quoted'[7] in
order to augment our knowledge of the Bard, recommending
medicinal injections of poisonous hedgerow ingredients, gleaned
from black-letter learning, to increase modern wisdom. His subsequent consideration of foolishness and rustic dancing is by
no means in homeopathic proportion to his Shakespeareanism,
however, and he fills his two volumes with romantic conjectures,
linking, for example, the struggle between Death and the Fool
'in old dumb shows at fairs and perhaps at inns' to 'the modern English pantomime'. It is not far from such barely concealed
fascination with the 'trash' of past times to his recording of 'modern instances' of morris dancing, 'because it is extremely prob-
able that from the present rage for refinement and innovation,
there will remain, in the course of a short time, but few ves-
tiges of our popular customs and antiquities'.[8] This is his final
word: a long way from his ostensible purpose of the illustration
of Shakespeare.

The ideological value of thus constructing the popular in juxtaposition both to the classic stage and to modern sophistications,
setting up an image of the people and the nation through a study
of entertainments, was soon recognised by writers of many hues.
At the opposite extreme, perhaps, from the annotating excuses
of the professional philologists working on Shakespeare, is the
work of William Hone, a working-class Londoner who became
a Radical supporter of Burdett, a member of the OP committee,
and a pamphleteer whose most biting satire, often in conjunction
with George Cruikshank's political engravings, is based on his familiarity with the language and imagery of showmen and street
and fairground entertainers. Hone was a notable figure to his
contemporaries, not simply a parodist and political writer with

antiquarian interests and extremist connections; he was a friend of Douce, and also of Hazlitt and Lamb, as well as of prominent Radicals like Spence and Burdett.[9] *The Every-Day Book*, written to cover every day of 1825, and dedicated by Hone to Lamb, is 'a series of five thousand anecdotes and facts' about 'popular amusements, sports, ceremonies, manners, customs and events'. In 1823 he had produced a book that in some ways resembles Douce's *Illustrations of Shakespeare*, entitled *Ancient Mysteries Described . . . including notices of ecclesiastical shows, the festivals of fools and asses – the English boy-bishop – the descent into hell – the Lord Mayor's Show – the Guildhall giants – Christmas carols etc.*[10] Simon Shepherd points out[11] that in subsequent scholarship Hone's focus on popular parodic and burlesque entertainments in his ground-breaking study of ancient performance has since been quietly sidelined by a predominantly conservative academic interest in the drama of the medieval period; he characterises Hone's approach as proto-Bahktinian, a class-based study of medieval drama which relates it to present popular amusements and also attacks the Catholic Church for attempting to enlist the people's games, their rough antics with bedecked asses and cross-dressed parades, to prop up corrupt and failing ecclesiastical power. Hone's characterisation of the English people in his evocation of popular pursuits is thus thoroughly political; but he cannot avoid a fascination, even covert delight, in some superstitions and practices, a feeling which is in some measure shared by most commentators. It is perhaps the same appeal of the culture of their erstwhile peers, from which they are excluded by educational upward mobility, that has driven left-leaning scholars who write about the unlettered ever since, from Mayhew's disapproving and lovingly detailed survey of the London gutters in 1850 to the 1960–70s fixation of the Birmingham Centre for Contemporary Cultural Studies upon black youth sub-cultures.

At the other end of the political spectrum in the nineteenth century is the unabashed participant–commentator Pierce Egan, a man of no scholarly pretension, whose prolific writing of and about popular entertainments is marked by no conflict except the zestful battles it precipitates, sponsors, umpires and celebrates. The son of a downwardly mobile member of an Irish gentry family, apprenticed to a printer in 1786, Egan wrote some of the most successful, and controversial, non-satirical popular texts of his time. He established himself as the voice of 'the Fancy' – the sub-culture of fashionable gentlemen, noblemen and men of no visible means whose passion was sport, gaming and, especially, pugilism, in the first quarter of the nineteenth century. His first great success was *Boxiana: Sketches of Ancient and Modern Pugilism*, a monthly part-work that began in 1812 with an elaborate history of his subject and substantiated his stories of bare-knuckle fights past and present with the claim that boxing 'came from Nature', is quintessentially 'manly', and, especially, characterises the Englishman. The world of sports spectatorship and gambling interlocked with the theatre at every level. In 1812 William Oxberry, publican, printer, theatre historian and legitimate actor also published a book about boxing, *Pancratia: A History of Pugilism*; the West End world of the Haymarket and the Opera was also the site of the Crockford's and the other upper-class gambling hells; race meetings were the occasion for showmen to gather along with the riders and gamblers; and, at the lower end of the social scale, fairgrounds always included not only shows and playbooths, but also Crown and Anchor – gambling – tents to part the gawping merrymakers from their money. Egan's later books about the entertainment world include *The Life of an Actor*, another part-work, issued in 1824 and dedicated to Edmund Kean. These books are not for the poor – *The Life of an Actor* cost 3s a part, and included hand-coloured illustrations by Theodore Lane – but they embody a populist culture that claimed to include all Englishmen in its performance of a national identity.

To explore the temporal, moral and literary cross-currents of the discourse of popular entertainment in the nineteenth century, the rest of this study will focus, through the work of Hone and Egan, on its most fertile and formative period, the years following the great upsurge of popular radicalism at the end of the Napoleonic wars, 1815–22. Radical publicity after Peterloo (1819) sparked a period of furious activity in the world of popular entertainment and also in its defusing and its diffusion. Hone is our witness for the latter days of Bartholomew Fair, and in his work and the writings of historians of entertainment who followed him, especially George Daniels, I trace its destruction in the flesh and appropriation into discourse. Egan (no doubt entirely unintentionally) was the originator of a medium through which new modes of popular performance surfaced in London theatre that were to prove irrepressible; a different history from that which we currently use would see this creative stream as an important part of nineteenth-century drama.

Bartlemy

Bartholomew Fair, called by the people of London who took part in it for half a millennium 'Bartlemy',[12] is ignored by modern theatre scholars; it has been consigned to the realm of popular custom, and is out of fashion even there. It is neither rustic nor the property of an authentically industrial working class, but rather an inconveniently commercial ancient holiday imbued with the least attractive qualities of the debased urban mob – drunkenness, chauvinism, ignorance, rowdiness, theft, cheating and whoring.[13] It was at first a permitted and officially set-up site of inversion and liberty, patronised by the great; but, as carnival will, it got out of hand and developed a recalcitrant life of its own, powerful enough to evade theocracy and enact dramatic fictions during the Commonwealth, and indeed to preserve debased religious drama in performance until the nineteenth century, as well as providing a period of good living to some of the leading comic actors during the seventeenth and eighteenth centuries and to entertainers, showmen, freaks, fakes, beggars, thieves, charlatans and prostitutes down the centuries. Then, in the early nineteenth century, at the point which Hone records, it was suppressed in the flesh, and banished to the imaginary of the English people, where it served a purpose during the imperial years; and now it is forgotten. In *The Cities of the Dead* Joseph Roach discusses the function of 'forgetting' in the imaginary of western culture; he has notably forgotten this most ancient event, which does not occur in his index even under its polite name; and so also has his source for the discussion of the ludic spaces in London, Steven Mullany's *The Place of the Stage*.[14] Stallybrass and White's *The Politics and Poetics of Transgression* is the only modern work to have given real space and serious attention to the Fair, and their understanding of its significance is the foundation of what follows; but even they have tended to substitute consideration of Jonson's comedy and Pope's evocation of 'the Smithfield muse'

in *The Dunciad* for close scrutiny of Bartlemy itself, and its performance of the popular. I am especially concerned here with how
that powerful site was foreclosed and its significance deliberately
occluded by the way in which it was memorialised.

The ground where Bartlemy materialised each year in the
thundery and stinking dogdays is soaked in blood. The Fair
was established by charter in 1123,[15] and from 1327 to 1854
shared its 'smooth field' – Smithfield – with a beastmarket sup-
plying the capital's butchers. The sale of animals for slaughter
ceased on Fair days at 10am, and the sheep pens, transformed
by green boughs and plank tables to masquerade, according to
Hone, under titles like 'Fair Rosamond's Bower' or 'the Imperial Hotel', became 'the great public cookery' full of 'steaming
abundance', offering in the early years roast pig, and later oysters and fat sausages of dubious meat content with plenty of
mustard and pepper.[16] But this was London's biggest daily food
market: during 1828, for example, 152,804 head of cattle and
1,582,530 sheep passed from the market down Stinking Lane to
the slaughterhouses next to Newgate prison (an institution also
founded in the thirteenth century).[17] It was notoriously 'that
sink of cruelty, drunkenness and filth':[18] as late as the 1980s
I saw the Smithfield gutters still running with offal and dilute
blood washed from the livestock market. Until 1855 the market
dealt in living flesh. As did the Fair: according to Sir William
Wilkinson Addison, '[e]very component of a fair was there from
the beginning . . . its feasting, its greed, its folly', and in the
middle ages '[s]laves were bought and sold here'.[19] The regular influx of drovers led to the early establishment of inns; for
their convenience and that of the citizens another sort of flesh
market grew up in and around their houses of call. Apparently
as a cockney joke, the brothels were eventually collected in Cock
Lane; their workers were often foreigners who could not get work
within the walls. The outsider women did a specially good trade,
of course, at Fair-time; and outsiders, emblematised by the black
population of London, remained a strikingly visible presence at
Bartlemy to the end. Rowlandson engraved a black huckster selling from a tray round his neck at the front of his famous engraving
of the Fair;[20] and a nostalgic flaneur of 1827 left this portrait of a
dancer:

Didst thou ever, dearly beloved reader, and fellow-visitant to Bartlemy, didst thou ever behold a black dancing girl at one of the minor shows at Smithfield? *We* saw her but for a moment, and it was many, many years ago; but that fine female image of breathing ebony, hath never passed away from the chambers of our brain. There she stands, statue-like and melancholy as when we beheld her in the flesh – beautiful in her darkness – apparently proud of her dingy brow – a living carcanet. She lacked the usual gloss of cutaneous swarthiness; her arched brows cast no shadow upon her cheek – it was black as midnight. Her lips alone partook – and that but slightly – of the northern hue; the jet and ruby seemed to struggle there for dominion; – they were as rosebuds seen at twilight – her heart's blood just blushed in them to claim kith with the great crimson tide of humanity.[21]

Human as well as animal blood fed the Smithfield grass. The twelfth-century fair for the sale of cloth and for pleasure was granted for the support of St Bartholomew's Priory, and the hospital founded by the ex-entertainer Rahere in 1102 still serves the city's sick and dying; a brown-enamelled 'heritage' plaque today marks the inn where the nineteenth-century resurrection men sold corpses to supply its dissecting theatres. The field beside which the Priory was built was already a horse fair and race-course; Rahere was given a muddy area previously used for gibbetings and other punishments.[22] All this continued, so that before the great gates of the church, the field remained a playground for rich and poor – the joust and the wrestling match – as well as for the performance of mystery plays by the citizens. There was a whipping-post for summary justice at the Fair standing for centuries in the midst of the field. And this place saw the great juridical spectacles that confirmed the power of Church and state: it was in Smithfield in 1381 that the Peasant's Revolt culminated in the dramatic confrontation of rebel leader and the young King Richard II, at the end of which Wat Tyler was hauled from sanctuary in the church and beheaded on the spot. He had conveniently taken his last stand at the place where traitors were customarily executed, dragged by the heels from the Tower of London to die beneath the Smithfield elms. William Wallace died in this way in 1305: according to the Victorian historian of the Fair, Henry Morley, Wallace suffered actually during Bartlemy days, although executions were normally suspended for the duration of the holiday. Morley imagines Wallace's hanging and disembowelling as a rare entertainment for the merrymakers.[23] Two more

Scottish freedom fighters were executed there in 1307, and Roger Mortimer died at Smithfield for murdering Edward II. In 1538 John Forest, Prior of the Observant Convent at Greenwich, was roasted alive in a cage there for refusing to recognise the king's supremacy. In the sixteenth century the fires of martyrdom for more than two hundred people, whose sectarian allegiances conflicted with those of the ruling power, were lit so that they roasted, like Bartlemy pork, with the church door before their eyes.[24]

Each year, notionally on 23 August, the eve of St Bartholomew's Day ('black Bartholomew' in the martyrology of the French protestant refugees who settled in London) the Lord Mayor brought the pomp of office to permit the festival of fools, processing on horseback from the Mansion House via Newgate, where he drank the governor's health, to the gate leading to Cloth Fair beside the church, accompanied by the Aldermen and a gaggle of appropriate officials, all in their violet robes of state. He uttered the set speech proclaiming the fair and warning its traders in goods and in liquor to give full measure. In the medieval period the patriarchs reappeared to take part in the fun next day, in red robes, and having this time proclaimed the games, they settled in to watch the wrestling and to throw prizes to victors, including the best of the disputing scholars under the monastery's tutelage. For the three days of cloth trading the traditional summary court of Pie Powder enforced the mercantile standards officially proclaimed; for the rest of the fortnight to which the fair soon extended the pleasure-seekers were expected to look out for themselves – or, rather, the expectation was that they would fail to do so. Bartlemy was a byword for excess, deception and robbery; it was for getting and spending, an initiation into the ways of the world, and a loss of savings, cares and innocence.

Its power to command attention and challenge other definitions of culture fluctuated. Hone records particularly lurid attacks upon it round the turn of the eighteenth century, when 'The Observator' of 21 August 1703 calls it 'this market of lewdness', but he also notes that by 1740 its length had extended to three or four weeks, and great booths were erected where actors from the Theatres Royal played seasons patronised by gentry as grand as Frederick, Prince of Wales.[25] Hone repeats this as a challenge to his reader's credulity, and it is clearly a distant memory by the turn of his own century. Preaching the Fair down in 1830, the

Rev. R. C. Dillon (who had been the Lord Mayor's Chaplain in 1826) proclaimed it was 'an annual exhibition of folly and iniquity in this great City, which does injury to thousands' many of whom are to be seen lying in the streets helplessly drunk,[26] while 'not less than five hundred females – servants in families, and in other similar situations – are every year entangled at this fair in those snares of artifice, from which a whole after-life has not the power to set them free!'[27] For Ben Jonson the London dramatist, writing in 1614 (the year the filthy mud of Smithfield was at last paved over, to match the now-surrounding streets and alleys) saturnalia was the emblematic centre of the play that he set in the fair, and like many other writers championing playing and plays, he defended that principle from puritanical attack. But the intellectual defence of Bartlemy was always an edgy performance, and often found its arguments undercut by the brutal materiality of the less articulate upholders of tradition. From some point in the seventeenth century, when the Fair's liberties were widely understood to be under threat, a burlesque proclamation of Bartlemy licence began to take place on the night before the official ceremony. A gang of the City's tailors met in a Cloth Fair pub (its namesake is also now provided with a heritage plaque) and, having drunk enough, issued forth into the street, shears in hands, to proclaim their rights. They triggered the waiting 'Lady Holland's mob'. This collection of, as Hone described them, 'the most degraded characters of the metropolis' then rampaged at will through the surrounding streets. In 1822 more than five thousand rioters in the early hours of the morning so alarmed the civic authorities that they took determined steps to confine them thereafter to the fairground itself.

Hone observed and recorded the forces by which this most rich and resonant liminal event in the British popular calendar was pushed over the edge into, simultaneously, material extinction and virtual recreation in the imaginary of the Victorian nation, Britain the imperial power. Marcus Wood claims that Hone 'conjoins, reinvents, but never drowns his sources' and so his texts are 'some of the most open in English'.[28] But here Hone speaks in the tones of the proto-Victorian working-class apologist and moralist, and if we regard Bartlemy as his source, then he has surely drowned and closed it down. He was avowedly in favour of the utter extinction of the Fair. To do this is not to 'interfere with the amusements of the people,' for the people of the metropolis do not require such amusements; they are beyond the power of deriving recreation from them. The well-being of their apprentices and servants, and the young and the illiterate, require protection from the vicious contamination of an annual scene of debauchery, which contributes nothing to the city funds, and nothing to the city's character but a shameful stain. Bartholomew Fair must and will be put down.[29]

However, the repressed will have its way. As Douce excused his detailed description of contemporary morris dancing as something about to be forgotten, and so in need of antiquarian preservation, so Hone notes that of course no respectable person still visits Bartlemy, and so creates for himself an excuse, as historian or anthropologist, to go there and record it. His *Every-Day Book* entry about the Fair in 1825 is extremely detailed and informative about the size, the placing, the design of the stalls selling sweets, chapbooks, cheap toys and fairings; his assiduous visiting of the offerings of the twenty-two show booths is a historical exercise undertaken 'rather to amuse the future, than to inform the present generation'.

We are indeed grateful to know what he saw. It included six shows chiefly offering performance – plays, slackwire-dancing, juggling, all of which he tolerates – and three menageries, between which he discriminates carefully, praising the clean and modern arrangements of Atkin's and printing its full self-description, while recording that the long-established Wombwell's was overcrowded and managed only for the money to be made. Wombwell himself offended modern sensibilities. He was a small man with a face reddened by drinking and 'feelings perverted by avarice', indifferent to the public outcry caused by his having exposed his lion Nero to be baited by bull-dogs on a recent occasion in Warwick. Most of the rest of the shows Hone records follow a single, ancient pattern: for a penny entrance, they offered the sight of a collection of human and/or animal marvels, anomalies whose contemplation, conventionally by gawping simpletons, could be said to define the boundaries of nature, and confirm the norm by their deviation from it.[30]

The objects in these 'raree shows' are of two kinds, usually presented together. Giants, dwarfs, learned pigs and learned horses, a seven-footed mare, a preserved dolphin (a fake, Hone says), a

mermaid, fat girls, a 'white negro girl', all astonish by trans-
gressing the physical norms. Intermixed with them, in the same
booths, are examples of the abnormalities of culture, the perhaps
even more 'amazing' deliberate and wilful differences gone in for
by other races, colours and human organisations. This was not a
new commodity; Stallybrass and White note 'increasingly from
the sixteenth century, the fair's "monsters" . . . were supple-
mented by a display of the exotic – i.e. the marketable wonders
of the colonized world' and they quote Trinculo's appraisal of
Caliban as an attraction which would part 'a holiday fool' from
his money in a showbooth. They argue that 'most important of
all in countering nostalgic, populist interpretations of the fair
is the recognition that it was a crucial point of intersection between the imperialist spoils of the nation-state and the European
citizen'.[31] Mullaney speaks of the renaissance theatre in general
as emerging from the 'dramaturgy of the margins . . . a liminal
breed of cultural performance, a performance *of* the threshold,
by which the horizon of the community was made visible, the
limits of definition, containment, and control made manifest'.[32]
By the nineteenth century such time-honoured performance of
culture and difference is to a modern eye very obviously impe-
rialistic. Hone details such figures as 'Two wild Indians from
the Malay Islands' turbanned and wielding scimitars, and an
'Indian Chief' of whom Hone says dryly that his abdication to
come instead to Bartholomew Fair was probably forced upon
him by his tribe. Hone describes as 'perhaps the very best' exhibit in the whole Fair a show bringing together 'The Black Wild
Indian Woman' ('a court lady of the island of Madagascar') –
'The White Indian Youth' ('an Esquimaux') – and 'the Welsh
Dwarf' (fifteen-year-old Mr William Phillips of Denbigh). These
are to be seen 'all alive!' and all exhibited by a 'young American'
juggler, whose skills, and even his props and his dress, reminded
the sage observer of an ancient Gleeman copied by Strutt from
a manuscript in the Cotton collection. Hone is no longer sufficiently a radical or a subversive to read as anything other than
rational and good the processes of colonisation going on here,
whereby 'the boundaries between high and low, human and animal, domestic and savage, polite and vulgar' are reaffirmed as
they are transgressed[33] and he adds his own layer of distanciation
by placing the showman in an antiquarian picture.

Its primitive educative function is not enough, on its own, to
save Bartlemy from general condemnation in the modern world.
Hone reassures his readers that the City managed the Fair well
in 1825: 'the Corporation of London appears seriously to have
engaged in considering the nuisance' and its end is near. He was
right. In 1830 the Corporation made their move: having bought
the rights to the rents from stalls and standings in the fair, they
began to price the showmen off the streets. A manuscript history
of the Fair – ironically preserved in the Guildhall library, though
the Corporation has not recorded how they came by it[34] – charts
the rapid extinction of Bartlemy by the authorities.[35] The compiler has copied out the known sources on the history of the
Fair, and also collected nineteenth-century journalists' reports;
one records that in 1832 the Fair was reduced by the forbidding
of booths and stalls 'in any of its avenues', only ten shows were
put on, with a few exhibitions in houses in Giltspur Street; custom was bad, and though one could buy rare fruits – peaches
and nectarines at two or three for a penny – scarcely anyone did,
fearing they would contract the cholera from such exotic fare.
In 1834 and 35 one 'JJF' reported on the rapidly shrinking Fair,
noting that Wombwell's beasts were pitiable, apparently starving
and injured, while lesser showmen were sharing pitches to keep
down expenses and could not afford any handbills or performers
outside to draw in the customers. A 'standing' cost £3. 15s by
1835, and Fido and Jose the learned dogs could not take enough
at 1d a head to afford to return on the second day. Even so, some
tried to draw custom by cutting prices – it only cost a halfpenny
to see a peepshow offering the Murder in the Red Barn plus
'the great meeting of the Trades Unions to petition His Majesty
to pardon the Dorchester Unionists'. But the main money was
being made by the gambling tables, occupying nearly the whole
length of Smithfield from Duke Street. Some shows hung on.
Clarke from Astley's, asserting he was to be seen 'any time these
twenty years', was still there, and his clown was still stripping
off eighteen waistcoats as his horse jogged round the ring, to
reveal himself in equestrian splendour; in 1835 Richardson, veteran theatrical booth-holder, was putting a brave face on things,
claiming the Fair was looking up; and the sun was shining.

But at this point the Guildhall manuscript plunges back into
historical mode, and confines itself to the palmy eighteenth

century until the very end of the book. There the compiler (or re-binder) has included a set of rough notes describing the Fair from 1837. The scrawled scraps make pathetic reading. In 1841 they are only able to list seven shows; under 1842 they declare 'All is over. Bartholomew Fair is alas no more; no one left to tell the sad tale of the downfall. A few peepshows . . . were all that was to be found remaining of this carnival, the [city authorities del.] Corporation being determined to abolish the fair . . .'[36] The entry for 1845 begins 'fallen fallen fallen' and records eight ginger-bread stalls and a few nuts and apples. In 1848 the Lord Mayor walked to the ceremony of the proclamation in plain clothes, 'the cattle sale was continued throughout the day and not as hereto-for closed at ten o'clock'. The account concludes 'the charge for standing was so enormous that owners could not afford to keep Bartholomew fair'. There are no more entries, though the recorder has set out blank spaces for the ensuing years until the Fair was actually abolished, in 1855. The live meat market closed in the same year.[37]

The rhetoric of appropriation: Bartholomew Fair and the historians

It may be that the Fair, from the point of view of its mute partic-ipants, did not dematerialise at all, but simply relocated. In the unofficial histories I have been seeking out via the memoirs of per-formers, there are clues that the closure of the Fair on its ancient site was not a finality. The clown Charlie Keith, for example, who wrote his life story for the low entertainment journal *The Magnet* in 1875–6, remarks that he was inspired to take up his career by a new fair at Britannia Fields, now New Hoxton, which was called the New Bartholomew and began 'the year after Smithfield was prohibited'.[38] But at hegemonic levels of consciousness it has been written out of the official histories, and into a textual realm. The Guildhall manuscript, complete with its theatre-historian's tone of the always-already lost, seems to exist as a substitute for the event it records, a harmless simulacrum safely stowed away in the Corporation's library. Antiquarian appropriation was one of the weapons for the suppression of Bartlemy.

For all his earlier Radicalism and satirical use of print to at-tack and subvert authority, Hone's work begins this caging-in.

The Every-Day Book as a whole is a work of management and control, a taming of the hitherto uncollected, unclassified, rampagious minutiae of British popular life and lore. As if to invoke the bookish autodidact and his classificatory predilections, each day's entry begins with the saints' days and the historical landmarks belonging to it, and ends with an item from the 'Floral Directory' – that which shares an entry with Bartlemy is the mushroom, Agaricus Campestris, 'dedicated to St Laurence Justinian': an image of the persistently ephemeral which has interesting resonances with the Fair. A major entry such as Bartlemy itself is copiously supplied with print. Hone seems to cocoon the dangerous matter in its own history, and in literary allusion – lengthy quotations from Jonson, and several other printed works down the ages – in histories of the Priory, the Hospital, the medieval games, the licensing of trumpeters; in broadside ballads; he even, straining relevance to the limit, includes Charles Lamb's whimsical essay on roast pig. And he includes line-drawings, from old manuscripts, and from the pen of 'an artist who accompanied' him on his field trip. Not only this plethora of textuality, but also the prodigal use of typefaces, the way he breaks up his pages, and the insertion of sketches, ballads and colophons, all work to convert his account of the shows from a bawdy and rowdy ordeal into a safe, bookish, solitary, and an intellectual experience. The blood and bestiality of Smithfield is safely packaged for family consumption; its fleshly satisfactions are transformed into antiquarian interest in the amusements of the poor.

This move is not peculiar to Hone and the Guildhall manuscript. It is adopted by the major historian of the Fair, Henry Morley, in 1859, and, in its most extreme form, by the theatre critic and playwright George Daniels, who in 1842 – the year when for the first time there were no shows at Bartlemy at all – produced an extraordinary work called *Merrie England in the Olden Time*. Daniels's two volumes, taken from articles previously published in *Bentley's Miscellany* and now augmented with notes and illustrations, are an extraordinary rhetorical display. They pretend a casual, relaxed, light-hearted history; but offer instead a reading experience of painful discontinuity, a tense and continually interrupted and weakened narrative. They intermingle texts in such a way as to create an almost impenetrable maze of print, that cannot be followed consecutively and persistently;

the reader is helplessly controlled by the author, whose anxiety to discipline both material and reader is palpably at odds with his avowed message of hearty pleasure and relaxation.

The authorial voice of the book begins by ventriloquising Shakespeare: 'Dost thou think because thou art virtuous there shall be no more cakes and ale?'[39] and it clings to such authorities for its assertions of freedom: before the text progresses half-way down the page the praise of good living, eating and drinking begins to ground upon antiquarian footnotes, in which suggestive songs, bygone hostelries of London, morris dances, puritan grotesques and sketches of rope-dancers materialise; before the end of the first chapter twenty-nine lines of note crowd the text into a five-line strip, and the authorial voice can only force them off the last page by silencing itself and printing a drinking song. In chapter 3 a rodomontade upon the text 'The Genius of Mirth never hit upon a happier subject than the humours of Cockneyland' seems to conjure up two characters who henceforth carry the sentimental values Daniels is advocating along a narrative line that seems barely under the authorial voice's control. They are epitomes of the London burgher, of the same class as Hone's citizens who 'do not require such amusements' as Bartlemy and have servants and apprentices who need to be protected. By Daniels, however, the idealised Londoner is treated with condescension, an air of amused patronage which is now sentimentalised, but which stems from the contemptuous Tory tradition of the 1817 *Blackwood's Magazine* attack upon the 'cockney poet' Leigh Hunt, where the term 'cockney' excoriated the vulgar, the opposite of all that was educated, genteel, of the court – capable of poetry. By 1842 this contempt has softened into sentimental amusement.[40] 'Mr Benjamin Bosky' presents his card, affirming that he is a 'dry-salter' with a business in Little Britain – just off Smithfield, and felicitously named for the home of a character emblematic of the little people of the land; his patronymic is, however, a slang euphemism for 'drunk'.[41] He introduces a figure scarcely displaced from the mythic, his 'Uncle Tim', the Cockney archetype as found in Dickens's early work. Daniels's book appeared the year before *A Christmas Carol*; Uncle Tim owes something to the Cheeryble brothers (*Nicholas Nickleby*, 1839) and much to Pickwick (1837). Bosky and Uncle Tim are in favour of the people's pleasures; and it is in their amusing company that the narrator patronises the quaint humours of a London citizen society sanitised by antiquity and tradition and blessed by a combination of nostalgia and utopianism, eventually leading to the textualised Bartholomew Fair.

Daniels's opinion of popular culture is the same as Hone's, but seen from the opposite ideological position: '[o]ur ancestors were wise when they appointed amusements for the people' which benefit the state and also the Church, which wisely recruits the people's heroes to its cause. He maintains that all such amusements should be kept up, despite Puritanism – which by the second volume is made to include the '[c]ant and utilitarianism' of 'political economy' and 'improvement'. He is aware, however, that for his purpose the history of Bartlemy will need to be carefully manipulated:

The stream of time, that is continually washing away the impurities of other murky neighbourhoods, passes, without irrigating, Smithfield's blind alleys and the squalid faces of their inhabitants. Yet was it *Merryland* in the olden time, – and, forgetting the days, when an unpaved and miry slough, the scene of *autos da fé* for both Catholics and Protestants, as the fury of the dominant party rode religiously rampant, as *such* let us consider it. Pleasant is the remembrance of the sports that are past . . .[42]

Perhaps the eighteenth-century pornographic usage that termed the female body 'Merryland'[43] is actively in Daniels's mind in this topographic evocation. Certainly the passion, dirt and violence he wishes rhetorically to set aside thrust themselves forward as he writes, finally undermining his syntax as he tries to master them facetiously with alliteration and archaism. The struggle mirrors on a small scale the battle he has, using the textual resources of narrative, authorial voice, character, illustration, fact, date and footnote, to dominate his whole subject and pen it into manageable textual spaces.

My evocation of Smithfield's bloody antiquity, above, is deliberately hot, *excited* by the idea of Bartlemy – its corporeal presence, its undeniable antiquity in a field where so few ancient records exist, its stirring potential as a site of the history of the people: the same excitement that moves Hone and Douce in their partially shamefaced evocation of the antiquity of morris dances and folk customs. The question that then suggests itself is why the Fair, with all its now-safe temptation to such engagement, has been so completely suppressed as to be forgotten, so put out of mind that while Smithfield has memorials to body-snatchers, the Fire of London, Rahere (in the church), even a resited pub called the Hand and Shears, there is nothing to mark the Fair, and no mention anywhere of Lady Holland's mob. The manuscript resides inside the Guildhall library; outside that library there is no marker – instead, a memorial to Hemming and Condell, Shakespeare's printers. Part of the answer is no doubt the way in which Londoners were made ashamed of Bartlemy, its thuggish, drunken, dangerous connections with sex and gambling serving to alienate all classes of Radical opinion. Equally, the modern interest in 'popular culture' is unprepared to deal with cruelty, ignorance, racism, prejudice and violence as recreational. So the suppression of Bartlemy was effected, and its textualisation played a part in the triumph of the new middle-class voice of reason and control. Stallybrass and White suggest, however, that because 'the mechanisms of identity-formation' only freed the middle-class subject from the 'vertiginous and disorienting calling of voices from above and below' by taking 'all this *clutter* and *mess*' into 'the bourgeois Imaginary', this mistaken manoeuvre inevitably 'forestalled its radical democratic project'.[44]

I will not follow the lead offered by this insight, a suggestion that might direct us to seek for the point in time when the clutter and mess began to erupt once more out of the bourgeois imaginary. That route inevitably takes the artistic manifestations under scrutiny a step further from their place and people of origin. Instead I would like to look for ways in which the suppressed forces of popular expression found other, immediate outlets, and how the rhetoric of 1840s social reform worked to deny these the status of art. The residual Bartlemy could be diffused into Merry England; but there were emergent popular voices that challenged the writers of the 1820s, 30s and 40s and would not be confined to the page, but burst out into and through performance. If Bartlemy was – or could be made to be – a story of loss and ending, suppressed in the flesh and diffused in the imaginary, there were phenomena of the 1820s that presaged a much less conclusive hegemonic victory for the middle classes. The intelligentsia of the right and the left had a much greater and more complex task in assimilating such emergent forces to a serious new model of culture and community.

Daniels's controlling characterisation of Bosky and Uncle Tim, substantial if vulgar citizens of London, was being overtaken by a different phase of cockney stereotyping, one that shows great anxiety over the cultural challenge posed by the new, and younger, more self-assertive, voices of the people. This panic surfaces very clearly in the 1820s controversy over *Tom and Jerry's Life in London*. A closer look at that immensely successful publication and its stage life suggests a different practical outcome to the attempt to control the entertainments of the people, in which the interests and even the caterers and customers of Bartlemy completely evaded suppression; but the rhetorical triumph of the discourse of the popular has so successfully shaped our understanding of their new manifestations, turning them into nothing but the Other of the art–entertainment binary, that such a continuity has been disguised and denied.

Tom and Jerry's life in London

During the nineteenth century characterisation of the metropolis of London developed into an important strand in Victorian proto-sociology as well a major theme in the novel. These representations have provoked a correspondingly large and various critical exegesis, which tends to focus, at least when considering fictions, on the relation of the narrating–writing individual to the cityscape described and inhabited or observed.[45] Pierce Egan is often cited as one of the Late Georgian writers whose practice, of coupling journalistic sketches with detailed prints (by Robert Cruikshank), is a crude forerunner of the metropolitan novels. But Egan, though his personal voice is everywhere in his writings, is not engaged, as they are taken to be, in an artistic agon with his material.[46] He could more accurately be seen as playing with it, allowing it to slip excitingly through his mind and his fingers. Following a structural principle of juxtaposition, which he optimistically suggests will be 'almost like the rapid succession of scenes in a play, which will tend to increase the effect'[47] he allows his sketches of London life to unfold, in loose-jointed flaps. He sometimes writes with great exuberance, but may still lazily refer the reader to the superior detail and verisimilitude of the plates, or insert blatant guidebook descriptions of tourist sights, and even excuse himself from writing the full amount required

by a number because he has lost his notes. His disorderly procedure and jocose tone tend to be seen, through the appropriative,
hierarchising procedures of canonical criticism, as raw material
which Dickens transformed, infusing it with his genius, endow-
ing its rich chaos with significant organisation. Egan, however,
is crucially unlike the Victorian novelists in that he is concerned
to claim not simply verisimilitude, but factual truth.

However, Egan's evocation of London is also strikingly unlike the deliberately detached, quasi-scientific discourse of
the proto-sociologists of the first Victorian generation. Henry
Mayhew attempts to explore the hidden depths and to reveal
the underclasses to respectable scrutiny by his exhaustive tax-
onomies of street life and crime; reformers who took Mayhew's
message to heart, like Andrew Mearns and James Greenwood,
issued lurid jeremiads warning their contemporaries to reform
'darkest London' before it was too late.[48] Egan is no prophet of
doom; his is a representation of things as they are, with named
individuals, real places – but described as an invitation, not as
a warning. He offers hot gossip, insider information about the
London he knows, seeming to celebrate and revel in the modern
city: its rapid change, its extreme manifestations of both high
and low life, and, most of all, its wildly heterogeneous visual and
social variety. The Tom and Jerry phenomenon was condemned,
like the Newgate novels by Ainsworth, Bulwer Lytton and others which shocked critical opinion by drawing stories from the
Newgate Calendar, for its use of vulgarity and for glamorising
reprehensible behaviour; but Egan's texts are emphatically not
about housebreaking and murder, and the criminal lower classes
are not the central actors in his sketches.

The condemnation meted out to Tom and Jerry was nevertheless very violent and extraordinarily emotional. *Life in London; or,
the Day and Night Scenes of Jerry Hawthorn, esq., and his elegant
friend Corinthian Tom, accompanied by Bob Logic, the Oxonian, in
their Rambles and Sprees through the Metropolis* appeared in parts
from September 1820, and in volume form in July 1821, and
was an immediate popular success: its spin-offs, imitations, pla-
giarisms and, especially, dramatisations flooded the town and
continued into 1823 with such pieces as *The Fancy's Opera* at the
Adelphi in January, and the revival of Pocock's *Hit or Miss* which
starred Mathews as a sprig of the upper classes besotted with

driving coaches, a genteel craze of the time, who is seen exploring the world of the Fancy. Theatrical versions of Egan's original
were mounted at illegitimate theatres all over London and in the
provinces; Stirling records that this 'extraordinary piece made
the fortunes of half the managers in England'.[49]

As soon as it was evident that Egan's invention had taken on
a life of its own in the popular imagination, critical notice began to be taken, especially of the performances. *Town Talk*, for
example, objected to the theatres mounting 'vivid representations of the vilest practices of the blackest sinks of iniquity' while
regretting that 'a decent man like Pierce should have done so
much mischief'.[50] The plays seem to have caused offence even
in the Lord Chamberlain's office, and to have been licensed in the
teeth of the officials of the examiner of plays: the Larpent Collection has on file, with the approved copy of Moncrieff's version
staged at the Adelphi and then at Covent Garden, several letters of protest. Two internal notes read 'your Grace cannot be
aware that the Lord Chamberlain gives his sanction to this obnoxious performance' and 'this poisonous and disgusting scene is
licenced by your Grace. Doubtless my Lord without your knowledge. P.W.'.[51] The sanction of the Lord Chamberlain, the Duke
of Montrose (a Scottish high Tory) was unequivocal, however,
and Egan's biographer records that he not only saw the play himself at the Adelphi but returned a second time with his wife. It
had an unprecedented run there, from 26 November 1821, of almost 300 nights. The royal Duke of York attended, and the wife
of the MP Charles Arbuthnot was introduced to the minor theatre for the first time, recording that it was 'a very pretty theatre,
but beyond anything vulgar I ever saw'.[52] *Blackwood's* informed
its readers that getting in to see the play remained a perilously
crowded experience months after the opening.[53]

The press condemnation, when it was not simply fulmination
about 'this obscene and contemptible production'[54] focused on
two things: the exhibition, in a place where women would be
bound to take notice of it, of that which is unfit to meet the
public eye (literally, in fact, the obscene) – journalists rhetorically demand whether their readers 'can . . . endure the thought
of making their wives and sisters acquainted with the disgusting
orgies of Saint Giles and Saint Catherines' 'where the characters in a drama are prostitutes, thieves and vagabonds'; and they

express their horror at the *language* heard on stage, 'a tissue of disgusting ribaldry and obscene jests' or, more tellingly, 'flash and indecency'.[55] Moncrieff, understandably elated by the success of his play, printed a triumphant self-defence in his preface to the published text, and focused upon the characterisation of the piece in terms of its linguistic stamp upon modern times: 'To those venerable noodles who complain that I and my prototype, Pierce, have made this an age of *Flash*, I answer – any age is better than the AGE OF CANT!'[56]

The critical focus upon the harm done by the plays is no doubt partly a response to the commonplace that while the print media carry the freedom of the press, a valuable liberty that requires us to tolerate, if not to read, all sorts of trash, the drama is charged with the duty of idealisation. The classic stage should be a display of manners and deportment that is a model for correct behaviour; so the representation of manifestly incorrect 'sprees and rambles', in which young men drink and rowdy in low-class haunts, is improper.[57] But such representations had long been tolerated or ignored; *The Beggar's Opera* was a stock piece to which no one any longer made serious objection, even though it had become a vehicle for all sorts of theatrical games, with impersonations, topical songs, introduced dances and wholesale cross-dressing. In the play versions of Tom and Jerry most of the dramatists have used stock devices to provide the through line of action which Egan omits; so the characters, already conceived one-dimensionally, slide in the direction of stage convention, and so, one might assume, of acceptability. Astley's Amphitheatre claimed to be the first to stage the story, on 17 September 1821, in a dramatisation by Egan's friend Barrymore, with which the author assisted.[58] It introduced Harlequin and Clown among the characters, and played various scenes of slapstick as they led Jerry into folly. Moncrieff's version used a venerable story-line to string the action together and provide some suspense, by having Jerry already affianced to Sue, who in Egan's book is a mere extra, a friend of Corinthian Kate, Tom's mistress. The women are transformed into old schoolfriends, one living in the country and one in town, where Kate agrees to help her friend keep an eye on Jerry and show him the dangers of getting into trouble in London. This predictably involves them in dressing up as young gentlemen themselves, a comedy device as old as the commercial stage. Jerry meanwhile, in this play and especially in Dibdin's version staged at the Olympic, slips away from Egan's picture of a fine young buck, an athletic huntsman who is soon initiated into town manners and becomes indistinguishable from his urban cousin Tom, towards the stereotype of the country clown, a comic butt who is fooled, fleeced, made drunk and stripped by the London sharks and sharpers. The minor characters include equally threadbare stage types: an Irish watchman derived from Dogberry, an old woman who keeps a sponging-house and is given to malapropism, and her good-hearted maid who helps the prisoners.[59] Recognisable intertheatrical transactions were going on: at the Adelphi John Reeve as Jerry and Benjamin Wrench as Tom created personae that were the basis of their career-long public images, in a reciprocity of popularity between the players and the roles. At the end of Moncrieff's version there is an elaborate masquerade, where Logic appears as Dr Pangloss from *The Heir at Law* and Tom as Don Giovanni: their layered intertheatricality is spelt out.

The London stage life of Don Juan/Giovanni, indeed, is a clear precedent for Tom and Jerry. As a reviewer in *The Drama*[60] remarked

Don Juan has appeared on the English stage in various forms from a serious opera to a ballet, pantomime and burlesque, and has been played at every Theatre in the metropolis. We have had him '*In London*' (at the Olympic and Drury) – '*In the Country*' (at the Coburg) – '*On Horseback*' (at Astley's). He has also been turned into an *Harlequin*, (at Drury) – and last of all 'A Vampire!' (at the Adelphi.) Mr Dibdin's excellent burlesque will never be forgotten.

The interaction of the Don and Tom and Jerry happens on multiple levels; there is, for example, a book of 1822 entitled *Don Juan; containing his Life in London, or, a True Picture of the British Metropolis* by one Alfred Thornton, in which lengthy guidebook descriptions of the tourist sites of the capital and glitzy excursions to its night spots are strung together with the adventures of an (unintentionally) comically reflective and strangely morally concerned Don, given to soliloquy about the wickedness of the world.[61] To compound the theft of Egan's idea, the copy I bought has accidentally bound into it one gathering of *Real Life in London*,[62] a rapidly issued imitation of *Tom and Jerry* which

Egan called 'a bare-faced piracy' of his own work. But the interaction goes both ways. In a plate for chapter 6 of Egan's own book
Cruikshank shows Vestris costumed for *Don Giovanni in London*,
a role which made her famous, in the dressing room at Drury
Lane. There are vital differences of effect and reception between
the two sets of rakish heroes, however. In the Don Juan/Giovanni
burlesques, the rake's profligate and entirely immoral behaviour
is found amusing, and defeated by humour, and certainly removed out of harm's way. As Hone remarked, his adventures
'seem but an amplified version of the adventures of *Punch*, the
libertine destroyed, in the puppet-show of the streets'.[63] These
relatively easy-going, mocking responses to the Don's stage adventures, as well as the ordinary theatricality of the structures
introduced in the dramatisations of Egan's work, suggest that to
cause such cultural alarm there must have been something exceptional, other than its mere dramatisation, its fleshly presence,
about Tom and Jerry.

I would suggest that the problem was rooted, firstly, in the perception that this representation had an extraordinary degree of
realism. This was not 'the adventures of Punch', but of men and
women, whose current everyday experience had not so far been
exposed by such unequivocal stage representation. At Astley's
the first dramatisation to reach the stage confined this aspect of
its innovation to picturing relatively harmless aspects of London
social life and leisure. The Amphitheatre regularly turned all its
big dramatic representations into horse drama; so the leading
scenes there were not the book's riotous fights in Temple Bar
or the visit of the cousins to an East End dancing room, but
the arrival of Jerry from the country on the Exeter Mail coach,
with four horses, at its London terminus, the White Horse Cel-
lar; a scene outside the Opera House in the pouring rain, with
people struggling to get to cabs or their own carriages; and 'the
scene of the *Epsom Races* . . . . it is a true and humourous [sic]
picture of real life, and exhibits post chaises, gigs, tilburys, car-
avans, hackney coaches, carts, and four-in-hand barouches, all
drawn by real horses.'[64] None of these scenes was actually in
the book. The Coburg weighed in with *Life in Paris* in April
1822, attempting a rival spectacle by showing the Boulevard –
Paris's minor-theatre district – by night, 'with all the various
exhibitions which characterize that scene of Gaiety – Rope

Dancers – Tumblers – Punch – *Boutiques Ambulans* – the whole Tribe of French Vendors of Flowers etc., Musicians, Promenaders'.[65] The Adelphi version included an elaborate display of waltzing – the latest dance craze – and culminated in a Venetian masquerade parading through Leicester Square, complete with clowns stealing poodles, a dwarf with a big head, and all the characters in fancy dress.[66] The idea that the play could be a vehicle for framing and presenting a picturesque version of popular amusements had crossed the mind of the critic who commended Astley's Epsom races: he wondered that the Amphitheatre's unique facilities had not been utilised in a scene 'which would have afforded a fine scope for Jerry and Tom to have exercised to the fullest extent their propensities for "*larking*" – we mean Bartholomew Fair!' At the Adelphi the smaller stage and lack of a circus ring did not, apparently, interfere with the excitement of presenting the audience with carnival pictures of the modern London outside its doors.

But some of the town's amusements that were shown were less picturesque, and less amenable to defusion by their framing on stage: their quotidian acceptability, indeed, depended on their not being named or seen. The hostile critic in the *Mirror of the Stage* quoted above expostulated, '[w]e know we shall be told, that this drama represents the every-day scenes of real life in London: but surely there are *some* scenes unfit to meet the public eye'. What exactly this means is made clear when in January 1823 the periodical congratulated itself on being of 'the respectable part of the public press' which has forced the managers to clean up Tom and Jerry. The new piece at the Adelphi, *Green in France, or Tom and Jerry's Tour*, which in fact still contains larks, fights, drunkenness, scenes in fairgrounds and women in breeches is, they claim, unobjectionable, because the women are now 'chaste' – Tom, Jerry and Logic have married them.

So the shocking element in the original plays was, it appears, that they showed active unmarried women; and this implied prostitutes. Interestingly, the scene in which this is most obvious is an intertheatrical one, a representation of soliciting, and fighting over women, in the lobbies of one of the patent theatres. This is directly taken from Egan, where the young men, already drunk, go to the saloon at Covent Garden and look on. In the book reviews it was not singled out by critics as offensive, possibly because although it was graphically realistic, with details of the nicknames and characters of prostitutes and the proclivities of certain of their customers discussed in detail and their likenesses shown in the plate, it was presented in the authorial voice, and, of course, only on the page. But on the stage, embodied in the flesh of actresses, the matter was entirely different. The Olympic version by Charles Dibdin the younger is a patent acting-out of the sexual traffic that uninvolved frequenters of the theatres, and all respectable women who went there, agreed to ignore.

Dibdin's character Sue is the sister of a sharper called Floss, and they set out to fleece Jerry. In the licenser's manuscript the fourth scene is set in the '*Lobby of the Theatre. Loungers etc going in and coming out of the Boxes*' where Tom, Jerry and Logic enter discussing being drunk. Then

JERRY: there's a pretty girl
(*Sue and Floss appear arm in arm*)
TOM: She *is* indeed – new too – even *I* don't know her –
LOGIC: Nor I, but I'll speak to her (*going towards her*)
TOM: (*stopping him*) Stay Logic; she is already engaged, and no true Corinthian will intrude himself upon the Engagement of another gentleman
JERRY: But he's an old Ephesian, and doesn't care what he does, – She's monstrous handsome.[67]

An improvised quarrel and fight ensues, to the accompaniment of a song with a chorus demanding that a constable or the box-keeper should come and 'turn them out' (the usual formula of the audience's demand for order to be restored in the theatre). A constable does appear, and takes bribes from all and sundry; and they exit on the lines: 'Nobody can hear the play if you be so uproarious / This is Life in London.'[68] In the printed version the dialogue is cut after Tom's first speech, presumably for decency: the brutal sexuality of the men's appraisal and the conclusions they draw still has the power to startle the reader. Scenes follow which appear to depict criminal activity very nakedly. Jerry is fleeced first by means of loaded dice, with the sharper, Nickem, confiding his contempt for the country booby to the audience; and then by Sue, who has persuaded him to bid in some kind of fraudulent auction, and accepts the jewellery he has bought with feigned reluctance, while 'laughing in her sleeve' at him. In this scene Floss commentates on the proceedings between them to the audience.[69] These scenes are toned down, or omitted entirely, in the published text, which again suggests that they were at the limits of acceptability. The attitude of the whole piece has an edge of rather dark cynicism about its revelations that would seem to me to go some way towards explaining the critics' shock; but the representation on stage of what happened in the lobbies may well have been enough to infuriate those determined to maintain the double standards by which they ignored the sexual traffic when they accompanied their wives to the boxes.

The problem about prostitution in the box lobbies is not the whole story. More general forces repressing sexuality on stage, or, more particularly, disempowering women in the name of decency, seem to me to be at work in the condemnation of the play. Moncrieff's version of the play, which was also violently attacked, is not nearly as cynical or as explicit as Dibdin's. The Adelphi bills at the opening of the second season assert that its 'series of pungent and minutely accurate Representations of HIGH and LOW LIFE' are strictly moral, and that this piece, which is 'the substance', should not be judged by its imitations, 'the shadows'. Early in its 1821 run, bill matter claimed on behalf of the author that the realism of the piece means it deserves to be seen as 'in the very highest class of Drama', an 'animated picture of every species of Life in London, deprived, through the filtering stone of the Proprietor's critical Care, of all that might disgust or offend even the most fastidious Imagination' and offering a lesson in life for the mere price of a ticket. Moreover, as they truly assert, the play provides a moral ending for all, and 'Sue and Kate are proved to be very different Characters from those they have been represented.'[70] In the final scene all three young men are declared to be about to be rescued and reformed by marriage to Kate, Sue and another new character, Jane. There is no box-lobby scene, and the women claim to do all they do by way of duping Tom as well as Jerry for their own good. Kate claims that 'to rescue Mr Corinthian from the vortex of riot, folly, ruin, into which he is plunging, is the most earnest wish of my heart'.[71] So either Moncrieff is right in thinking he is being condemned for the more explicit scenes risked by other adapters, or, more interestingly, the critics concerned about the representation of women in modern society are disturbed by his work on a less conscious level. I suggest that in the case of his version the repressive response has more to do with the powerful agency of the women. In Moncrieff's added structuring, Kate, Sue and Jane drive the plot, and manipulate the men; they both literally and figuratively wear the breeches. This is perhaps enough by 1821 for shying critics to condemn them as offensive to decency and virtue.[72] The freedom of women seen in earlier comedy was curtailed; from this decade on the display of female power, emblematised in female flesh, was steadily excluded from sight, and confined to the 'popular' stage, away from the respectable audience, unless it was very cleverly and carefully framed to disguise its potency.

The second area of cultural importance in the Tom and Jerry plays and their spin-off productions is in the critical response to the language they employ and propagate. This too signalled a significant moment in the closing-down of what was acceptable on the stage that was to become the voice of middle-class Victorianism. Olivia Smith suggests that '[i]deas about language and ideas about suffrage shared the central concern of establishing which groups of people merited participation in public life. Civilization was largely a linguistic concept, establishing a terrain in which vocabulary and syntax distinguished the refined and the civilized from the vulgar and the savage.' She fixes upon the moment of 1819–22, and the work of Hone, as the point where 'writers and readers released themselves from previous constraints. They were incessantly aggressive and wilfully, hilariously rude. The manacles were broken and the people laughed and laughed.'[73] I would extend consideration of the anxieties this generated to its focus upon the stage, as an issue of specifically class definition. Deborah Vlock, in her study of the nexus of popular theatre from which, she argues, Dickens's novels grew, focuses on the politics of voice and its particular urgency in the early years of the nineteenth century.

As the external marks of nobility were embraced by a middle class with the taste – and the capital – for living stylishly, the voice was increasingly perceived as a more reliable social register . . . which eventually dominated the field of popular stereotypes, blessed with the ability to embody truth . . . the socially inscribed voice was woven into antitheatrical discourse, with working-class voices raising respectable blood pressures. Early modern and modern European statements about performance frequently centred on insolent or subversive voice.

This importance makes the actor a threatening figure, for she or he may assume voices not indicative of real standing.

'False speaking' is empowered with the potentiality to destroy old worlds or create new ones. It is as if dramatic voices hold the essence of human behaviour inside of them, germs of being and action, and threaten to loose the dangerous, the eccentric, the deviant of these into the world.[74]

This argument casts an interesting light on the otherwise rather puzzling intrusion of the figure of Green, in Moncrieff's play, who becomes the title character in its sequel, *Green in France*, and similar London citizens in other adaptations – Dibdin has the family of 'Lustre, glass-man of Temple Bar' – who have no point of origin in Egan's book.[75] They derive from the Court/City contrast used by dramatists from the Renaissance onwards, but here they are modulating from being simply the destined victims of courtly rakes to acting as one reference point within a world of middle-class self-definition. Such a dramatisation of the vulgarian as comic cockney butt is hegemonically acceptable; but the plays also allow other voices to be heard, to which the critics are extremely hostile.

Part of the problem is that the leading characters are shown allowing their own voices to be subverted by vulgarity: slang, flash, non-standard speech is offered to the audience as fashionable and desirable. Egan's scene (Book 2, chapter 1) in which Jerry arrives in Tom's house, and in his 'chaffing crib' – parlour – is fitted with a fashionable coat by Primefit the tailor and with a fashionable vocabulary by Tom and Logic, is picked up enthusiastically by the dramatisers, who reproduce the slang very fully. Moncrieff also uses it later in the act to pull in the scenes he has not been able to stage, having Jerry exclaim:

'Now, my dear Jerry, to introduce you to another scene of Life in London; – you have taken a ride among the pinks in Rotten Row, have dipped into the Westminster pit, sported your blunt with the fly fakers and gay tyke boys on the phenomenal monkey – seen that gamest of all buffers, Rumpty-tum, with the rats; and now you can make an assignation with some of our dashing straw-chippers and nob-thatchers in the Burlington Arcade – this is the very walk of Cupid . . .'

Here he is interrupted by Jane passing him a note, and the men exit in pursuit, uttering hunting cries.[76]

Vlock suggests that critical concern about such gleeful departures from standard English feeds into contemporary concerns 'among the privileged classes, about the insidious powers of subversive speech, and the confusion of identity that could result from the "master" language failing to maintain its proper relation to other languages'.[77] She sees this as middle-class anxiety about the nether world; but in my view the dark region of the popular, the vulgar, is not only lower class; it is an alternative model of behaviour and identity that challenged the aspirant middle classes in the 1820s–30s, derived from the cross-class alliance that was the world of popular amusement. It was in the effort to pull clear of that debased aristocratic value system that these anxieties arose.

At the opening of his third act – the point where the half-price audience came in, and a reprise of the plot so far was advisable – Moncrieff gives the young men a slang panegyric on the cross-class, all-inclusive delights of the fast life. It is derived from what Egan calls a 'crambo Chaunt' which he puts into the mouth of Logic, the dissolute 'Oxonian', who in both book and plays is represented as chiefly learned not in Latin and the classical lands, but in the town's secret languages and secret places:

> Life in London! With us, is a round of delight,
> Larking all day, sprees and rambles all night;
> Tom, Jerry, and Logic, have ever the best
> of the coves in the East, of the swells in the West:
> such pals in a turn-up, so bang up and merry,
> As Jerry, Tom, Logic – Tom, Logic, and Jerry,
> Ne'er were seen, since the World first by Noah was undone,
> So here's Logic's, Jerry's, and Tom's, life in London!
> Drinking, dancing, pinking, prancing,
> Milling, billing, wetting. betting,
> Playing, straying, bumbling, tumbling,
> Smoking, joking, swagg'ring, stagg'ring,
> So up to all, downy, there's ages of fun done!
> In Logic's, and Jerry's, and Tom's, Life in London![78]

The aspirant Toms and Jerrys of the audience are thus offered great temptations to unseriousness, and can acquire apparently first-hand experience of the fun to be had in low life.

Again, realism is the great threat. Don Juan was clearly a puppet aristocrat, whose fall was to be relished along with his adventures; but here was real life. For the first time audiences were witnessing the appearance of the lowest elements of society, speaking their own virtually unintelligible languages, on the stage. Anxiety about hearing the siren voices of the abyss intersects with the anxiety about the realism of the plays, for they not only claimed to be about real people and the latest languages, but in some cases introduced named individuals from the London streets, in the flesh. The Adelphi's scene in 'the back slums in the holy land' featured Little Jemmy Whiston, a drunken beggar with deformed legs whose pitch was Blackfriars Bridge, and Billy Waters, a one-legged former slave who was an accomplished violinist and dancer.[79]

One scene which is the focus of much of the hostile comment is set by Egan in All Max in the East, but by Moncrieff in a real boxer's pub, 'Mr Mace's crib'. The female characters in the scene are working women (not a category often featured on the West End stage) and are all either black or, in some cases, perhaps, making a point of not being so: they are called African Sal, Mahogany Mary and Mrs and Miss Lillywhite. There is also a black child, to whom Logic feeds gin. The central figures are African Sal, played by a man, Sanders, and Walbourn's Dusty Bob, a low-class man whose dirty job (Egan specifies that he is 'a coal-vhipper',[80] and gives him the epithet 'nasty' rather than 'Dusty') symbolically blacks him up. While their scene is, on the comic level, crude carnivalesque grotesquery, it is also sufficiently independent and aggressive to be alarming, especially since it was the most popular episode, and took on a life beyond the play, danced as a sketch or interlude in other bills.

The first speech, by Dusty Bob, offers the challenge of the secret language and also marks the scene as displaying grotesque consumption and abandon

Now, Landlord, arter that 'ere drop of max suppose we have a drain o' heavy wet, just by way of cooling our chaffers – mine's as dry as a chip – and, I say, do you hear, let's have a two-penny buster, half a quartern o'bees'vax, a ha'p'oth o'ingens, and a dollop o'salt along vith it, vill you?

The gentlemen enter; when Logic calls Sall 'my snow-ball' Bob says 'come, let's have none of your sinnywations, Mister Barnacles; she's none the vurser, though she is a little blackish or so!' Logic calls for drink, in response, and Sal speaks for herself:

'Massa Bob, you find me no such bad partner; many de good vill and de power me get from de Jack Tar.' The climax of the scene is their dance, a

comic pas deux – Dusty Bob and Black Sal, accompanied by Rosin, on his cracked cremona, and Jerry on a pair of tongs, to the air – 'Jack's alive' – she twirls about the stage in the fullness of her spirits and Bob runs after her with his hat in his hand, crying 'Sarah! vy, Sarah! 'ant you well!' The black child seeing this, and thinking there is something the matter with its mother, also squalls violently; stretching its arms towards her.[81]

The Londoners comically but self-confidently taking the stage here are no feeble and pretentious cockney butts; the grotesque black woman, played by a man and therefore with physical aban-don, eats two pounds of beefsteak at a time, and dances drunk-enly, all over the stage, leading her man a merry dance; they have an insistently visible, vocal and dark-complexioned child. This display can only be admired by the gentleman who ventures into their space, who finds he is playing second fiddle on the plebeian spoons. They suggest that cockney voices are not the product of Merry England, but the miscegenated consequences of the spread of Empire. Here, as clearly as in the scenes bringing box-lobby solicitation onto the stage, is a display of the previously marginalised and hidden or unacknowledged life in London, presented as unashamed and self-sufficient, and so beyond respectable control; and it became a huge popular success.

Conclusion

Can one therefore say that in the case of the Tom and Jerry per-formances discursive mastery of the people of London failed, and that, unlike the historicisation and antiquarian appropria-tion of Bartholomew Fair, the strategy of containment within the discourse of the popular could not diffuse/defuse the cultural strength of modern London? Such a conclusion is not borne out by the accepted accounts of what followed. Tom and Jerry be-came a memory, a point of reference in the autobiographies of Victorians like Sala; but it was Dickens – an avowed enemy of Moncrieff, whom he hated for his stage appropriations of his novels – who imposed his reading of Victorian London in the imaginary of its inhabitants and its posterity; and his reading, while comic and grotesque, has not the cynical vision of Bob Logic nor the materiality of African Sal. The post-Dickensian discourse interpellates the Londoner as the vulgarian with the heart of gold, and suppresses the gatherings of industrialisation and the Empire into a patronised set of comic characters. The history of popular entertainment, whether it was the story of Bartholomew Fair or Grimaldi's memoirs as 'edited' by Dickens, followed the route set by Bulwer Lytton's *England and the English* and became part of the textualisation of 'the olden days' within a new English self-consciousness. In the theatre, this meant that plays in which the modern cockney was represented by such feeble and insulting comic representations as Sam Gerridge in Robertson's *Caste* or by dangerous villains like those in Tom Taylor's *Ticket of Leave Man* were celebrated as a new realism.

However, a stage history not dominated by writers – journalists, critics and novelists – might have a different balance. Logic's word-chopping and Sal's dance could not actually be repressed. Young men and women continued to seek entertainment, song and dance and spectacle; and Londoners at large did not take to Lytton's attempts to revive the Drama. Class segregation set in, and classes who had brought it into being immediately became beset with worries about what the others, the lower orders, might be doing, out of their sight. The legal and economic shake-out in the entertainment world that followed on the hegemonic initiatives I have been pursuing resulted in the banning of lower-class bloodsports, of Bartlemy, and, after the 1843 Act, the dispersal of the Drama through all the metropolitan theatres that chose to submit their plays to the licenser's office. But that same act also regularised the issuing of licences to premises for singing and dancing, by magistrates who did not take responsibility for what was seen there; and the Victorian music hall emerged.

The halls were without doubt the single biggest success story of Victorian entertainment. So the solution to 'the Decline of the Drama' was the segregation of the vulgar, the creation of the music halls and of the musical theatre – the whole world of burlesque and extravaganza. The notion of 'the popular' as opposed to 'the Drama' in fact vitiated dramatic writing, and turned all the exuberant life of the theatre in the early nineteenth century into 'entertainment'. A new history would seek the lost drama of

the Victorians – the parodic, the experimental, the alternative –
in the halls, and I hope in future to begin this exploration; others, I hope, might undertake similar work in the burlesque and
the musical extravaganza, for example, in the raffish theatres that
continued to serve the young men of the metropolis; and in the
lower reaches of the sensational and melodramatic offerings of
suburban and provincial companies beyond the construction of
the conventional story of the stage.

7   Claiming kin: an experiment in genealogical research

Among the faces I saw among the portraits of actors at the Garrick Club had been that of Edmund Kean. I could have sworn he tipped me a wink. I returned him a bow, for here too I could claim a distant kinship. My mother's grandfather, John Walter Bowden, in 1846 married Ellen Theresa McCarthy, whose aunt had married into a well-known theatrical family, the Darnleys, one of whose members was the father of Edmund's stepbrother Henry and stepsister Phoebe. Their mother, Ann ('Nance') Carey, was never, I'm sorry to say, married to the fathers of her children, but she took young Edmund on tour with her to exploit his talents as a prodigy in the fit-ups of Richardson and Saunders, performing melodramas and pantomimes in the fairs and markets. Edmund therefore learnt to act, sing, tumble and walk tightropes from a very early age, before maturing into the greatest Shakespearean actor of his day.[1]

Jack Le White, whose proud reminiscence this is, was a minor actor. At New Year 1978/9, aged sixty-six, already sixty years in the business, he and the other members of the stage company in a West End dramatisation of *Under the Greenwood Tree* had been invited to entertain Princess Margaret at a theatrical dinner. When he set eyes on the Princess, he records, he wished he could tell her that he still possessed the envelope in which his grandfather had received forty guineas for performing for her great-grandfather 120 years before. Jack was 'born into a speciality act', a member of the hundreds-strong Whiteley family of circus, music-hall and bit-part performers whose only claims to fame are their ubiquity within the profession, and the awareness they have of themselves as significant because of their belonging in that pattern. Neither of these attributes is peculiar to them. The all-encompassing spread of family or quasi-familial links within show business could be exemplified right across the spectrum of success and

171

fame: take, for example, the links that can be traced from Sarah
Siddons into the twentieth century. Sarah's son Henry Siddons
(1774–1815)[2] was the only one of her children to act. In 1802
he married Harriet Murray (1783–1844), granddaughter of Sir
John Murray of Broughton, Bonnie Prince Charlie's secretary,
whose son Charles had become an actor. The Henry Siddonses
managed the Theatre Royal Edinburgh, and in 1815 the beautiful widow Harriet became joint proprietor there with her brother
William. She was a very successful matriarchal manager, wor-
shipped by admirers as various as young Fanny Kemble and Sir
Walter Scott.[3] Harriet's sister Maria married 'Joe' Leathley Cowell, actor, author, artist (1792–1863), the errant son of a middle-
class service family (his father was a Colonel Witchett). Their
younger son Joe became a scene-painter, while the elder was
Sam Cowell (1820–64), a comic singer who was one of the leading stars of early music hall – the song 'Vilikins and his Dinah', a
cockney folksong in the cod gothic mode, was his biggest hit. Sam
married the actress Emilie Marguerite Ebsworth, grandchild of
the pantomimist Robert Fairbrother, 'friend of Sheridan and Mrs
Jordan', and therefore cousin to Louisa Fairbrother, sometime
dancer, who became Mrs Fitzgeorge, i.e. the morganatic wife
of George, Duke of Cambridge. Half-sister to Joe and Sam, by
Joe Leathley Cowell's second marriage to the actress Frances
Sheppard, was Sydney Frances Cowell (1823–81), actress, who
by marriage brought into the profession the son of an American Methodist mother, one Hezekiah Linthicum Bateman. He
became an actor–manager, responsible for Irving's debut at the
Lyceum, and their children were a journalist and five actors, including the famous Victorian child stars Kate and Ellen Bateman.
Their sister Virginia in 1882 married Edward Compton, actor,
so linking this family to the Compton/Mackenzie/Symonds tribe
which included John Addington Symonds, Victorian man of letters, whose connections included Sir Rowland Hill and five generations of doctors and whose cousin, the Rev. Samuel John,
wrote the hymn, 'The Church's One Foundation'. Its many theatre people include, in an eighteenth-century generation, the
famous light comedian Henry 'Bath' Montague and his wife
Emmaline Hetling, actress; in the twentieth century, the novelist
and dramatist Compton Mackenzie. Virginia and Edward's children included Viola and Ellen, joint managers of Nottingham

Rep 1920–3, Frank Compton, whose daughter Jean married Leslie Howard's brother Arthur, and Fay Compton (b.1894), whose marriage to actor Lauri de Frece, brother to Henry de Frece who married the male impersonator Vesta Tilley, links this group, via the de Freces' mother Marian Fitzwilliam, back up the generations to the Buckstone/Copeland clan, which included John Baldwin Buckstone and William Robert Buckstone, who married the actress Elizabeth Sarah Jerrold, sister of Douglas and thence related by marriage to the Mayhews. I have picked and chosen still-recognisable names from these endlessly ramifying family trees, but many more working performers, at every level from music-hall singer to royal mistress, could be added to this single list. They are not a unique group – except in the sense that diligent searching out of links might well render them and most of the other British performing families above the level of supernumerary into one network, a single tribe that derives Jack Le White from Edmund Kean and embraces all these individuals on the way.

This case study attempts to engage anew with theatre history by beginning at the level of interest – interest in who begat whom, or how they were related – that motivates research into family history. There is a strong, almost instinctive academic resistance to the acceptance of the importance or validity of such an interest, which in itself signals the possibility that this might be a deconstructive and potentially subversive approach that could change our understanding of the theatre and its use of its own traditions. As in the case of anecdote and mimicry discussed above, non-academic generations of writers in the field have found family links to be a significant kind of information: *The Green Room Book* and its successor in the twentieth century, *Who's Who in the Theatre*, from which the pattern of people in the paragraph above is derived, saw fit to print many pages of family trees. Performers themselves have often had a sense of show business as a family 'tapestry', as Jack's mother Leonora Catalina Whiteley called it when she dictated her version of the story in 1942; sometimes a sense of the importance or simply the beauty of that pattern has led them to publish their family history.[4] I think this is more than a casual interest; and should be distinguished from the ache for knowledge about ourselves and our connections that characterises the western individual since the shift was made from a theocentric to an anthropocentric vision of the significance of life. That wish to understand who and what they are in human terms may be what drives the hordes of ordinary people 'doing their ancestors' who constitute the majority of users of national and local archives in Britain today. But there is something more material as well as more rhetorically explicit about the family of performers. Theatre families like the Whiteleys hardly need to go in for research. Their history is still active, a vital part of their sense of themselves and a practical dimension of their daily experience. It seems logical, therefore, to look to genealogy, in the pre-Foucault literal sense, for a method in theatre history. The structure of feeling that underlies Jack Le White's apparently exorbitant memory for, and valuation of, professional and sanguineous kinship and patronage is the subject of this case study. I hope not only that it may tell us how theatre families themselves have used and valued their history, but also perhaps reveal important people and patterns which have been missed by the more orthodox tracing of dramatic links and literary precedents. This is about the dynamics between the people in the profession; and particularly about a way to approach the special position of women in the nineteenth-century theatre. If one looks carefully at the Sarah Siddons heritage sketched above, the significance of women as the carriers of the line, managers of theatres and, perhaps, possessors and transmitters of theatrical talent – as prime custodians of cultural capital – can be brought into focus in quite a new way. This approach offers something, therefore, for feminist historiography. I shall return to a closer examination of that possibility below.

What is does it mean to be born into the profession?

In order to understand theatre genealogy more precisely, I shall look first at the passage quoted at the head of the chapter. Something that immediately strikes the modern reader is the extraordinary tenuousness of the links it invokes. Jack's connection to Kean involves no blood relationship at all, but goes by way of his great-grandfather's marriage (possibly not the one from which Jack actually descends) to a woman whose aunt was married to 'someone' who was married to Edmund Kean's stepmother. But while Jack would not have dreamt of speaking up to tell the royal patron about his great-grandfather, he did bow to the portrait of the actor, and imagined that Kean tipped him the wink – he thought, in other words, that the kinship would have been recognised by the man who was 'the greatest Shakespearean actor of his day'. The assumption links him to the humble showmen quoted in chapter 5 who claimed professional brotherhood with Charles Mathews and Garrick. That vision of the profession, as shaped in a hierarchy with obvious gradations and orders of success, but also having a shared core of skill and experience that forms a meaningful, unbroken continuum of recognition from the bottom to the top, also emerges in, for example, the writings of the twentieth-century members of the famous Lupino family. Stanley Lupino called his autobiography *From the Stocks to the Stars* because he belonged to 'the oldest theatrical family in England', which had risen from vagabondage, when an ancestor 'way back in Shakespeare's days' was put in the stocks for illegal performance, to his niece Ida's Hollywood stardom. He adds that his is 'a family whose boast it was that no wife, mother, son, or daughter ever deserted the profession' and that the story of their descent is 'not ancient history to us – it was part of our living work. Lupinos have been kings of comedy for over two centuries.'[5] Lupino Lane tells the same tale in a curious little volume called *How to Become a Comedian* and offers there a list of the training course through which 'each member of my family, male or female, has been put . . . by the elders of the family'. It includes 'Ballet, Tap, National dances, Fencing, Boxing, Acrobatic tricks, Juggling, Building and painting scenery, Shakespeare and acting, Designing costumes, Composing music, How to produce plays, How to produce Ballets and Dances, How to "light a production", Singing and elocution, The art of miming or expressing the emotions, in "dumb show"'.[6] Not the least extraordinary thing about this compendious list of all the theatre arts rolled into one is the sandwiching of 'Shakespeare and acting' between building scenery and costume design, well below dancing and acrobatic tricks.

The need that the theatre child has to learn so much, and so much of it physical, is an obvious reason for the importance of a broadly defined family in the living history of the profession. Returning to the passage quoted above, it is notable that this is the point to which Jack works round in his claiming of kinship with Kean. Like the preserved grandparental envelope in which royal patronage was received, the chain of generations could be regarded as merely the wrapping around a relationship of fellow-feeling: the reality the elderly Jack shares with 'young Edmund' is of being trained, and in Edmund's case exploited, as a child performer. The unchanging experience of entry into the profession is a kinship that bound all those trained for physical performance, and before the twentieth century this meant everyone whose family intended to put them on the stage. The 'step' relationship of Kean to the Careys is a part of that particular familial experience. Earlier in his memoir Jack recounts his own childhood fostering in a collier's family, a routine procedure for lowly touring performers who farmed out infants until they could be sent for and trained, from the age of three or four – coming into their own family to start work; Jack was trained by his father and his two nearest siblings. He does not record ill-treatment; but it was hard work, and a premature responsibility often recalled in such memoirs in terms of rebellious escapades and beatings as well as anxious pride in developing skills.[7] Kean, 'the wretched offspring of poor players', was toted round the fairs and made to work hard, and contemporary anecdote censoriously mythologised his ill-treatment at the highest theatre in the land: 'Kean was nursed in poverty and suckled in distress . . . his infant powers being called into action in sundry devils, cupids, monkeys, serpents, etc, at the old Theatre Royal, Drury Lane, where the instruction of a posture-master tortured his unfortunate victim.'[8]

So training is a part of the importance of family, and looking at the family links that can be established may tell us about a frequently omitted or obscured aspect of theatre history: induction into the profession and the transmission of skills. In turn, this consideration may partly explain the stretching of the definition of family in entertainers' accounts. It is in any case a predominantly twentieth-century view that narrows 'family' to include only blood relations and acknowledges only a small selection of additional bonds through marriage or cohabitation. Before the mid-nineteenth century the biological basis of the household was less important than its functions in establishing hierarchy and mirroring the authority patterns of the larger society. Early Modern Catholic society stressed the household of the order or the fraternity, which was eternal while the individuals within it came and went; and with the establishment of the Protestant household the master of the house was cast as a father to all, including servants, apprentices, long-term visiting younger kin and adoptees, and seen as likely to be a better, more objective God-substitute to them than a biological father. The following advertisement by an experienced Riding Master for a female pupil for the equestrian business appeared in the 'wanted' columns of the *Era* in 1866, where it would be noted chiefly by the lowly travelling performer:

she must be about Seven or Eight years of age, of good appearance, healthy, good head of hair, and active. She will be treated as one of the family, and diligently instructed in her profession. One that has been brought up to the business preferred . . . NB A good house and home to come to.[9]

This was an ancient practice, and would explain the adoption of Elizabeth Barry into the Davenant family and of Ann Bracegirdle into the Bettertons, where they each received the instruction that made them able to take their places as the leaders of the second generation of British actresses. In the course of the eighteenth century 'the emerging merchant classes became increasingly reliant on family and kin to accumulate skills and capital', but even in the early nineteenth century they 'could not depend exclusively on their own offspring to build their family futures. They remained dependent on the circulation of children to perpetuate themselves.'[10] This pattern can without strain be detected in the economy of the theatre, with the 'family' mapping partly onto the company, especially where a manager like Tate Wilkinson or Sarah Baker, giving a start to very many performers, took a long-term interest in them, determining their roles and chances and having a measure of control over their placing within the profession; while the lesser circuit or strolling company was obviously, if sometimes evanescently, familial. In tracing the work and influence of the widely defined theatre family, therefore, one may hope to find out something about the internal dynamic of skill transmission or, to put it another way, the control of cultural capital. The place that theatre as a profession has in the imaginary within the developing discourse of modern class and culture is as important in this discussion as the role of theatre families in strictly economic relation to the accumulation of capital; for one thing, in theatre the link between money and status and artistic recognition and achievement is especially unstable, and it may well be that the caste value of one's theatrical ancestors outweighed – indeed, still outweighs – their ability to bequeath funds. The extra inherited dimensions of firstly talent, and secondly mysteries and skills complicate the already subtle cross-currents of class and status.

Genealogy as women's history

The tracing of families as engines of induction, training and inheritance within the profession, and the exploring of the internal, sometimes hidden, power structures that reveals, brings into focus the historical contribution of women to theatre. But in linking family to class to gender in this discussion, it becomes necessary to revisit certain definitions and consider current reconceptualisations of gender and class in the nineteenth century. Tracy Davis's economic analysis[11] has made clear to us the dangers of applying culturalist/Marxist categories to Victorian theatre in Britain without taking account of working women – working-class women – not only via consideration of their actual employment, but also in the discursive evidence of attitudes towards them and their values. In order to build upon her perceptions, and to look at the tension between work and womanhood in the higher reaches of the theatre where families were or aspired to be respectable, I propose to look next at theatre women, their training and their family support structures, in the first half of the nineteenth century, to discover what was thought about their entry into the profession, suggesting the contemporary conception of a stratified society that was in play and to extrapolate how such discourses were being actively used to place theatricals within it. A tool for the deconstruction of this social imaginary is Davidoff and Hall's *Family Fortunes*,[12] which uses case studies of families in the city of Birmingham and the rural eastern counties to beat out an economically based understanding of middle-classness as it grew in Britain in this period, and as it related to women, via the interrelationships of commerce, capital and family. I shall use this approach to consider the life stories, particularly those of women, offered in Catherine Oxberry's *Dramatic Biography and Histrionic Anecdotes*, 1825–7.

Davidoff and Hall detail at some length[13] the disincentives to female participation in economic life that grew up in this period.

A striking difference between their sample and mine is that in the theatre the confinement of the female members to non-executive participation in the family business is not really possible. The ineluctable necessity for full female participation in performance makes the profession almost unique amongst middle-class occupations. Some aspects of theatre could evolve as other businesses did, with, for instance, the exclusion of women from power because they had no access to the male domains that handled capital investment. Jane Scott of the Sans Pareil/Adelphi needed an exceptionally complaisant father to enable her to build a theatre, inherit it from him, and pass it on in her own will, despite the fact that she died married. Such financial independence was very unusual, as Davidoff and Hall show. They argue 'for the centrality of the sexual division of labour within families for the development of the capitalist enterprise'[14] demonstrating that exclusion from the workplace, and all the class-building pressures of which that was a part, removed women from active participation in business and reduced their input in family firms to the reproductive rather than the productive use of capital. This argument highlights discursive issues that cause extreme tension in the theatre biographies of the period, especially, for fairly obvious reasons, in those by or about female performers. In theatre families, women were still going on stage, participating in the business end of things, at a moment when all social pressures told them that if they were to be middle-class, they should not be doing so; and, in addition, they were participating in a profession that actually exploited and shockingly revealed their femininity as a saleable commodity. Like the commercial middle-class worlds Davidoff and Hall explore, the theatrical milieu was involved in a complex and overlapping transition from patronage to commercial relations, negotiating conflict between aristocratic dynastic and middle-class religious values, and struggling with the move towards a separation of work and home. Narratives of women in the theatre all worry away at these concerns, against the background of what we understand, through Marxist and post-Marxist analysis, as the production and reproduction of the ideology of capitalism. The discourse is fraught with contradiction.

These ideological narratives tell one story, while the women themselves are living another. Hazlitt's praise of Eliza O'Neill, for example, is often contradictory: writing of her as Elwina in Hannah Moore's *Percy*[15] he says '[h]er great excellence is extreme natural sensibility; that is, she perfectly conceives and expresses what would generally be felt by the female mind'. His grammar seems to fight with what he feels compelled to say, his initial assertion attributing to nature what the following subjunctive construction immediately acknowledges to be conscious art. Consider also Helen Faucit's construction of herself. She was the offspring of a complex, often successful but personally unhappy theatrical family, and, presumably on the basis of a fortunate conjunction of genes, she became one of the great performers such groups do throw up.[16] But she asserted that she was a good actress in spite of her family; especially she denied the training aspect of her inheritance. She told the story of having escaped all that as a child, and having communed with nature upon the seashore, not learning but living, feeling she actually *was* each of Shakespeare's heroines. Writing a book about the characters as if they are real people, in a grotesque effort of self-justification and appropriation, she describes this process, saying she 'lived again and again through the whole childhood and lives of many of Shakespeare's heroines'.[17] Her husband's biography of her points out with satisfaction that as a young person she was not allowed to go to the theatre, so this natural and magical merging was 'never warped by the impersonations of the actresses'. Such was her preparation for 'success in my art, . . . the preservation of the freshness and freedom of spirit which are essential to true distinction' on the stage.[18] One cannot but add that it was even more essential to her being able to *leave* the profession sufficiently unsullied to become Lady Martin and Queen Victoria's personal friend. And there is of course the major example of Fanny Kemble's writings and her career, from princess of a doomed theatrical dynasty to self-supporting Shakespearean lecturer, a position in which she could at last exercise her art while maintaining her class and gender roles – living one story, while telling us, and herself, quite another. I shall return to the example of the Kembles below.

Catherine Oxberry's biographies

One series of nineteenth-century popular publications provides an interesting example of the rhetorical work that had to be done to appropriate the story of the actress to the emerging doctrines of work and gender. The publication of *Oxberry's Dramatic Biography and Histrionic Anecdotes* in 1825–7 relates to the explosion of self-consciousness and self-definition that the British theatrical profession underwent as part of its 'class' transition in the first third of the century. It was successful enough to be imitated by another publisher and continued without the consent of its original owner. Its first five volumes consisted of material gathered by William Oxberry, actor/printer/publican, who died of a stroke in mid-career in 1824. The New Series, two volumes published in 1827, relies on additional materials donated and purchased from other actors. Oxberry's widow, much his junior, who had also been a performer, was left with more children than assets at his early death, and so undertook the editing of these lives of their contemporaries. She asserts in her preface her freedom to publish truths that her husband's friendship with his subjects made him unwilling to reveal. Her bold claiming of ownership and responsibility has not prevented the normative masculinisation of her product by the master narrative of theatre history: the *Oxford Companion to the Theatre* asserts that her second husband, Leman Rede, 'was responsible for' everything published in her name. In fact the (unremarked) female voice of the biographies, especially in the first volume, is an important element in their rhetoric; there is no reason to suppose it ventriloquised. I would argue for the evidence, and the importance, of Catherine Oxberry's hand in the biographies, whoever wrote them with or for her in their later phases. The first volume in particular concerns itself with the description and coercion of moral behaviour, and especially of that of women. In the imaginary of the theatre world, the moral position of women was a crucial site of tension in the redefinition of class. The importance of the actress in this rhetorical endeavour is signalled by her disproportionate representation in the biographies, as compared with the gender distribution of roles in plays, and therefore of leading performers in the profession in general. The first five Oxberry volumes attempt an even distribution of biographies, eight men and eight women, though volumes 2 and 4 have only seven women, and therefore nine men. Volumes 6 and 7 are the spurious continuation, and here the distribution changes: volume 6 has ten men and six women, and the seventh only manages twelve biographies, of which eight are of men. The New Series has in volume 1 nine men and seven women, in the short final volume seven men and three women.

In the biographies, a complex and tense rhetoric surrounds the exploitation of young women's sexual attractiveness on the stage, which is linked to their accession to the profession. The problem most often attaches to the stories of girls from humble, non-theatrical backgrounds whose beauty causes their parents to have stage ambitions for them, and to have them trained as singers (or occasionally dancers). In the biography of Ann Maria Tree in volume 3 there appears the following diatribe about the musical actress:

Really, the situation of a young actress, in the present day, is little better than that of a slave. Just review the life of one. From twelve years of age until eighteen, kept eight hours a-day, singing and playing the piano; dieted, and kept to particular hours, from eighteen to twenty-five; hurried from theatre to theatre, and from town to town, to fulfil engagements, at the imminent hazard of her health, and the certain sacrifice of comfort. All this while carefully excluded from any intercourse with one of the other sex, who might render her happy. Her every movement watched by her anxious relatives, lest, by taking a husband of her own choice, she should defeat their hopes of subsistence on her exertions. At twenty-five, *they* begin to look out for her; and the very person who is to perform the principal character in this drama of matrimony, is little consulted about it. At length, the musical victim is sold off to some rich booby, who she heartlessly weds – she is raised into a circle of society to which she is unused, and for which she is unfit; for her studious and industrious existence has allowed her little chance of mixing in company. What are the results? Taken from a station where, as an exhibitor, she was delightful, to one in which she is a novice, and consequently aukward, and where she has no means of display – she disgusts the very being she should charm – he curses his folly – she, her parent's cupidity – and the great dramatic alliance becomes the fruitful source of lasting misery.[19]

This is an acute manifestation of the problem about the division of labour, and the concealment of aspects of the female role in respectable marriages. Domestic accomplishments such as music are, in middle-class circles, cultivated in order to distinguish the girl's education from the commercial training given to boys; they are 'deliberately paraded as being the opposite of business duties'.[20] But here they are outrageously, to the misery of the trainee and her false positioning in the class above that of her friends, turned into a business for profit. However, elsewhere the Oxberry volumes speak obsequiously of actresses elevated by marriage to rich men and peers, which is after all, as the novelists remind us, the goal of every middle-class girl to whom marriage is the only trade. The exposing of that trade, via the professional stage, is the discursive problem, acutely seen in volume 5 in the biography of Susannah Paton, who moved from child prodigy to being the mistress of a peer. Paton's sexual life is raked over in her Biography, and she is roundly blamed for being so silly as to live with Lord William Lennox without his supporting her – the writer tartly remarks that as she's still working she must be his wife, rather than his mistress.[21] Several others among the women described left the stage when they entered into a non-theatrical marriage or liaison, becoming a conventional upper-class woman in the sense of being supported by a man, and then returned to the stage when financial support from him began to fail.[22] As had been the case from the days of the first actresses, gentlemen wanted exclusive possession of the actresses they made their own, but were not always able to maintain that expensive position.

One might seek evidence in the nineteenth century for the growth of feeling within theatre families, amongst fathers and husbands and also mothers and daughters, as opposed to genteel lovers, that they too would prefer the women not to participate in the family business. This is not easy to read from the biographies, since they obviously include only women who did have a stage career, offering no sight of women from theatrical backgrounds who did not enter the profession actively. Something may be extrapolated or inferred, perhaps, from the difference between the men and the women described in terms of how far this sample of successful performers originated in theatre families. It would seem, from what the biographies say about the families of their subjects, that of the 59 men and 49 women described, 43 men and 20 women had no theatrical family background; of the 16 theatre-family men, only 6 had siblings and/or other relations besides their parents in the profession, while 12 women had wider family links than simply theatrical parents. Of those not in some way born into the trade, 11 men and 5 women married within it. Thus in the case of the men, 73 per cent came into the job from outside, though 19 per cent of these then married in it, while only 30 per cent of the women were not personally as well as professionally embedded in the group; and several of these were peripherally involved, being introduced like Susannah Paton when their childish talents were recognised by craftsmen or tradesmen associated with the theatres. Virtually the only respectable route in for women, except for those from a theatre family, is via musical apprenticeship.[23] Many men found they had talent, needs, inclinations or passions which carried them into theatrical life from their employment elsewhere, in printing or haberdashery or the army; girls from beyond the theatre either ran away with actors or with other men and are represented as taking to performance out of necessity; or they were sufficiently remarkable as children – either musical or beautiful – to be put to the trade by designing parents. Thus theirs seems always to be represented as a passive route to fame.

And once they are present in an active role on stage, the biographies often strain to represent the actress as not naturally a worker and wage-earner, not a mercenary woman motivated by personal aggrandisement or gain. A particularly melodramatic trope repeatedly suggests itself for the defence of the actress as worker. The New Series declares: 'The first step towards the exaltation of the drama, is the removal of the ancient prejudice, that actresses are generally of light reputation. Some of the best wives, the tenderest mothers, and, decidedly, the *best daughters*, we have ever known, are actresses.'[24] Accordingly women like Maria Lacy (vol. 4), child of an old theatre family that had got into difficulties, whose earnings contributed to the support of aged parents, respectably placed brothers, or their own children, are especially praised; such earnings, unwomanly in themselves, are redemptively used. This is equally praiseworthy in such cases as that of the unfortunate Mrs Glover (vol. 4) where the families they support consist of rapacious errant husbands or abusive fathers, whom the biographies luridly represent and censure, while still regarding their women as vindicated as class members and females by their sacrifices.

These various insights are perhaps not very unexpected. As work for women became increasingly problematic within middle-class self-definition it is not surprising that women seem most likely to go on the stage when their families are in the business, or that once there their hard work and calculation should need to be excused and their exploitation of their femininity camouflaged as part of the mythologising work of such class-defining publications as the Oxberry biographies. But are there other things that can be gleaned, from Oxberry and other biography and autobiography, that will reveal a different, more active aspect of the part played by the theatre family in history? Are there other discursive elements that might have been part of the experience and self-perception of these women in the theatre, but which are automatically veiled in their self-presentation?

I think there is a case to be made, from a reading of Oxberry against the grain, for the theatre as a site in which there was more than usual continuity of female networks, female direction of events and consequent power, because of the particular realities of the theatrical family unit and its structures of inheritance (of talent rather than simply property) and training (in skills that had to remain essentially physical and manual, and were not capable of scientific industrialisation and abstraction from the family setting to the factory). Such talent and skill therefore remained distributed across the whole family group, and women remained mobile, full-time employed, and seen to be going about the business; they were not able to retire to the domestic sphere, working only 'behind the scenes'.[25] The biographies display the discursive tension thus created in contradictory statements about the role of the family in training for the stage, and the appropriation of women's work and earnings. Davidoff and Hall stress that it was the *family* that mediated between the public and private, and connected the market with the domestic – the model is one of the 'family enterprise'. In their case studies of provincial businesses, '[f]ar from the market being separate from the family, the two were locked into a set of elaborate connections'.[26] In the biographies, despite their rhetorical unease, one may see these elaborate connections, the family working in the theatre to pass on inherited skills and talents and to enable the smooth running of the enterprise, through women as much or more than through men.

There is a pattern within high-ranking theatrical families of boys leaving, to gain an education that will take them away from the stage, some returning under an impulse normally regarded as the irrepressible vocation of talent; in humbler theatre families the boys are said to work the provincial circuits while learning their trade apprentice-wise and thoroughly. Girls are described as going onto the stage very early, within the family business to which they make an essential contribution. The 'Children of Thespis' are a tribe, a self-generating and perpetuating community; admission is by birth, talent and work, and if there is any discrimination by gender, it is towards the inclusion of women rather than men. The biographies are censorious or equivocal or self-contradictory around a series of moral and behavioural problems that make the social position of the theatricals difficult to elevate, and they often appear to be awkwardly imposing external values. But when it comes to this issue, of the possession of expertise, traditional knowledges, of theatre talent, by women as well as by men, the social imaginary with which they work is strikingly at variance with the world of business explored by Davidoff and Hall. The rhetoric both claiming and defying respectability resounds through the volumes, particularly towards their close.

The life of Matilda Ray (Mrs Horn) in the final volume of the original series is a fallen-woman story, and one on which the writer cannot decide a stance: Miss Ray was the daughter of a provincial manager (at Cheltenham) but was in the view of the writer a shrinking and delicate creature in danger on the stage, in need of protection; but her actor husband Mr Horn was not himself faithful or caring; but love conquers all; but she has left the stage and gone into protection . . . Before the writer tangles with these contradictions, however, the piece begins with apparently unconnected speculation about why actresses sometimes conceal their station of birth, as if they are ashamed not to be born the daughters of barristers or clergymen but of 'vulgar chandlershop people'. They should not be so concerned: the greatest actress of all time was born at a low Pothouse, the greatest actor threw summersets in a public house, one leading lady of the stage was a servant in a cookshop twelve years ago and another a servant turned away for theft – all of which except the last is reason for praise. The conclusion is that 'Birth is the work of fate; station is generally the result of industry or talent – when accompanied by virtue always so.'[27] It remains a matter of speculation how far the writer was aware of the discursive struggle going on here; but the underlying message is clearly that a combination of birth into the profession, application and talent are what matter in the theatre business; all the rest – gender, class, personal behaviour – is an unfortunate complication.

Family fortunes revisited: a new view of the role of women in the nineteenth-century theatre

From the broad pattern of professionalism crossed with the imperatives of nature suggested in the biographies, and scattered clues there about the lives of certain women, I want to return to genealogy, using information about relationships and inheritances to tease out the otherwise occluded stories that indicate the importance of women in theatre history. Women in management can be traced through their patterns of inheritance and marriage. There are instances of women in the eighteenth and nineteenth centuries who not only transmitted but in some cases built and bequeathed provincial circuits.[28] Sarah Baker of Kent, who inherited little but her skills from her mother and built a series of theatres upon them, is by no means alone. Mrs Gosli inherited and worked her father's Nottingham–Derby circuit in 1781. By 1786 this theatre group was being managed by William Perkins Taylor. He was snapped up by the widow Hannah Richardson, née Prichard, an experienced and successful actress somewhat his senior, the daughter and sister of country managers called David; their sister married Henry F. Thornton, proprietor of theatres in the south of England. Taylor died in 1800 and Hannah managed at Nottingham in his stead. In 1805, according to Oxberry, as a 'judicious and experienced . . . matron'[29] now managing the Stamford circuit, she trained a young actor called Benjamin Wrench and launched him on the stage, and married him, despite the fact that he was previously engaged to her daughter. Oxberry suggests that Wrench, who went on to a considerable London career, married an 'elderly lady' cynically for his own advancement; but one might read Hannah Prichard's supporting of her own long career as performer and manager through three marriages to younger men in a different light.

Whatever the cloaked reality that generates a faintly scandalous sense of a sexual dimension to women in power, it is evident that theatrical women are often teachers, in the generation described in Oxberry; and their position in chains of kin can be read as pivotal. They can be seen as acting as the stabilising good sense, the managerial and organisational infrastructure, in positions of power long after their days as window-dressing. In a business where there was little possibility of a stable domestic life separate from and foundational to the business enterprise, where men could not provide single-handed for their families as middle-class men should, the female leading light might well have been as important as the male, even though their names have not entered eponymously into the master narrative. Take, for example, the cousins who became Harriet Waylett and Mrs W. West, who were major London performers in the 1810s and 20s, one as a singer in ballad opera and musicals, who had a spell in illegitimate management at the Strand Theatre, and was a regular star at the patent houses, the other a leading tragic actress who played opposite Edmund Kean at Drury Lane. Their uncle James Cooke was a provincial actor, and Mrs West's father was first cousin to the tragedian George Frederick Cooke. Mrs West had a niece Peggy whom she trained for the stage and took on tour with her; Peggy's daughter Jane Elizabeth Thomson (1827–1902), appearing first in Australia as a child prodigy, married a minor comedian, Charles Frederick Young, and then, having established herself as a leading London actress, married the leading actor Herman Vezin in 1864. The end of this female line was her daughter's death, which is supposed to have caused her own suicide in 1901. The ever-changing names disguise the transmission of such talent.[30]

The family tree is also often evidence for the artificiality of the division into high and low art, the distinction made between the entertainment world and the Drama: there are links within families of entertainers from Drury Lane to the showman's tent; and the movements of women, in particular, can be traced to make this clear. Take, for example, a woman called Ursula Agnes (1740–1803), patronymic unknown, who had two actress daughters, Ann and Elizabeth Field. Ursula married John Booth, a tailor who worked at the Theatre Royal, Drury Lane. She played small parts, finishing her long career as a professional 'aged crone' in Drury Lane dramas; she and Booth lived in the courts and alleys around Covent Garden, and raised the Field girls and also Julia, Elizabeth's daughter by her first husband, one Dr Granger. Julia, having escaped the clutches of a dancing-master relative of Booth's named Burghall, married a Robert Jones in 1800 and went with him to the USA, acted there 'briefly but brilliantly' and died at the age of twenty-four, leaving behind a line of American actresses. Her mother Elizabeth, born 1760, rose in the profession by taking to the minors, in the fashionable new form, the hippodrama. She became an Astley's star, 'the best actress that ever trod the boards of the Amphitheatre',[31] and in 1787 married another equestrian actor, William Wallack (1760–1850). Their many children included Henry (1790–1870), who married actresses and fathered two more, as well as an actor son; James William Wallack (1791–1864), a Kemble imitator who managed major theatres in both London and New York and fathered the US actor Lester Wallack (1820–88), Mary, who became Mrs Stanley and was a leading performer at the Coburg, and Elizabeth, who appeared at the English Opera House and married a British fairground showman called Pincott. Elizabeth's daughters included Ellena Elizabeth Pincott, whose 1814 stage debut was in the time-honoured child role of the Duke of York in *Richard III*, and Leonora (1805–84), who started in life as a rope-dancer and stilt-walker and a pantomime chimpanzee, but about 1839 married Alfred Wigan, an ex-public-schoolmaster who had drifted into theatre via a job as secretary to the Dramatic Authors' Society. By 1842 they were making a name for themselves in the West End; Joseph Knight opines that 'to her husband and his associate and partner, Robson, she was of great service, as she had stage knowledge and *flair*'.[32]

These examples demonstrate, I hope, the fruitfulness but also the difficulties of tracing the specifically female lines that played a part in the transmission of talent and skills in nineteenth-century theatre. There are three important ways in which attention to family patterns modifies the received understanding of theatre history by making possible greater attention to and estimation of the importance of women, as well as modifying the *Family Fortunes* model of the function of women in the family business. Firstly, it is sometimes worth seeking for women within theatrical families who did operate backstage, supporting and enabling the public activities of the business, in perhaps a rather more active way than the average middle-class family matron: acting as teachers and facilitators, rather than simply sending out their sons to man the shop. Secondly, one might seek evidence of long-lasting theatre families whose patriarchal pride in the family name actually hides the way in which the family has been perpetuated and its success renewed by bringing in talented women by marriage. Most importantly, I think Knight's attribution of 'stage

knowledge and *flair*' to Mrs Alfred Wigan suggests significant
ways in which women might be the source as well as the repos-
itories and transmitters of theatrical achievement. Evidence can
be sought of women who were the driving forces that brought a
stage partnership or family to success and eminence, either by
their sense of the business or simply their innate abilities, their
stage presence and acting talent. For such a search within one
family a well-documented and eminent clan is necessary, and I
therefore turn back to a rereading of the family history of the
Kembles.

The descendants of Sarah Ward: three ways to dynastic domination

The first shift I would suggest in our reading of the Kemble story
is in its point of origin. Hershel Baker's classic account of John
Philip Kemble makes something of a joke of beginning with his
subject's 'pedigree', and dwells at length on the modest gentry
family of Catholic recusants, a humble branch of which produced
Roger Kemble in 1721, 'the first actor (so far as we know) in a
family that was to adorn the English stage'.[33] However, Baker
himself, using the account of the family written by Ann Kemble
Hatton, the sister of John Philip and Sarah, goes on to tell a story
which demonstrates that this is not true, except in the narrowest
name-centred conception of 'family'. Roger Kemble, having left
home and his apprenticeship to a barber, attached himself first
to an actress called Furnival and then to Sarah, daughter of John
Ward, the manager of a Midlands strolling company. Ann Hatton
writes:

There was something remarkable in John Ward's choice of a wife . . . for
Mrs Ward had little pretension to beauty: her figure was tall and masculine, she had a stern countenance, and was very near sighted – but she
possessed a retentive memory, and had a mania for the Stage – yield-
ing to her persuasions, John Ward the ci devant officer commenced the
management of an itinerant company of comedians, of which himself
became the grand attraction and support, for he possessed a majestic
person – eyes of uncommon brilliancy formed 'to threaten or command,'
features of Roman mould, a voice of great power and flexibility, with the
most distinct and correct pronunciation, and these, united with classic
taste, strong sense, and sound judgement, rendered him a declaimer

of first-rate merit – from John Ward a gentleman and scholar, has descended all the genius acknowledged and admired in his grandchildren. To a player a large family must on many accounts be an encumbrance, but luckily for John Ward, out of a numerous offspring only three survived, William, and Stephen, who had no theatrical talent, and Sarah who married Roger Kemble the father of Mrs Siddons – Sarah Ward inherited the strong mind and genius of her father, she had his dark intelligent eyes, his handsome haughty countenance with the tall and masculine figure of her mother – while a mere child her abilities as an actress were highly appreciated.[34]

In other words, the Kemble effect was created by the mingling of the physical attributes of John and Sarah Ward senior, under the command and direction of Sarah's will – her 'mania for the Stage'. It descended through Sarah Ward junior, the brilliant mainstay of her father's company in her teens, wooed by several unlikely suitors beyond the profession, from a noble lord who died of grief when her parents rejected him to a wealthy Quaker whom they preferred. She chose the fledgling actor Kemble, whose 'person was his only recommendation, it was obvious to them *he had no talent for the stage* his education had been circumscribed, he had a good plain understanding but no genius, and to anything more than being a handsome, spirited, good tempered man, he had not the remotest pretension'.[35] The point of origin, then, is Sarah Ward: the Kemble family genius is founded on this woman.

The two had numerous children, and in the most famous firstborn daughter and son, Sarah (b.1755) and John Philip (b.1757), the Ward blood is clearly the strongest determinant: both charismatic, tall and proud, with commanding, brilliant eyes in the unsmiling 'stern countenance' of their grandmother; Sarah certainly had her mother's talent, though John Philip's narrow range of tragic poses and sonorous declamation was not universally admired. Both parents were handsome; the youngest brother Charles (b.1775) may, perhaps, have had more of his father's easy charm and 'polish' and less of the high temper that the maternal grandparents and his older siblings possessed. He was to transmit the genes; but before turning to Fanny, his daughter, it is worth considering the fate of the others of the generation of John Philip and Sarah. Winston recorded the family as twelve.[36] When Sarah, now Siddons, made her sensational reappearance at Drury Lane in 1782, four of them followed her to London: Covent Garden engaged Stephen (b.1758), to the amusement and exasperation of the town, since he had far less appeal than she; but John Philip, already an established provincial actor, soon joined Sarah at Drury Lane, as did their sisters Frances (b.1759) and Elizabeth (b.1761). These two were possessed of the looks and a measure of the acting talent of the family: Frances made a successful upper-class marriage and retired from the business, but Elizabeth and her theatre-proprietor husband Charles Whitlock were very successful in theatre in America. Ann (b.1764) also came to London in 1783 and attempted to join the family, but finding herself rejected took to giving public lectures on the subject of 'Woman' and other publicity stunts. The later-born children were less robust than these, and several died young, with at least one more, Jane (b.1777), becoming, like Ann, an impoverished pensioner of the family elders.

Two younger brothers, Stephen and Charles, can be interpreted as pursuing the second family-building expedient I have suggested: they recruited distinguished women to the clan via marriage. Stephen was not a good enough actor for Covent Garden, but as a man was better placed than his sisters to control his own fortunes. So he married Elizabeth Satchell, daughter of the Prince of Wales's musical-instrument maker, whose 'early inclination for the stage' was, according to *The Thespian Dictionary*, 'impossible to subdue' so that she had entered the profession via training in music and made a great success.[37] She and Stephen appeared together at the Haymarket for ten seasons before retreating to manage the Theatre Royal Edinburgh and then to manage the North of England circuit based on Durham. Charles meanwhile married Marie-Thérèse de Camp, the daughter of a French émigré who had been a pet and plaything of the Prince Regent's social circle as a beautiful and gifted child performer. Her 'surpassing beauty' provoked the adoration of all the town when she appeared as Polly in *The Beggar's Opera*; John Philip attempted to rape her in her dressing room.[38] Safely married to Charles, she later wrote and, with her husband, acted in fashionable and successful afterpieces at Covent Garden – farces and musical plays.

These two reinforcements of the Kemble genes resulted in the next generation in two cousins called Fanny, and in their stories one sees a much greater compromise with the class ideal. In one case the Victorian womanly impulse to retreat into private life was at odds with her training, temperament and family obligations. As I have discussed elsewhere,[39] Fanny Kemble Butler's writings play out that tension at great length. She was Charles's daughter, and having mistakenly married the American slave-owner Butler and left him for his politics, she wrote extensively and vividly about her experiences on the stage and the plantation, and made herself a peculiarly Victorian performance career 'lecturing', that is, performing, from Shakespeare, solo and without costume or scenery: thus working out a personal means of avoiding the limitations and dangers attaching to being a woman on stage. Stephen's daughter Fanny took the opposite path away from conflict. She was a beauty, and a gifted composer and singer; appearing on the family stage, she attracted and married the son of the wealthy inventor Sir Richard Arkwright. Settling into Victorian matronhood at his 'fine mansion', and in a social circle that included the Dukes of Rutland and Devonshire, the other Fanny records that she never lost her 'transparent and child-like simplicity and sincerity', 'she thought wives were bound implicitly to obey their husbands, for she believed that at the day of judgement husbands would be answerable for their wives' souls'.[40]

Meanwhile Marie-Thérèse's sister Adelaide, who had been this Fanny's inseparable companion in the Durham company, offers a rare glimpse of the theatrical family woman making the strictly backstage contribution to the family business. After Fanny's marriage 'Dall' went to live with her sister's family as unpaid help, and brought up Fanny Kemble Butler, who speaks of her with enormous affection and compassion. She records that her aunt arrived from Durham in 'a bitter bankruptcy of love and friendship, happiness and hope'. Aunt Dall became an indispensable person, the main carer for the children and the only anchor within a wild London household and on tour in America:

She had a robust and rather prosaic common-sense, opposed to anything exaggerated or sentimental, which gave her an excellent judgement of character and conduct, a strong genial vein of humor which often made her repartees witty as well as wise, and a sunny sweetness of temper and soundness of moral nature that made her as good as she was easy and delightful to live with.

She tended young Fanny, and Charles and Marie-Thérèse's other children, with 'unremitting care . . . without any joys or hopes but those of others . . . in a serene, unclouded, unvarying atmosphere of cheerfulness, self-forgetful content that was heroic'.[41] So Adelaide, as a nineteenth-century woman, contributed behind the scenes as a manager and facilitator in the Kemble family business: it was a kind of dramatisation, a staged version, at least as Fanny Kemble transmits it to us, of the domesticated role of the Victorian middle-class female.

The Victorian woman in the theatre: putting up a family front

The self-concealing management of the fortunes of the theatre family was to become a Victorian norm, but one which still differs significantly from the standard middle-class model. Women who inherited and wished to develop theatre talents and skills learnt to use their family and marital position as a cloak for their professional leadership. For a Kemble example of the way in which theatrical women continued to act as the driving force that shaped the path to business success, I would cite the Sarah Siddons descendant, Sydney Frances Cowell (1823–81), whose life is described above, p. 172: she married a respectable (in this case, exaggeratedly respectable, a strict Methodist) man from outside the business, and he became the financial front, the means by which the burgeoning talent of his wife and children could operate in Victorian theatre. I would argue that in the mid-Victorian period, as the impulse to respectability bites deep, entrepreneurial women of a theatre background and family marry 'out', but marry men who will provide them, in effect, with a respectable name behind which they can continue to work. The aristocratic raid on theatrical beauty gives way to a canny middle-class alliance between old talent and skills, and new money and class connections.

Consider for example Ellen Tree, one of a family of girls who succeeded on the London stage in the early 1830s by talent, enterprise and a degree of exploitation, both of the unstable situation and of their own attractions. Ellen was the woman whose impersonation of the hero in Talfourd's *Ion* improved on the efforts of Macready, for whom the part had been written: he registered his malign disgust ('if it is the author's feeling that it is the nasty sort of epicene animal which a woman so dressed up renders it, I am very loth to appear in it').[42] She would appear to have seen that to compete in the theatre world, as it was being remodelled by this very Macready, was difficult for a woman operating in her own name – so she annexed the most prestigious one available, and became Mrs Charles Kean, and a powerful force in his highly respectable enterprise of educational Shakespeare. One might read this the other way round, and take it that the younger Kean, without his father's talent, was lucky to be able to support his family business with her abilities; either way the alliance serves the purpose of modernising the theatre within a middle-class setting.

A similar point can be made about many theatre marriages in the Victorian period: George Taylor lists 'Mrs Wigan, Mrs Kendal, Mrs Boucicault, Mrs Herman Vezin and Mrs Bancroft' as actresses who supplied the 'professional experience' their middle-class husbands lacked, and 'manipulated' their husband's careers to create success.[43] One might well put this in reverse. Mrs Wigan was Leonora Pincott (see above for her family). Mrs Kendal was Margaret Robertson, great-granddaughter of James Robertson, leading comedian at York under Tate Wilkinson, granddaughter of the stepdaughter of the Wrench who played Corinthian Tom, daughter of another Robertson and the actress Margaret Marinus, sister of Tom Robertson the dramatist. Mrs Herman Vezin was Jane Thomson (see above, p. 188) and Mrs Bancroft was Marie Wilton, child of provincial actors, infant prodigy, star performer of boy roles and lessee and manageress of the theatre, the Prince of Wales's, for which she hired Bancroft as a performer. I would argue that these are women whose sense of the theatre business and of their capacity to get to the top within it suggested to them the usefulness of a man from outside, with a good education and financial connections. They married respectability, and brought their catches into the business. Mrs Boucicault was Dame Irene Vanbrugh, and is in some sense an exception, since she and her actress sister Violet were daughters of a prebendary of Exeter Cathedral whose wife belonged to an old Exeter family of theatre patrons. Dame Irene might be said to have engaged the junior Boucicault as her manager and husband to help her negotiate the complexities of the theatre world

into which she made such an unprecedented entry from the upper middle classes. It is interesting that she created the part of
Rose Trelawney in Pinero's play about the transformation of the
theatre into a respectable middle-class business, *Trelawney of the
Wells*. The piece is most obviously a fictionalisation of the story
of Tom Robertson's plays and the 'realism' they pioneered at the
Prince of Wales's Theatre. But it also tells how Rose Trelawney,
child of the theatre, who carries with her the glamour of ancient
stage connections – the memory of Edmund Kean's Richard III –
captures a young man of the upper classes and carries him into
her world, her charm and taste and talent making the theatre acceptable to his relations. The models for Rose as the guiding force
for theatrical change are Madge Robertson and Marie Wilton,
buying in class credentials in the shape of gentlemen to front their
ancient family business. Such a reading reverses the valence of
the polarisation identified by Davidoff and Hall in their study of
family fortunes.

Conclusion

Family history is important in an anthropocentric understanding
of self, and the theatre is an extreme example of a professional
group for whom family, very broadly understood, is a central
structure of feeling and practical support. I have been attempting in this chapter to use genealogy to unpick some of the previous academic narratives of power within this professional world,
and in particular to open up a point of view which allows the
importance of women's theatre work to become visible. Following the suggestion of Davidoff and Hall's *Family Fortunes*, I have
looked at the part played in theatre families by women not simply
as consumers, progressively separated from production, but as
equal sharers in the work and also sometimes as the major creators and transmitters of cultural capital. The internal dynamic
of skill transmission, as well as the pragmatic need for women to
continue to appear upon the scene, enabled some women to control not only their own lives, but those of husbands and children.
Looking through personal stories at the social imaginary of the
early nineteenth century, I have attempted to look beyond the
theatre itself to its place in the emerging cultural pattern, and to
use the understanding that actresses had of their own position,

and the conflicted rhetoric of Catherine Oxberry's commentary upon them, to discover an aspect of the social imaginary of the Victorian middle classes in process of formation. But the woman in the theatre remains in an exceptional position; and the latter part of this discussion has focused upon the successes in that unusual milieu of some remarkable women, the driving forces in outstanding families like the Kembles and also in their own networks of kin and influence, which I have tried to pick out from behind the patriarchal family names. Much remains to be done in tracing such patterns across the period and beyond.

Perhaps the most important aspect of the structure of the profession in the nineteenth century still to be pursued from this approach is the matter of training and preparation for the stage. In practical terms, I have noted how important physical training of young children was in determining the pattern of induction to the profession. More discursively important is the tense position of young women, in particular, who were professionally trained for the stage because they exhibited beauty or musical talent beyond the norm. The middle-class girl practised her singing or her piano-playing in order to distinguish herself from her brother, solidly learning mathematics and Latin; and she hoped to please a husband by her pretty accomplishments. But the actress could potentially use those same accomplishments, trained hard for seven years even if still masked as natural gifts, to win big prizes in the marriage market. Such professionalisation of marriage was problematic. I have only touched upon the mechanisms of apprenticeship and training that family history reveals in relation to these discursive problems; and other equally interesting implications remain to be teased out. The ways in which people become actors, how they are trained, the relation of a perception of personal talent to the learning of the traditions of interpretation and skills or representation, are central issues in the conception of theatre. Family history may be useful in tracing changes to the formation of the actor along quite a different axis from the intellectual history of theories of representation. An alert and imaginative pursuit of family history, then, might be a useful academic tool in redressing the received emphasis upon texts, and upon the genius of writers intervening in or compelling the service of the theatrical culture. It throws the stress back upon trained, material skills – on acting, singing, dance; and on co-operation and management. Following the lead provided by Davidoff and Hall's analysis of the family roots of successful British capitalism, it shows that in show business 'capital' consists in these skills and that its exploitation depends upon their conservation and transmission, by women as well as by men. It reveals the interactive role of women before and behind the scenes; thus the business is feminised, but also hard-headed.

There is a final point to be made, that contrasts with that grounded, material understanding of the family profession. A consideration of family history may also restore to a place of importance in historiography ideas about the 'magic' or 'romance' of the stage which, however we may deprecate them, are an important part of most people's perception of what is important about theatre: important enough to make us want to know its history, its hidden secrets. This combination – an emphasis upon blood, inherited magic, on the one hand, on the other upon skilled management – circumvents more masculine and cerebral idealisations (the genius of the playwright) in favour of feminine ones (the power of the family).

Just such a story is embodied in a theatre history text which dates from 1931, a novel which is a good example of history written in the popular tradition, outside the 'rigour' demanded by *Theatrewissenwchaft*. *Broome Stages* is by the experimental West End playwright Clemence Dane, a very successful but, of course, largely forgotten woman of the theatre.[44] The long novel is exuberantly and deliberately melodramatic. Generations of a theatre family triumph, build, act, fight and love each other, pass on their blood and their theatres and die lurid deaths – on stage, incognito in the pit as the curtain falls, touring on the high seas, in the greenroom set alight by the candles of the first-night party. The grasp of the cultural mutations of 150 years of London theatre that underlies the tale is, however, very material and grounded. Dane's theatre family begins when a dreamy and handsome young countryman falls onto the stage through the roof of a barn, and marries first another strolling teenager and then, after her death giving birth to their talented daughter, an upper-class heiress whose money and connections fuel the family dominance of the stage ever after. Their repertoire always combines Shakespeare, in inherited family editions, with melodrama and modern comedy written by family members; the theatres they buy and build are two West End houses and one on the south bank. Branches of the family pioneer into America and, in the last chapters, into motion pictures, founding both a studio and a string of cinemas. This is the substance. But the spirit, passed on strictly from one gender to the other, down the generations, is the charm of the Broomes, contained in a rhyme which the original boy learnt from a village woman who was killed as a witch:

> Dickon! Dickon! Cats and mice!
> Crook your finger and beckon thrice!
> By the Father and the Son,
> Reckon up and beckon on!
> Reckon, beckon –

Then came the two secret lines that set the Broome charm working.[45] Dane, charming her readers, does not tell us what these lines are. Their dream-casting possessor cherishes the rhyme because he understands that 'Lucy Godfrey's wicked fairyland may be mere muck-heap by honest sunlight. All the same, by touchwood-light the muck-heap must be beyond desire beautiful.' Thus Dane romantically sums up the illusion, the glamour of the stage, Rosamund Gilder's 'devil's way';[46] but the combination of qualities touched on in the verse itself, the charm that makes the theatre family successful, is the combination that makes commercial theatre work. They must beckon – lure and enchant the audience, foster the illusion; but they must also reckon – stay aloof, be alert, manage their businesses with no illusions at all. Theatre history should try to understand and consider both sides of their story.

Notes

I THEATRE HISTORY TODAY

1. See R. W. Vince, 'Theatre history as an academic discipline', in
Thomas Postlewait and Bruce A. McConachie, eds., *Interpreting the
Theatrical Past* (University of Iowa Press, 1989), pp. 1–18, pp. 12, 1.
For discussion of the crisis of direction and the impact of new the-
orisations see, for example, Joseph R. Roach, 'Introduction' to the
Theater History and Historiography section in Janelle G. Reinelt and
Joseph R. Roach, eds., *Critical Theory and Performance* (Ann Arbor:
University of Michigan Press, 1992), pp. 293–8; and Marvin Carlson,
'The theory of history', in Sue-Ellen Case and Janelle Reinelt,
eds., *The Performance of Power* (University of Iowa Press, 1991),
pp. 272–9. Thomas Postlewait's latest work in this area is expected,
in the shape of *An Introduction to Theatre Historiography* (Cambridge
University Press, forthcoming [2003]), and soon afterwards a book
on the historiography of the English Renaissance theatre (private
communication). For a survey of recent writing on nineteenth-
century performance and historiography see Jane Moody, 'The state
of the Abyss: nineteenth-century performance and theatre historiography in 1999', *Journal of Victorian Culture* 5.1 (Spring 2000),
112–28. Interest is, however, very strong in new kinds of cultural
history that include performance and the pervasive category of 'the
performative' as elements in understanding identity, self-definition
and community. The London Theatre Museum, having problems
with falling ticket sales for its conventional exhibitions, is pioneering
a large new interactive theatre history experience on-line and in its
galleries, which will, one assumes, lock into the new demand in the
British National Curriculum for the inclusion of theatre history in
A-level English studies. The academic writing that feeds on/feeds into
the expansion of the field of theatre study into inextricable combination with studies of race, gender and the widest possible definitions
of cultural studies underpins this book.

2. See the historiographical discussions exemplified by the work and
legacy of Hayden White, who suggests that 'the most difficult task

which the current generation of historians will be called upon to perform is to expose the historically conditioned character of the historical discipline'. *Tropics of Discourse: Essays in Cultural Criticism* (Baltimore: Johns Hopkins University Press, 1978), p. 29.

3. Robert D. Hume, *Reconstructing Contexts: The Aims and Principles of Archeo-Historicism* (Oxford: Clarendon Press, 1999), p. 5.

4. 'It is not the insistence that facts exist that makes positivism vulgar, but, rather, the insistence that facts can remain neutral'. Roach, Introduction, *Critical Theory*, p. 294; Hume takes Roach to task for generalising from only one cited reference, and for what he calls 'conceptual imposition' – reading backwards from the perceptions of a modern sensibility to interpret slender factual evidence. (Hume, *Reconstructing Contexts*, p. 173.) In his review essay, 'Writing history today', *Theatre Survey* 41.2 (November 2000), 83–106, Thomas Postlewait condemns Hume for promulgating too narrow a definition of evidence, invoking Bloch's *The Historian's Craft*, trans. Peter Putnam (Manchester University Press, 1954), for a more liberal understanding. See also Carl E. Schorske, *Thinking with History* (Princeton University Press, 1998) and Georg G. Iggers, *English Historiography in the Twentieth Century* (Hanover and London: Wesleyan University Press, 1997).

5. 'REED is an international scholarly project that is establishing for the first time the broad context from which the great drama of Shakespeare and his contemporaries grew. REED examines the historical MSS that provide external evidence of drama, secular music, and other communal entertainment and ceremony from the Middle Ages until 1642, when the Puritans closed the London theatres.' http://www.chass.utoronto.ca/~reed/reed.html quotation taken 08/08/02. The publisher has used its best endeavours to ensure that the URLs for external websites referred to in this book are correct and active at the time of going to press. However, the publisher has no responsibility for the websites and can make no guarantee that a site will remain live or that the content is or will remain appropriate.

6. William Van Lennep et al., eds., *The London Stage 1660–1800, A Calendar of Plays* . . . 5 Parts (11 vols.) (Carbondale: University of Southern Illinois Press, 1960–70). A new version of Part 2, 1700–29, is currently being prepared by Judith Milhous and Robert D. Hume. Two draft volumes 'to be published by the Southern Illinois University Press' appeared in printout form in 1996 and are deposited in major research libraries.

7. Alfred L. Nelson and Gilbert B. Cross, gen. eds., *The Adelphi Theatre Calendar, Part 1, 1806–1850* (New York: Greenwood Press, 1988).

8. http://www.emich.edu/public/english/adelphi_calendar; http://www.backstage.ac.uk

9. The International Federation for Theatre Research colloquium 'Re/writing national theatre histories', Finland 1997, centred upon this issue; and see Bruce McConachie, 'Theatre history and the nation-state', *Theatre Research International* 20.2 (1995), 141–8, and 'Cultural systems and the nation-state: paradigms for writing national theatre history', *New England Theatre Journal* 8 (1997) and Steve E. Wilmer, 'Reifying imagined communities: nationalism, post-colonialism and theatre historiography', *Nordic Theatre Studies* 12 (1999), 94–103.

10. Simon Shepherd and Peter Womack, *English Drama, a Cultural History* (Oxford: Blackwell, 1996).

11. The most recent suggestions relate to an alternative to the 'antinomous spheres' of art and commerce which Modernism set up, turning instead to 'engagement with theatre's place in a culture of commodification'. These formulations are culled from Christopher Balme's keynote speech to the International Federation for Theatre Research XIV World Congress on 1 July 2002, 'Stages of forgetting: theatre history and the dynamics of cultural amnesia'. Apart from the volumes already mentioned, there is already a body of new-style work about twentieth-century theatres which can be traced through Dan Rebellato, *1956 and All That: The Making of Modern British Drama* (London: Routledge, 1999), and volumes in the Cambridge Studies in Modern Theatre series, especially Clive Barker and Maggie B. Gale, eds., *British Theatre Between the Wars, 1918–1939* (Cambridge University Press, 2000). Feminist studies have often ranged more widely than such periodisations, beginning with Sue-Ellen Case, *Feminism and Theatre* (London: Macmillan, 1988) and developing analytical power to shed light on many aspects of history, representation and reception: see, for example, Mary Anne Schofield and Cecilia Macheski, *Curtain Calls: British and American Women and the Theater, 1660–1820* (Athens and London: Ohio University Press, 1990); Jill Dolan, *The Feminist Spectator as Critic* (Ann Arbor: University of Michigan Press, 1991), and Maggie B. Gale and Viv Gardner, eds., *Women, Theatre and Performance: New Histories, New Historiographies* (Manchester University Press, 2000). An example of feminist criticism's reach is Janelle Reinelt, ed., *Crucibles of Crisis: Performing Social Change* (Ann Arbor: University of Michigan Press, 1996). There has been a particular hot spot for work on women in the theatre in the British Restoration period, with important work by, for example, Elizabeth Howe, *The First English Actresses: Women and Drama, 1660–1700* (Cambridge University Press, 1992) and Jacqueline Pearson, *The Prostituted Muse: Images of Women and Women Dramatists 1642–1737* (New York and London: Harvester/Wheatsheaf, 1988). In the eighteenth and nineteenth centuries cultural materialist/New Historicist/*annaliste* reading from below is variously exemplified, with shifting foci between

stage, text, cultural and political history, by Marc Baer, *Theatre and Disorder in Late Georgian London* (Oxford: Clarendon Press, 1992); Jane Moody, *Illegitimate Theatre in London, 1770–1840* (Cambridge University Press, 2000); Gillian Russell, *The Theatres of War, Performance, Politics and Society, 1793–1815* (Oxford: Clarendon Press, 1995); George Taylor, *The French Revolution and the London Stage, 1789–1805* (Cambridge University Press, 2000); Julia Swindells, *Glorious Causes: The Grand Theatre of Political Change, 1789–1833* (Oxford University Press, 2001) and Jim Davis and Victor Emeljanow, *Reflecting the Audience: London Theatregoing, 1840–1880* (University of Iowa Press, 2001). Materialist/economic history is comprehensively served by Tracy C. Davis in *The Economics of the British Stage, 1800–1914* (Cambridge University Press, 2000). J. S. Bratton et al., *Acts of Supremacy: The British Empire and the Stage, 1792–1830* (Manchester University Press, 1991) begins upon such readings of the imperial stage; Jennifer Devere Brody's *Impossible Purities: Blackness, Femininity, and Victorian Culture* (Durham and London: Duke University Press, 1998) blends feminism with the influence of Joseph Roach's wide take on performance, race and gender.

12. See Michael L. Quinn, '*Theaterwissenschaft* in the history of theatre study', *Theatre Survey* 32 (November 1991), 123–36. Quinn makes a case for complicating and extending our understanding of the scope and spread of the German theatre history scholarship. See *Journal of Dramatic Theory and Criticism* 3.2 (1989) for a special section on theatre history.

13. Hume, *Reconstructing Contexts*, p. 62 and passim.

14. Judith Milhous and Robert D. Hume, eds., John Downes, *Roscius Anglicanus* (London: Society for Theatre Research, 1987), p. v.

15. Jean-François Lyotard, *La Condition Postmoderne*, trans. Geoff Bennington and Brian Massumi (Manchester University Press, c. 1984).

16. Reinelt and Roach, *Critical Theory*, p. 293.

17. Joseph Roach, *Cities of the Dead: Circum-atlantic Performance* (New York: Columbia University Press, 1996).

18. Ibid., p. 1.

19. Milhous and Hume, *Roscius*, p. x.

20. Roach, *Cities*, p. 93.

21. Davis, *Economics*, p. 5.

22. Carlson, 'The theory of history', p. 276.

23. Rosamund Gilder, *Enter the Actress: The First Women in the Theatre* (1931, reprinted Freeport, NY: Books for Libraries Press, 1971), pp. 8–9.

24. Jonas Barish, *The Antitheatrical Prejudice* (Berkeley: University of California Press, 1981), p. 475.

25. Modern music-hall scholarship is led by Peter Bailey, whose publications so far include *Leisure and Class in Victorian England: Rational Recreation and Social Control, 1830–1885* (London: Methuen, 1978); *Music Hall: The Business of Pleasure* (Milton Keynes: Open University Press, 1986); and *Popular Culture and Performance in the Victorian City* (Cambridge University Press, 1998). See also J. S. Bratton, ed., *Music Hall: Performance and Style* (Milton Keynes: Open University Press, 1986). A synoptic view of work done so far is usefully supplied by Dagmar Kift, *The Victorian Music Hall: Culture, Class and Conflict* (Cambridge University Press, 1996). For melodrama, see below pp. 12–14.

26. For discussion of this phenomenon in theoretical terms, see Morag Shiach, *Discourse on Popular Culture: Class, Gender and History in Cultural Analysis, 1730 to the Present* (Cambridge: Polity Press, 1989), and David Harris, *From Class Struggle to the Politics of Pleasure* (London: Routledge, 1992); for its effects upon politicised theatre work and history see Baz Kershaw, *The Politics of Performance: Radical Theatre, a Cultural Intervention* (London: Routledge, 1992), and especially chapter 5, 'The death of nostalgia: performance, memory and genetics', in *The Radical in Performance: Between Brecht and Baudrillard* (London: Routledge, 1999). The most useful theoretic work on the issues for the theatre historian is, in my opinion, Peter Stallybrass and Allon White, *The Politics and Poetics of Transgression* (London: Methuen, 1986).

27. For discussion of these foundational theatre historians and a list of their publications see below, chapter 3.

28. This is a deliberate simplification of the issues: for an acute detailed discussion, see Rebellato, *1956 and All That*, chapters 2–4; for the disputes between London professionalism and new conceptions of theatre in political and educational contexts, see Kershaw, *Politics of Performance*.

29. See, for example, Ira Hauptman, 'Defending melodrama', in James Redmond, ed., *Themes in Drama 14: Melodrama* (Cambridge University Press, 1992), pp. 281–9.

30. Frank Rahill in *The World of Melodrama* (University Park and London: Pennsylvania State University Press, 1967), p. xiii, starts his recuperative – or, rather, excusatory – attempt on the topic by quoting from Fowler's *Dictionary of Modern English Usage*: 'A term generally used with some contempt'.

31. William Archer, *The Old Drama and the New* (London: Heinemann, 1923), p. 246.

32. Augustin Filon, *The English Stage, being an account of the Victorian drama*, trans. Frederic Whyte (London: John Milne, 1896), pp. 37, 35.

33. Ibid., p. 66.

34. Ibid., p. 63.

35. Michael Booth, *English Melodrama* (London: Herbert Jenkins, 1965); Jerome K. Jerome, *Stage-land: Curious Habits and Customs of its Inhabitants* (London: Chatto and Windus, 1889). For more recent but still often defensive works, see Redmond, ed., *Melodrama*, and, in a recent and much more highly theorised instance, Michael Hayes and Anastasia Nikolopolou, *Melodrama, the Cultural Emergence of a Genre* (New York: St Martin's Press, 1996).

36. Martin Meisel, *Realizations: Narrative, Pictorial, and Theatrical Arts in Nineteenth-century England* (Princeton University Press, 1983), p. 436.

37. Critical work on stage melodrama had, at the end of the twentieth century, become indebted to the maturing appreciation of the genre of melodrama in film for new ways of breaking out of this binary: see Jacky Bratton, Jim Cooke, Christine Gledhill, *Melodrama: Stage, Picture, Screen* (London: British Film Institute, 1994).

38. Peter Brooks, *The Melodramatic Imagination: Balzac, Henry James, Melodrama, and the Mode of Excess* (New Haven and London: Yale University Press, 1976).

39. Elaine Hadley, *Melodramatic Tactics: Theatricalised Dissent and the Market Place, 1800–1885* (Stanford University Press, 1995).

40. See, however, the beginning of work on the revival of Jane Scott's Romantic melodramas by academic historians working with professional performers, funded as a research innovation by the AHRB and reported in a special issue of *Nineteenth Century Theatre and Film* 29.2 (Winter 2002), ed. Jacky Bratton and Gilli Bush-Bailey.

41. Hume, *Reconstructing Contexts*, p. 47.

42. Peter Burke, *Varieties of Cultural History* (Cambridge: Polity Press, 1997), p. 2.

43. It is worth noting here John Docker's remark that '[a]lways, in modernist cultural history, there is the same unfailingly reproduced narrative of decline'. *Postmodernism and Popular Culture: A Cultural History* (Cambridge University Press, 1994), p. 40.

44. Feminist theatre history directly concerned with this period is exemplified by Ellen Donkin, *Getting Into the Act, Women Playwrights in London 1776–1829* (London: Routledge, 1995); Tracy C. Davis and Ellen Donkin, eds., *Women and Playwriting in Nineteenth-century Britain* (Cambridge University Press, 1999); Catherine Burroughs, ed., *Women in British Romantic Theatre: Drama, Performance and Society, 1790–1840*) (Cambridge University Press, 2000).

45. It also had an important life beyond the established leading nations of Europe in the nineteenth century – see Laurence Senelick, ed., *National Theatre in Northern and Eastern Europe, 1746–1900* (Cambridge University Press, 1991).

46. See Peter Burger et al., *The Institution of Art* (Lincoln: University of Nebraska, 1992), p. xv, for this definition of positivism.

2 BRITISH THEATRE HISTORY: 1708–1832

1. James Wright, *Historia Histrionica: an historical account of the English Stage* [by James Wright] (London: W. Haws, 1699); and John Downes, *Roscius Anglicanus, or an historical review of the stage* (London, 1708).

2. Milhous and Hume, *Roscius*, pp. xiii–xiv.

3. David Erskine Baker et al., *The Companion to the Playhouse: or, an historical account of all the dramatic writers (and their works)* . . . 2 vols. (London, 1764); this was extended from 1764 to 1782 as Isaac Reed, ed., *Biographica Dramatica, or a companion to the playhouse* . . . 2 vols. (London, 1782). There is no readily discernible point of origin for such works, however, and Baker and Reed relied heavily (and ill-advisedly, in point of accuracy) upon the publications of Gerard Langbaine, published in the 1680s and 90s, which are themselves derivative: see James Arnott and John Robinson, *English Theatrical Literature 1559–1900, A Bibliography* (London: Society for Theatre Research, 1970), items 3 to 11.

4. BL cat. no. 641 i 22–25.

5. BL cat. no. HLR822.009 has Charles Burney's notes, while 11795.df and k has those of T. H. Lacey together with volumes of his collected materials for a new edition. Malone's copy is in the Bodleian: see James Arnott and Robinson, *English Theatrical Literature*, for this and listings of other editions.

6. Printed by Thomas Richards 'for strictly private circulation'.

7. John Payne Collier, *An Old Man's Diary, Forty Years Ago*, part 1, p. 20.

8. Ibid., part 3, p. 27.

9. Benjamin Victor, *The history of the theatres of London and Dublin, from the year 1730 to the present time, to which is added, An annual register of all the plays etc performed at the Theatres-royal in London, from the year 1712* (London, 1761); Walley Chamberlain Oulton, *The History of the theatres of London: containing an annual register . . . from the year 1771 to 1795*, 2 vols. (London, 1796). For other editions and titles in this genre see Arnott and Robinson, *English Theatrical Literature*, items 829–48.

10. Hayden White, *Metahistory: The Historical Imagination in Nineteenth-century Europe* (Baltimore: Johns Hopkins University Press, 1973), pp. 59–60. *Annales* began as *Annales d'histoire economique et sociale*, published in Paris in 1929, appearing under its current title since 1946.

11. R. Dodsley, *A Select Collection of Old Plays*, 11 vols. (London, 1744), vol. 1; his Preface occupies pp. i–xxxix, the section on pre-Shakespearean drama pp. viii–xxi.

12. *Egerton's Theatrical Remembrancer* (printed for T. and J. Egerton, London, 1788), p. iv.

13. The books not already noted are Rufus Chetwood, *A General History of the Stage* (London, 1749); Thomas Davies's edition of and additions to *Roscius Anglicanus*, edited by Francis Godolphin Waldron (London, 1789); Francis Godolphin Waldron, *The Origin of the English Stage* (London, 1802), and *A Compendious History of the English Stage* (London, 1800), which compiles materials from Chares Dibdin and other writers; and Ralph Wewitzer, *A Theatrical Pocket Book, or brief dramatic chronology* (London, 1814), and *A brief dramatic chronology of actors etc.* (London, 1817) etc.

14. Charles Dibdin, *A Complete History of the English Stage*, 5 vols., printed for the author (London, 1797–1800).

15. Milhous and Hume, *Roscius Anglicanus*, p. x.

16. Biographical information derives from Philip H. Highfill Jnr, Kalmin A. Burnim and Edward A. Langhans, *A Biographical Dictionary . . . 1660–1800*, 16 vols. (Carbondale and Edwardsville: Southern Illinois University Press, 1973–93).

17. Michael Kelly, *Reminiscences of Michael Kelly, of the King's Theatre and the Theatre Royal Drury Lane . . .* , 2 vols. (London: Henry Colburn, 1826), vol. 2, p. 37.

18. *Prompter*, no. 1, Tuesday 12 November 1734, printed for J. Peele, London, [p. 1].

19. *Satirist* quoted in Alfred L. Nelson Jnr, 'James Winston's *Theatric Tourist*, a critical edition with a biography and a census of Winston material', unpublished PhD thesis in 2 vols., George Washington University, 1968, a copy of which is deposited in the Theatre Museum, London, vol. 1, p. liv, and Alfred Bunn, *The Stage: Both Before and Behind the Curtain*, 3 vols. (London: Bentley, 1840), vol. 1, p. cxxxix.

20. Sometimes the prompter also acted as employment agent for minor players – see Thomas Dibdin's first step onto the stage, which he achieved by application to Booth, prompter at Covent Garden, who wrote him a recommendation to the manager of a small theatre in Margate (*The Reminiscences of Thomas Dibdin*, 2 vols. (London: Henry Colborn, 1827), vol. 1, p. 40).

21. O'Keeffe, *Recollections*, vol. 2, p. 422, quoted in Van Lennep, *The London Stage 1660–1800*, Part 5, vol. 1, p. clxiii.

22. W. R. Chetwood, *The British Theatre. . together with the lives of most of the principal actors . . .* (Dublin, Peter Wilson, 1850), p. 1.

23. W. R. Chetwood, *A General History of the Stage* (London: W. Owen, 1749), Dedication: unpaginated.

24. Quoted in Arnott and Robinson, *English Theatrical Literature*, p. 88.

25. Chetwood, *General History of the Stage*, p. 244, about Richard Wetherilt.

26. Quoted in Milhous and Hume, *Roscius Anglicanus*, p. xii.

27. Chetwood, *British Theatre*, p. i; Egerton, *Theatrical Remembrancer*, pp. iii–iv; Oulton, *Annual Register*, p. iii; on the Waldron/Davies

edition of *Roscius Anglicanus* see Milhous and Hume, pp. xxi–xxii; Jones, *Biographia Dramatica*, 1812, p. lxxiii.
28. Collier, *Old Man's Diary*, part 1, p. 24.
29. Ibid., p. 54.
30. Smith collection, BL shelf mark 11826r, s; Haslewood, BL shelf marks 11795.k.31 and 1179.dd.18, the latter being the collection augmented by Smith. Haslewood published collections and compilations, including some of theatrical anecdotes: *The Secret History of the Green Rooms: containing authentic memoirs of the actors and actresses in the three Theatres Royal* (London, 1790).
31. Copies of the catalogue of the sale, by Puttick and Simpson of London, are preserved in the Harvard Theatre Collection, Boston Public Library and the Bodleian, Oxford. A census of the Winston MSS and their ultimate destinations is appended to Nelson, 'James Winston's *Theatric Tourist'*.
32. Nelson, 'James Winston's *Theatric Tourist'*, vol. 1, p. xxxi.
33. See Charles Beecher Hogan, 'The manuscript of Winston's *Theatric Tourist'*, *Theatre Notebook* 1.7 (1947), 86–95.
34. John E. Cunningham, 'The origin of *The Theatric Tourist'*, *Theatre Notebook* 4.6 (1949), 38–40, p. 40; the letters are in Birmingham Reference Library.
35. Nelson, 'James Winston's *Theatric Tourist'*, vol. 1, p. lii.
36. See the census of MSS in Nelson, 'James Winston's *Theatric Tourist'*, vol. 2, pp. 168–210.
37. Twenty-three huge folio volumes of the Drury Lane materials are at BL shelf mark C.120.h.1; they are being rebound, courtesy of Marks and Spencer plc. The cash books are BL Add. MSS 29709–11.
38. Letter to C. B. Smith, 27 March 1835, bound in volume 7 of 'Original letters of dramatic performers collected and arranged by C. B. Smith' held at the Garrick Club.
39. Quoted in Nelson, 'James Winston's *Theatric Tourist'*, Appendix b, vol. 2, p. 177.
40. Held at the Garrick Club.
41. *The Diaries of W. C. Macready, 1833–1851*, ed. William Toynbee, 2 vols. (London: Chapman and Hall, 1912), vol. 1, p. 28, vol. 2, p. 433.
42. Nelson, 'James Winston's *Theatric Tourist'*, vol. 1, p. xxv.
43. See above, p. 29, on their encounters.
44. [John Genest,] *Some Account of the English Stage, from the Restoration in 1660 to 1830*, 10 vols. (printed by H. E. Carrington for Thomas Rodd, Bath and London, 1832)
45. Quoted in Arnott and Robinson, *English Theatrical Literature*, p. 90.
46. Genest, *English Stage*, vol. 1, p. 390.
47. Ibid., p. 27.
48. Ibid., p. 314.

49. Ibid., p. 29.
50. Ibid., pp. 154, 193.
51. Sir Leslie Stephen and Sir Sidney Lee, eds., *The Dictionary of National Biography*, 22 vols. (reprinted Oxford University Press, 1973), vol. 7, p. 998. Entry by J.K., i.e. the theatre historian Joseph Knight.

3 THEATRE IN LONDON IN 1832: A NEW OVERVIEW

1. See Jane Moody, *Illegitimate Theatre in London, 1770–1840* (Cambridge University Press, 2000), for a full and up-to-date reading of this history.
2. 6&7 Vict c.68, 26 July 1843, which repealed 3 Jac 1, c.21; 10 Geo 2, c.19,28; 28 Geo3, c.30.
3. Richard Schechner, *Performance Theory* (revised and expanded edition, New York and London: 1988), p. 72.
4. Ibid., p. 93.
5. See D. R. Gowan, 'Studies in the history and function of the British theatre playbill and programme, 1564–1914', unpublished D.Phil thesis, University of Oxford, 1998.
6. No more precise figure can be given, since it is not really possible to define a theatre at this time or, therefore, to separate it from other places of entertainment. There are several interesting contemporary lists of venues: on 27 March 1831 the low periodical *The Age* listed fourteen theatres that would be open in the coming week, and four dark or occupied by visitors: open were the Theatres Royal – the patented houses – plus the Queen's, previously called the Tottenham (and later under the Bancrofts to become the famous Prince of Wales's), the Coburg, the Surrey, Astley's, Sadler's Wells, the Garrick ('a beautiful new theatre'), the Pavilion, previously called the East London, the City in Milton Street, previously called Grub Street (this was a converted Methodist chapel), the City Vaudeville, Smithfield ('manager and author, on dit, Alderman Waithman' – who presented one of the petitions about the dramatic laws and sat on the 1832 Select Committee) and the New East London 'somewhere down Radcliffe Highway'. Not currently occupied by their companies were the Adelphi, the Olympic, the English Opera (the Lyceum) and the Theatre Royal, Haymarket, where, however, the French company were currently performing. The lofty journalistic ignorance of the location of the East End venues is interesting; it is repeated in a different way by O. Smith, the actor, in his collection of materials towards a theatre history, where he lists for 1831 the venues above plus the Italian Opera House, Cooke's Equestrian Circus in Great Windmill Street, the White Conduit House, the Union in King Street, Holborn, the Eagle in the City Road, Davis's in Bagnigge Wells Road, the Sloane Street, Chelsea, the Eyre Arms,

St John's Wood, the Peter Street, Westminster, the Horns at Ken-
nington, the Bell Street, Edgware Road, the Bayswater, the Bath
Street, City Road, the Battle-Bridge, the Cow-Cross, the Stepney,
and 'three others, names unknown, in that neighbourhood' (see the
British Library collection of Smith's papers, shelf mark 11826r, s,
discussed in chapter 2 above). This very interesting list clearly contains places operating under a licence for music and dancing, some
of which – the Eagle, for example – were to have a long history but
to choose a non-dramatic route, often as music halls; but at the time
of compilation they were seen by Smith as all in the same bracket,
as providers of entertainments. Four years earlier Thomas Dibdin,
who also had good professional reasons to know, had compiled a list
of current and recent places of entertainment which gives some of
these other names – the White Conduit Street venue he designates
'New Vauxhall', for example, and he offers 'the West London' as
a name for the future Prince of Wales's – but also adds the operas
and French plays performing at the Argyle Rooms, Bermondsey
Spa, Bagnigge Wells (but this may be 'Davis's'), Islington Spa, the
Minor Theatre in Catherine Street, the Pantheon, the Royalty, the
French Theatre in Tottenham Street, and Vauxhall Gardens. (*The
Reminiscences of Thomas Dibdin*, 2 vols. (London: Henry Colborn,
1827), vol. 2, p. 395). There are more than forty identifiably separate venues named here, within a four-year span.

7. Return from the Sessions-House, Clerkenwell, 8 October 1832;
   copy appended to the copy of the Report of the 1832 Parliamentary
   Committee held at Garrick Club.
8. *Report from the Select Committee on Dramatic Literature: with the minutes of evidence*, 1832; reprinted in the Irish University Press Series
   of British Parliamentary Papers, with an introduction and index
   by Marilyn L. Norstedt, Shannon, Ireland [1968]. Question and
   answer numbers 1994, 1996 (numbers subsequently cited are preceded by 'S.C.Q.').
9. See Frances Ann Kemble, *Records of a Girlhood* (New York: Henry
   Holt, 1883), pp. 503–4, 509, 511, 518; Henry Gibbs, *Affection-
   ately Yours, Fanny: Fanny Kemble and the Theatre* (London: Jarrolds,
   1946), p. 71.
10. See, as one example among many, H. Barton Baker, *The London
    Stage: Its History and Traditions from 1576–1888*, 2 vols. (London:
    W. H. Allen, 1889), vol. 1, p. 153.
11. *Satirist*, 8 May 1831, p. 38, 22 May 1831, p. 56, 29 May 1831,
    p. 62, 23 October 1831, p. 228, 30 October 1831, p. 238.
12. For the accepted story of this confrontation, see J. C. Trewin, *Mr
    Macready* (London: Harrap, 1955), pp. 110–24.
13. See, for example, Leigh Hunt's vindication of 'the state of public
    taste' and its abuse by spectacular productions in his critique of

Quadrupeds at the English Opera House, July 1811, reprinted in Houtchens and Houtchens, *Leigh Hunt's Dramatic Criticism, 1808–1831* (London: Oxford University Press, 1950), pp. 50–1; or *The Theatrical Observer*, a daily pamphlet begun in 1821 and intent from the first upon vilifying the patent houses for failing 'the Genius of the Stage' and especially great authors: see, for example, no. 3, 26 September 1821, asserting that the 'great national Theatre is being converted into a School for Scene-painters, Tailors, and the training of Theatrical Horsemen'.

14. Marc Baer in *Theatre and Disorder* has used a New Historicist focus on the 1809 OP riots at Covent Garden to refute Filon's crude conception of the nature of the protesting audiences, who were by no means an illiterate mob; and Julia Swindells has explored the political dynamic and controversial edge of theatrical materials hitherto dismissed as vulgar (*Glorious Causes: The Grand Theatre of Political Change, 1789–1833* (Oxford University Press, 2001)). See chapter 5 for two further ways of looking again at the battle for the patent houses.

15. See, for example, Theatre Museum, London, Haymarket File, bill for Monday 4 June 1832 – Kean's Richard III.

16. 'Farren was emphatically the representative of gentlemen.' George Henry Lewes, *On Actors and the Art of Acting* (London: Smith, Elder, 1875), p. 56.

17. The Theatre Royal, Haymarket, was rebuilt in Regency high style in 1820; on the assumptions of the clientele and the theatre servants at the Opera House, including having no fixed price and no copper change given for refreshments, see *Times*, 5 and 12 March 1832; and for the state of its drainage, see Tracy C. Davis, 'Filthy – nay – pestilential: sanitation and Victorian theaters', in Della Pollock, ed., *Exceptional Spaces: Essays in Performance and History* (Chapel Hill and London: University of North Carolina Press, 1998), pp. 161–86, p. 174.

18. *Figaro in London*, no. 27, 2 June 1832, and no. 69, 30 March 1833.

19. See M. Willson Disher, *Pleasures of London* (London: Robert Hale, 1950), pp. 96–7.

20. H. M. and G. Speight, 'The Minor Theatre in Catherine Street', *Theatre Notebook* 18 (1963), 117–20, p. 119.

21. Catherine Oxberry, ed., *Oxberry's Dramatic Biography and Histrionic Anecdotes*, 7 vols. (London: George Virtue, John Duncombe, 1825–7), vol. 5, p. 54; David Kerr Cameron, *The English Fair* (Stroud: Sutton, 1998), pp. 204, 206.

22. Dibdin, *Reminiscences*, vol. 2, p. 395.

23. On the prosecution of the Orange, see *Morning Chronicle*, 2 January 1832; and see the bill for Rayner's benefit there, BL shelf mark 376(3).

24. *Morning Chronicle*, 23 and 28 January, 6 and 21 February 1832; Watson Nicholson, *The Struggle for a Free Stage in London* (1906, reissued New York: 1966), pp. 314–17.

25. See Nicholson, *Struggle*, pp. 281–6.

26. For a narrative of Arnold's work, see A. E. Wilson, *The Lyceum* (London: Dennis Yates, 1952), pp. 28–66; for his high profile in the patent wars, see Nicholson, *Struggle*, pp. 214–16, 258–9, 272–5 and passim.

27. See *Tatler*, no. 131, 3 February 1831, for a letter about the need for an early curtain: the cost of seats being high, 'those whose habits of business would render the late hours the most inconvenient, are the very persons who would be most bent upon having their "pennyworth for their penny"'.

28. See the Select Committee's repeated commendation of Buckstones' *Victorine*, S.C.Q. 746, 2950, 2982, 2995–3003.

29. Opened 24 October 1831; quoted bill is that for November 14/15/16, from copy in Theatre Museum, London, Adelphi File.

30. Cameron, *The English Fair*, pp. 153–223, on London's metropolitan and suburban fairs and their suppression; see also the collection of cuttings about individual legal battles in the 1820s and 30s assembled by Francis Place, British Library microfilm set 41, vol. 1, reel 25.

31. See the case of the Southampton Arms in Camden Town, which made the only successful application to the Middlesex sessions of 30 October 1829, solely because one of the magistrates, the otherwise silent Colonel Bird, declared that he himself took his dish of tea there, and that he wanted a licence exclusively for the recreation of the middle classes. Place cuttings, British Library.

32. *Morning Chronicle*, 28 May 1832.

33. Newspapers of the 1820s and 30s often contain notices of these mushroom venues, such as that in *The Times*, 12 June 1832, reporting the opening of the Royal Clarence Theatre at King's Cross, under the management of Mrs Fitzwilliam and W. H. Williams; a vivid impression of the range of their clientele and ambitions can be gleaned from playbills collected in the British Library (see for example shelf marks 376 (1, 2 and 3)) which advertise everything from clog dancing and dog dramas at the Bower Saloon in Stangate Street to concerts with 'petites pièces' including legitimate light opera (*Love Laughs at Locksmiths*) at the City Vaudeville).

34. *Oxberry's Dramatic Biographies*, new series, 2 vols. (London: G. Virtue, 1827), vol. 1, no. 4, pp. 55–72, p. 64; *Satirist*, 8 May 1831.

35. *Tatler*, no. 4, 8 September 1830. For the prosecution, see Nicholson, *Struggle*, pp. 309–11; but the Tottenham Street Theatre soon reopened – by the 1860s it was the Prince of Wales's, the most fashionable theatre in London.

36. See opening night bill, Monday 4 April 1831 (BL 736 (3)).

37. A. E. Wilson, *East End Entertainment* (London: Baker, 1954), p. 80.

38. Harold Scott, *The Early Doors* (London: Nicholson and Watson, 1946), pp. 72–4.

39. For an account of the 1843 Act, Nicholson, *Struggle*, pp. 412–20.

40. Raymond Williams's groundbreaking interpretation of television and how it is received in terms of 'flow' is relevant to the discussion of such a theatrical event; he recognises that variety bills existed before television, but assumes that we have learnt to go with the flow specifically in connection with TV. I would suggest that his analysis of sequences of programming could profitably be applied to nineteenth-century theatre. See Raymond Williams, *Television: Technology and Cultural Form* (1974, New York: Schocken Books, 1975), pp. 78–118.

41. *Morning Chronicle*, 18 October 1827, report of a memorial presented to the licensing hearings at the Surrey Quarter Sessions.

42. See Iain D. McCalman, 'Popular irreligion in early Victorian England: infidel preachers and radical theatricality in 1830s London', in R. W. Davis and R. J. Helmstadter, eds., *Religion and Irreligion in Victorian Society* (London: Routledge, 1992), pp. 51–67.

43. See reports of licensing hearings at Surrey Quarter Sessions, *Morning Chronicle*, 18 October 1826 and 18 October 1827. Haslewood's collection of materials for a theatre history (see chapter 2, p. 29), includes a handbill for the auction of Vauxhall in March 1822, describing part of its 11 acres as useful for speculative building. The bill gives a very full description of the premises by that date.

44. See the bill for 23 April 1832, copy in British Library Playbills 170, Astley's Amphitheatre 1791–1843.

45. *The Times*, 26 December 1831, report of the first protest meeting of the minor theatres on Christmas Eve at the Albion Tavern, Russell Street.

46. S.C.Q. 710 – in the evidence given by Charles Kemble.

47. See Jane Moody, 'The silence of New Historicism: a mutinous echo from 1830', *Nineteenth Century Theatre* 24.2 (Winter 1996), 61–89, p. 62.

4 THEATRE HISTORY AND REFORM

1. *Tatler*, no. 329, 23 September 1831, p. 288.

2. For a different but related approach to Reform and the London stage in this period, see Julia Swindells, *Glorious Causes: The Grand Theatre of Political Change, 1789–1833* (Oxford University Press, 2001); for a detailed and extremely persuasive analysis of the economic theory of free trade as applied to the theatre in this moment,

see Tracy C. Davis, *The Economics of the British Stage, 1800–1914* (Cambridge University Press, 2000), pp. 17–41.

3. He was at this point publishing two novels a year, having leapt to prominence with *Pelham* in June 1828; *Paul Clifford*, August 1830, a tale of a chivalrous highwayman, had caused considerable controversy. The advances of more than £1,000 each which he received for these works were greatly in excess of anything dramatists could expect to earn at this time. He published his very successful *Eugene Aram* (1832) in play form in the *New Monthly Magazine* in August 1833. For his fast life, see Michael Sadleir, *Bulwer and his Wife, a Panorama, 1803–1836* (London: Constable, new edition 1933), especially pp. 128–60.

4. Charles W. Snyder, *Liberty and Morality, a Political Biography of Edward Bulwer-Lytton* (New York: Peter Long, 1995), pp. 27–45.

5. Ibid., p. 31, quoting *Hansard's Parliamentary Debates* (London: T. C. Hansard, 1832), third series, vol. 6, pp. 608–10.

6. Snyder, *Liberty and Morality*, p. 45 n. 44, citing Edward Bulwer to Albany Fonblanque, 1 May [1832], Lytton papers, Lytton Archive, Knebworth House, Herts., D/EK C26.

7. Plans for this unwritten volume are printed in Lord Lytton: *The Life, Letters and Literary remains of Edward Bulwer, Lord Lytton, by his Son*, 2 vols. (London: Kegan Paul, Trench, 1883), see vol. 1, p. 266. The improvement of the 'Condition of the Drama' is to be achieved by 'bring[ing] all theatres under one control, and pay[ing] rent of one of great national theatres'.

8. Dewey Ganzel, 'Patent wrongs and patent theatres: drama and the Law in the early nineteenth century', *PMLA* 76 (1961), 384–96, provides the accepted historical overview of Lytton's efforts, which is still of use and interest; he founds his discussion, however, on an acceptance of Lytton's view that there was a need for a *literary* revival to save the theatre (p. 384).

9. Bulwer Lytton, 'The state of the Drama', *New Monthly Magazine* 34 (1832), 131–5, pp. 131, 133.

10. *Mirror of Parliament*, vol. 3, p. 2154.

11. See, for example, the report in the *Tatler*, no. 344, 10 October 1831, p. 347.

12. *Tatler*, no. 347, 13 October 1831, p. 359, and no. 351, 18 October 1831, p. 374.

13. Review of *The World Turned Upside Down, or, Harlequin Reformer* at the Queen's, *Tatler*, no. 412, 28 December 1831.

14. Reported in *The Times*, 26 December 1831.

15. The meeting was reported in the *Morning Chronicle*, 4 January 1832.

16. See A. E. Dyson, *The Inimitable Dickens* (London: Macmillan, 1970), p. 82. Dickens pronounced Hall and his wife 'the most terrific humbugs known on earth at any period of history'.

17. *Morning Chronicle*, 25 February 1832.
18. Ibid., 23 March 1832.
19. Ibid., 12 June 1832.
20. *Mirror of Parliament*, vol. 3, p. 2154, 22 May 1832.
21. Hansard, 3rd series vol. 13, cols. 239–47; the report in the *Morning Chronicle*, 1 June 1832, gives the audience reactions. For the responses to Lytton's speech, see the following columns, 248–59.
22. *Morning Chronicle*, 1 June 1832.
23. See Charles Shattuck, *Bulwer and Macready* (Urbana: University of Illinois Press, 1958), Ganzel, 'Patent wrongs', and Jane Moody, *Illegitimate Theatre* in London, 1770–1840 (Cambridge University Press, 2000), for further discussion of the years 1832–43.
24. It was chaired by Edward Lytton Bulwer, with Thomas Slingsby Duncombe as his vice, and had twenty-two other members, though it was rarely attended by more than a handful of them, partly because it met during the election campaign: *Morning Chronicle*, 30 July 1832; see Ganzel, 'Patent wrongs', pp. 384–5, for a complete list.
25. Christina Crosby, *The Ends of History* (London and New York: Routledge, 1991), pp. 1–2.
26. Hayden White, *Metahistory*, p. 39.
27. *Report from the Select Committee* reprinted with an introduction by Marilyn L. Norstedt, Irish University Press Series of British Parliamentary Papers, Shannon, Ireland, 1968, p. 5.
28. S.C.Q. and numbers in parenthesis in this chapter refer to the question numbers of the Committee evidence, as reproduced in the 1968 printing above.
29. *Dictionary of National Biography*, entry on Collier, vol. 40, pp. 348–56; and see above, chapter 2.
30. Norstedt, *Report*, p. vii.
31. John Payne Collier, *The History of English Dramatic Poetry to the time of Shakespeare; and Annals of the Stage to the Restoration*, 3 vols. (London: John Murray, 1831), vol. 1, p. 1.
32. See S.C.Q. 278; and his *An Old Man's Diary Forty Years Ago; for the first six months of 1832* (Privately printed for the author, London, 1871), p. 92, where he talks of his good memory at the hearing.
33. *An Old Man's Diary*, p. 49.
34. Hansard, 3rd Series, vol. 13, col. 247.
35. Michael Dobson, *The Making of the National Poet*, Oxford University Press, 1992), pp. 3, 1. See also Jonathan Bate's brilliant encapsulation of the meanings of 'Shakespeare' and their ideological roots in the eighteenth century in *The Genius of Shakespeare* (New York and Oxford: Oxford University Press, 1998), especially pp. 165–70.
36. For the disputed history of which this is a summary, see Gary Taylor, *Reinventing Shakespeare* (London: Vintage, 1991); Simon

Jarvis, *Scholars and Gentlemen: Shakespearean Textual Criticism and Representations of Scholarly Labour, 1725–1765* (Oxford: Clarendon Press, 1995); Dobson, *Making of the National Poet*; and, especially on the textual construction of Shakespearean biography, Bate, *Genius of Shakespeare*.

37. Margreta de Grazia, *Shakespeare Verbatim: The Reproduction of Authenticity and the 1790 Apparatus* (Oxford: Clarendon Press, 1991), p. 6. Note, however, that Jarvis, *Scholars and Gentlemen*, p. 6, suggests that the editorial practices of Capell undermine de Grazia's stress upon Malone's work as the point of change. The opposition of 'authenticy' and anecdote as ideological is taken up by Bate, *Genius of Shakespeare*, and also in my chapter 5, below.

38. Edmond Malone, *The Plays and Poems of William Shakspeare . . . collated verbatim with the most authentick copies . . . to which are added . . . an historical account of the English Stage*, 10 vols. (London: Rivington and Sons, 1790), vol. 1, part 1, p. lx; vol. 1, part 2, pp. 119–21, 28, 32.

39. *Report*, pp. 3, 5.

5 ANECDOTE AND MIMICRY AS HISTORY

1. 'The challenge, then, is not simply to reject them but to analyze anecdotes carefully in order to establish their historical authenticity . . . in terms of the concepts of possibility, plausibility, probability, and certainty.' Thomas Postlewait, 'The criteria for evidence: anecdotes in Shakespearean biography, 1709–2000', in Peter Holland and Bill Worthen, *Redefining Theatre History – Theorizing Performance* (Basingstoke: Palgrave Macmillan, forthcoming, 2004).

2. Unlike scholars in the neighbouring areas of cultural studies, or film; see, for example, the work of Richard Dyer and others on celebrity and film stardom, which is interesting in the context of nineteenth-century stage performers.

3. See also the gutter press of the time, the cheap, partisan papers such as *The Age* and *The Satirist* which included theatre columns, often scurrilous, lying and over-excited. At the 2002 North American Society for the Study of Romanticism, in London, Canada, Jonathan Mulrooney (University of Vermont) presented a paper analysing the recuperative, hegemonic work being done on behalf of the literary orthodoxies by the daily publications that presented patent house playbills alongside critiques of the plays and players.

4. Catherine Oxberry, ed. *Oxberry's Dramatic Biography and Histrionic Anecdotes*, 7 vols. (London: George Virtue, John Duncombe, 1825–7); see also anonymous publications such as *The Biography of the British Stage; being correct narratives of the lives of all the principal actors and actresses . . . interspersed with original anecdotes . . .* (London: Sherwood, Jones, 1824).

5. In the 'Advertisement' prefacing the first number, 1 January 1825.
6. Oxberry's biographies are discussed at length in the case study on genealogy, pp. 180–6.
7. James Boaden, *Memoirs of Mrs Siddons. Interspersed with anecdotes of authors and actors*, 2 vols. (London: Henry Colburn, 1827), vol. 1, p. 32.
8. James Boaden, *Memoirs of the Life of John Philip Kemble, esq.*, *including a history of the stage, from the time of Garrick to the present period*, 2 vols. (London: Longman, Hurst, 1825), p. v.
9. See the analysis of this autobiography in Mary Jean Corbett, *Representing Femininity* (New York and Oxford: Oxford University Press, 1992), pp. 109–14.
10. *The Reminiscences of Michael Kelly*, 2 vols. (London: Henry Colburn, 1826); and see George Raymond, *Memoirs of Robert William Elliston, Comedian*, 2nd edn (London: John Ollivier, 1846), p. xv.
11. Letter of 5 March 1829, Hook to Mathews, in Anne Mathews, 'Theodore Edward Hook', 1841, printed in her *Anecdotes of Actors* (London: T. C. Newby, 1844), pp. 274–92, p. 289–90; Anne Mathews tells the story of the estrangement as part of her memoir of 'an extraordinary man', a genius whose 'talent was essentially oral' – she illustrates this with anecdotes of apparently quite heartless practical jokes that he played on stage and off. The publication which upset Charles Mathews was *Gervaise Skinner*, part of the nine-volume publication *Sayings and Doings*, 3rd series, 9 vols. (London: Henry Colburn, 1824–8), 1827.
12. Edmund Yates, *The Life and Correspondence of Charles Mathews, the elder, Comedian. A new edition, abridged and condensed* (London: Routledge Warne and Routledge, 1860).
13. Unidentified cutting, Strand Theatre file 1833, Theatre Museum, London.
14. Anne Mathews was Fanny's half-sister by their mother's previous marriage to an actor called Jackson. Basil Francis, *Fanny Kelly of Drury Lane* (London: Theatre Book Club, 1950), pp. 4–5.
15. See Shari Benstock, ed., *The Private Self: Theory and Practice of Women's Autobiographical Writings* (London: Routledge, 1988); Bella Brodzki and Celeste Schenk, eds., *Life/Lines: Theorizing Women's Autobiography* (Ithaca and London: Cornell University Press, 1988); Corbett, *Representing Femininity*.
16. Jane Marcus, 'Invincible mediocrity: the private selves of public women', in Benstock, *Private Self*, pp. 114–46, p. 115.
17. Brodzi and Schenk, Introduction, *Life/Lines*, pp. 1–15, pp. 8, 9; Susan Friedman, 'Women's autobiographical selves: theory and practice', in Benstock, *Private Self*, pp. 34–62, p. 38.
18. William Van Lennep, ed., *The Reminiscences of Sarah Kemble Siddons, 1773–1785* (Cambridge, MA: printed at the Widener Library, 1942), pp. 1–2.

19. George Raymond, *Memoirs of Robert William Elliston, Comedian*, 2nd edn (London: John Ollivier, 1846), pp. xiv–xv.

20. Jonathan Bate, *The Genius of Shakespeare* (New York and Oxford: Oxford University Press, 1998), p. 5; Philip H. Highfill Jnr, Kalman A. Burnim and Edward A. Langhans, *A Biographical dictionary . . . 1660–1800* (Carbondale and Edwardsville: Southern Illinois University Press, 1973), vol. 1, p. viii.

21. For Kant's assertion see E. J. Hundert, 'The European enlightenment and the history of the self', in Roy Porter, ed., *Rewriting the Self: Histories from the Renaissance to the Present* (New York and London: Routledge, 1997), pp. 72–83, p. 81.

22. Maurice Halbwachs, *On Collective Memory*, ed., trans. and with an introduction by Lewis A. Coser (Chicago and London: University of Chicago Press, 1992), pp. 141, 164.

23. Jerome Bruner and Carol Fleisher Feldman, 'Group narrative as a cultural context of autobiography', in David C. Rubin, ed., *Remembering our Past* (Cambridge University Press, 1996), pp. 291–317, p. 293.

24. Paul Connerton, *How Societies Remember* (Cambridge University Press, 1989), pp. 16–17.

25. Ibid., p. 3.

26. Joseph Roach, 'Culture and performance in the Circum-Atlantic World', in Andrew Parker and Eve Kosofsky Sedgwick, *Performativity and Performance* (New York and London: Routledge, 1995), pp. 45–63, p. 45; he quotes from Kwame Anthony Appiah, *In My Father's House* (New York and Oxford: Oxford University Press, 1992), p. 132.

27. Who *pays* and how much is always a preoccupation of actors – see below, pp. 124, 127.

28. For a discussion of this point see Shearer West, *The Image of the Actor: Verbal and Visual Representation in the Age of Garrick and Kemble* (London: Pinter Publications, 1991), pp. 58–61.

29. Quoted from an interview by Anthony Holden in his *Olivier* (London: Weidenfeld and Nicolson, 1988), p. 4.

30. Holden, *Olivier*, pp. 1–2.

31. Prod. John Fisher, Channel 4 1994.

32. Citations from the life of Mathews that follow will be either from Edmund Yates's 1860 abridged version of the life (see note 12 above) in the form 'Yates, pp. 6–7, 9,' (the childhood account here) or will be from Anne Mathews's original edition, *Memoirs of Charles Mathews, Comedian*, 4 vols. (London: Bentley, 1838), in the form 'A. Mathews, vol. 1, pp. 173–84' (the Lee Sugg story).

33. A. Mathews, vol. 3, p. 344.

34. Ibid., p. 114.

35. Yates, p. 104.

36. See A. Mathews, vol. 1, pp. 144–5.
37. B. W. Proctor (Barry Cornwall), *The Life of Edmund Kean* (1835, reprinted New York and London: Benjamin Blom, 1969), 2 vols. in 1, vol. 2, pp. 157–8.
38. Yates, p. 168.
39. W. J. Macqueen Pope, *Theatre Royal Drury Lane* (London: W. H. Allen, n.d. [1945]), p. 30; he adds that similar tales of performers getting into trouble for such things continue 'for years'.
40. Yates, p. 166.
41. S.C.Q. and numbers in parenthesis in this chapter refer to the question numbers of the evidence to the Select Committee, 1832 – see chapter 3, note 8.
42. A. Mathews, vol. 2, pp. 12, 13, 16.
43. Ibid., p. 478, vol. 2, p. 77.
44. Yates, p. 203; Hazlitt in *London Magazine* 5 (May 1820), reprinted in *Dramatic Essays by William Hazlitt*, ed. William Archer and Robert W. Lowe (London: Walter Scott, 1895), pp. 179–83, pp. 179–80.
45. James Boaden, *The Private Correspondence of David Garrick . . . And a new biographical memoir*, 2 vols. (London: Henry Colburn and Richard Bentley, 1831), p. v; see also Brian Dobbs, *Drury Lane* (London: Cassell, 1972), p. 101, on Kitty Clive's determined puncturing of the pretensions of Garrick and Macklin by, amongst other things, imitating well-known lawyers of the day when she played Portia to Macklin's famous and very serious Shylock.
46. Boaden, *John Philip Kemble*, vol. 2, pp. 532–4, vol. 1, p. 308.
47. Yates, p. 196.
48. See Thomas Sadler, ed., *Diary, Reminiscences and Correspondence of Henry Crabb Robinson*, 2 vols., 3rd edn (London and New York: Macmillan, 1872), vol. 2, p. 4.
49. Letter to H. B. Gyles 9 March 1827; Anne Mathews, vol. 3, p. 587. Foote's solo shows included an 'Auction of Pictures' – see Boaden, *Private Correspondence of Garrick . . .*, p. xxii.
50. Sotheby and Son, *Catalogue of the miscellaneous and dramatic library . . . of the late Charles Mathews*, 19 August 1835.
51. A. Mathews, *Anecdotes of Actors*, p. 184.
52. Part of Mathews's conflicted creative process is recorded in the contradictory statements that Anne Mathews makes about his material. She records his gratitude to helpful writers, but she also describes his pride in having nothing written down, and repudiating all published versions of the scripts; he told the Committee he did not need a licence; and there is certainly no record of his text in the Lord Chamberlain's collection. But published accounts exist, and this, from *Sketches of Mr Mathews . . . entitled The Home Circuit* [1827] printed by J. Limbird at the Mirror Office, 143, The Strand, seems

a very close description of the gallery monopolylogue as it appears in Anne Mathews and the letters and bills she prints.

53. Thomas Campbell, *Life of Mrs Siddons* (London: Moxon, 1839), p. 74. A. Mathews, vol. 1, pp. 382–3.

54. Proctor, *Edmund Kean*, vol. 2, pp. 244–5.

55. Bracketed citations from this text refer to the pages of the licenser's copy, British Library Add. Ms. No. 42920 ff. 120–210v.

56. Francis, *Fanny Kelly*, p. 28, quoting a letter from Lamb to the Wordworths.

57. *Diary . . . of . . . Crabb Robinson*, vol. 2, p. 135.

58. The 'Old Price' riots, which began on 18 September 1809 and continued for 61 nights, were a famous instance of self-assertion by the theatre public. An organised crowd violently but also wittily demanded that manager John Philip Kemble revert to the pricing structure that had prevailed before his rebuilding of Covent Garden. They carried their point: a demonstration of the national importance of the patent theatre as a public space, more answerable to the nation than to profitability.

59. L. E. Holman, *Lamb's 'Barabara S' – The Life of Frances Maria Kelly* (London: Methuen, 1935), p. 18.

60. An anecdote retailed by Macqueen Pope, *Drury Lane*, p. 12.

61. Michael Kelly, *Reminiscences*, Vol. 1, p. 329; such stories are not uncommon: they would seem to reflect practice. Downes recounts the traditional chain of performance instruction for the role of Hamlet, which links Betterton back to Shakespeare.

62. Baron Laurence Olivier, *On Acting* (London: Sceptre, 1987), p. 25.

63. Charles Dibdin the elder, *A Complete History of the English Stage*, 5 vols., Printed for the author and sold by him at his warehouse, Leicester Place, Leicester Square, London 1801, pp. 386–7, 381, 379–80.

64. Anon., *Biography of British Stage* (London: Sherwood, Jones, 1824), p. ix.

65. Thomas Dibdin, *The Reminiscences of Thomas Dibdin*, 2 vols. (London: Henry Colburn, 1827), p. 10. The invocation of Garrick's quasi-paternity is common to several of these sets of memories – Mathews records the great man's being introduced into his father's shop in the Strand and patting his own unconscious baby head; presumably part of the sense of 'the world we have lost' that pervades the invocation of the Garrick stage is to do with his generational positioning in relation to the writers. He died in 1779.

66. Oxberry, *Dramatic Biography*, vol. 1, 1825, pp. 11–12.

67. A. Mathews, vol. 2, pp. 369–70, letter from Colman to Mathews, 7 April 1815.

68. Boaden, *Life of John Philip Kemble*, vol. 1, p. 29.

69. Michael Dobson, *The Making of the National Poet* (Oxford: Clarendon Press, 1992), pp. 176–84.

70. A. Mathews, vol. 2, p. 432.

71. Ibid., vol. 2, p. 442.

72. See ibid., vol. 2, pp. 458–9, 462–7; and S. J. Arnold, *Forgotten facts in the Memoirs of Charles Mathews, Comedian, recalled in a letter to Mrs Mathews, his biographer* (London: Ridgewood, [1839]). On the ideology of the professional, see Corbett, *Representing Femininity*, p. 26: it 'mystifies the relations between producer and consumer by specifying knowledge, rather than a particular work product, as the commodity to be exchanged on the market; that commodity can only be produced by the professional body . . . a professional sells himself, not an alienable product, as the possessor of that specialized knowledge . . . the professional cannot be alienated from his labor because his own body is literally invested in it'.

73. See Thomas Marshall on Miss Somerville's Drury Lane audition, *Lives of the Most Celebrated Actors and Actresses* (London: E. Appleyard, [1847]), p. 74, and the Oxberry biographies passim.

74. Yates, p. 144.

75. William Hone, *The Every-Day Book: or the Guide to the Year, relating the popular amusements, sports ceremonies, manners, customs, and events . . .* , 2 vols., pub. in 1 vol. (London: William Tegg, 1826), 5 September col. 1244; George Daniels *Merrie England*, vol. 2, p. 118.

76. Mathews, *Anecdotes*, p. 191. Oxberry's *Dramatic Biography*, vol. 3, p. 175, offers a version in which Garrick, 'incog.' in the audience of a Yorkshire theatre, is recognised from the stage and his money refunded by a deputation of actors; for an elaborated version of recognition at the door, told as if from personal experience, see the memoirs of the actor William Abbott, edited by Buckstone and printed by John Kemble Chapman, who turned printer and publisher in 1843, after his theatrical problems. In *Chapman's Weekly Magazine*, no. 6, November 1843, pp. 333–4, Abbott recounts a visit to a theatre booth in Bristol fair, where he and a Mr Brunton (one of an important theatre family of the time) not only had their money refused, but were led to the best seats by a man shaking sawdust before their feet – like the manager of a Theatre Royal backing up the red carpet, carrying candles, before visiting royalty – and electrifying the country audience with their importance.

6 THEATRE HISTORY AND THE DISCOURSE OF THE POPULAR

1. For a convenient way into the issues underpinning British cultural studies that are briefly indicated here, see John Storey, *Cultural*

Studies and the Study of Popular Culture: Theories and Methods (Edinburgh University Press, 1996), *Cultural Theory and Popular Culture: An Introduction* (Athens, GA: Prentice Hall Europe and Georgia University Press, 2nd edn 1998), and *Cultural Theory and Popular Culture, A Reader* (Athens, GA: Prentice Hall Europe and Georgia University Press, 3rd edn 2000).

2. Florence Emily Hardy, *The Early Life of Thomas Hardy 1840–1891* (London: Macmillan, 1928), pp. 25–6.

3. See, for example, George Augustus Sala, whose *Twice Round the Clock or the hours of the day and night in London*, 1859, was one of a multitude of books through which the reader could vicariously enjoy the delights and dangers of the metropolis; he was an admirer of Egan, and claimed to have been 'an outrageous young Mohock' in his 'old days of Tom and Jerryism'. (Quoted by Philip Collins in his edition of *Twice Round the Clock* (New York: Leicester University Press, 1971), p. 15.)

4. Richard Hoggart, *The Uses of Literacy* (London: Chatto and Windus, 1957).

5. Morag Shiach, *Discourse on Popular Culture: Class, Gender and History in Cultural Analysis, 1730 to the Present* (Oxford: Polity Press, 1989), pp. 3–5.

6. J. White, London 1801.

7. Francis Douce, *Gesta Romanorum: Illustrations of Shakespeare and of ancient manners . . .* 2 vols. (London: Longman, Hurst, Rees and Orme, 1807), vol. 1, p. ix.

8. Ibid., vol. 2, p. 481.

9. For Hone's political and literary importance see Marcus Wood, *Radical Satire and Print Culture, 1790–1822* (Oxford: Clarendon Press, 1994) and Olivia Smith, *The Politics of Language 1791–1819* (Oxford: Clarendon Press, 1984), pp. 170–4.

10. Printed for William Hone, London 1823.

11. Shepherd and Womack, *English Drama*, pp. 33–52, especially p. 43.

12. Probably with a glottal stop – Bar'lmi.

13. Peter Stallybrass and Allon White, *The Politics and Poetics of Transgression* (London: Methuen, 1986, pp. 30, 31) note that even Bakhtin 'succumbs to that separation of the festive and the commercial which is distinctive of capitalist rationality'. 'It is a gravely over-simplifying abstraction', they point out, 'to conceptualise the fair purely as a site of communal celebration' and not concerned with money-getting; but this is the tendency of most subsequent writers about fairs and festivals who wish to sanitise and protect the people's 'authentic' leisure activities: 'the emergent middle classes *worried away at it*, particularly striving to separate and consolidate the binaries which the fair so mischievously seemed to intermix and confuse'.

14. Joseph Roach, *The Cities of the Dead: Circum-atlantic Performance* (New York: Columbia University Press, 1996), p. 6, on forgetting; Bartholomew Fair is not mentioned in the book. Steven Mullany, *The Place of the Stage, License, Play, and Power in Renaissance England* (Ann Arbor: University of Michigan Press, 1988), is concerned with locating the Shakespearean flowering of the stage in an anomalous place, the Liberties of London, 'an ambiguous realm' (p. 21) on the fringes beyond City jurisdiction, where the first playhouses were built. He sets these festive sites and their activities over against the City's own ritual calendar, within which church and civic ceremony took place within the City walls; this he says occupied only the first half of the year, from Midsummer's Eve to Christmas being given over to commercial concerns (p. 20). But Bartlemy was not in a Liberty – Smithfield was between the walls and the bars, within and without; and its ceremonials happened in the heart of the commercial half of the year. Mullaney does not discuss the Fair.

15. Ben Weinreb and Christopher Hibbert, eds., *The London Encyclopaedia* (London: Macmillan, 1983), p. 789.

16. William Hone, *The Every-Day Book: or the Guide to the Year, relating the popular amusements, sports, ceremonies, manners, customs, and events* . . . 2 vols. (London: William Tegg, 1826), entry for 5 September, vol. 1 columns 1168–1252, col. 1171.

17. Francis Sheppard, *London 1808–1870: The Infernal Wen* (London: Secker and Warburg, 1971), p. 189; see also Alec Forshaw and Theo Bergstom, *Smithfield Past and Present* (London: Robert Hale, 1980 – 2nd edn 1990), p. 54.

18. Quoted in Sheppard, *London 1808–1870*, p. 189.

19. William Wilkinson Addison, *English Fairs and Markets* (London: Batsford, 1953), quoted in David Kerr Cameron, *The English Fair* (Thrupp: Sutton Publishing, 1998), pp. 155–6. Henry Morley, *Memoirs of Bartholomew Fair* (London: Chapman and Hall, 1859), p. 70, citing 'the statement of Bartholomaeus de Glanvilla, an Englishman writing at the end of the fourteenth century', would seem to be the source for this, though he makes it a general assertion about medieval fairs rather than a particular characteristic of Bartlemy.

20. See Jane Traies, *Fairbooths and Fitups* (Cambridge: Chadwyck-Healey, 1988), pp. 32–3.

21. *Every night book; or a life after dark*. By the author of 'the cigar'. (London: T. Richardson, 1827), p. 30.

22. Christopher N. L. Brooke and Gillian Keir, *London 800–1216: The Shaping of a City* (London: Secker and Warburg, 1975), pp. 326–7, quoting the twelfth-century Foundation Book of the hospital.

23. *Memoirs*, pp. 71–2.

24. Forshaw and Bergstom, *Smithfield Past and Present*, pp. 23–5, 39; Weinreb and Hibbert, *London Encyclopaedia*, p. 790; they note that

charred human bones were recovered from excavations at the door of the church in 1849.

25. *Every-Day Book*, vol. 1, cols. 1240, 1242; Stallybrass and White, *Politics and Poetics*, p. 103, have shown that the renewed vitality went hand in hand with new investment in its suppression, until in 1750 the period of the fair was again cut back to three days; they add 'as the realm of Folly was being restructured within bourgeois consciousness as precisely that *other realm* inhabited by a grotesque body which it repudiated as part of its own identity and disdained as a set of real life *practices and rituals*, so it seemed to become more and more important as a set of *representations* . . . The Smithfield Muse was on the move' and invaded polite poetry.

26. The impossibility of eradicating ritual moments when the young will pass some boundary, whether that of Smithfield or of public examinations, and be taken up by the authorities helplessly drunk in the street, was confirmed in June 2000 by the Prime Minister's son. The universally sympathetic reaction to Euan Blair's transgression showed that such moments are regarded as inevitable.

27. *A sermon on the evils of fairs in general and the Bartholomew Fair in particular: preached at Charlotte Chapel, Pimlico on Sunday August 22 1830*, 2nd edn, Cochran and Key, 108 Strand, London, pp. 118–21.

28. Wood, *Radical Satire*, p. 269.

29. Hone, *Every-Day Book*, vol. 1, col. 1252. In his most radical days, during 1817, the year of his triumph over repression when he defended himself successfully against prosecution three times, Hone had used Bartlemy in the manner Wood suggests, for an attack on the Prime Minister, Sidmouth. A pamphlet entitled *OFFICIAL ACCOUNT: BARTHOLOMEW FAIR INSURRECTION; AND THE PIE-BALD PONEY PLOT!* (London; printed by and for William Hone. Reformists' Register Office, 67, Old Bailey, 1817 price two-pence) builds upon a hoax reported in the press that had led to the deployment of large bodies of troops in the streets around the Fair to suppress a feared revolution. It suits Hone's mocking purposes to represent this as a ludicrous idea, because the Fair is nothing but a treat for children, all about gingerbread and roundabouts; he ironically fantasises about the freaks revolting, the armless woman taking the Lord Mayor captive. He does incidentally admit, however, that were there any such plot, the impossibility of controlling 'fifty thousand people' in Bartlemy mood might well alarm the Prime Minister. The serious consequence of jittery authority calling out the dragoons for fear of a crowd was demonstrated two years later at the Peterloo massacre in Manchester.

30. Richard D. Altick, *The Shows of London* (Cambridge, Mass.: Harvard University Press, 1978), details the history of the commercial showing of rarities – the 'raree show' – as it developed in

England after the foreclosing of church displays of relics, and notes that from the sixteenth century onwards objects and people which were the fruits of distant exploration and conquest mingled with home-grown marvels; he dates an early example of such a show at 1578, p. 7.

31. Stallybrass and White, *Politics and Poetics*, p. 40.
32. *The Place of the Stage*, p. 31, emphasis original.
33. Stallybrass and White, *Politics and Poetics*, p. 41.
34. MS 1514. I am endebted to Sharon Tuff of the Guildhall Manuscript room for her researches into the origin of the MS, which only revealed that the book, possibly supplied by the Covent Garden bookseller Jacob Henry Bunn, had stood on the shelves there for years before it was rebound, to include some extra materials about the Fair which were 'found in the Committee Room,' in 1906. No one has recorded how it arrived at the Guildhall.
35. See also *Report of the Market's Committee relative to Bartholomew Fair, delivered into the Court of Common Council of the City of London 2nd July 1840*, preserved in the City of London record office, which proposes expedients for 'reducing the nuisance' arising from the Fair which will lead to its 'natural death,' regarded as a desirable objective for the City.
36. He adds the strange information that the food on sale had switched from the old oysters and sausages to 'a new delicacy, *fried fish*'. It would appear that British fish and chips were born as Bartlemy died.
37. Under the 1852 Smithfield Removal Act the old market closed 11 June 1855; Forshaw and Bergstrom p. 57. The Gilspur Street Compter, the jail for petty offenders in the market and fair, closed in the same year.
38. 'Circus Life and Amusements . . .', in the *Magnet* week ending Saturday, 10 July 1875, p. 5.
39. George Daniels, *Merrie England in the Olden Time* 2, vols. (London: Richard Bentley, 1842), vol. 1, p. 5. It is perhaps worth noting that to the readers of the book and of *Bentley's Miscellany*, 'Merrie England' probably had some of its modern connotations, but might also have carried overtones of the earlier usage by which 'Merryland' meant the female body, as explored in erotic texts. See Karen Harvey, 'Gender, space and modernity in eighteenth-century England: a place called sex', *History Workshop Journal*, 51 (2001), 159–79, p. 171.
40. Daniels, *Merrie England*, vol. 1, p. 45. For the phase of cockney stereotyping which envisaged 'the London burgher as comic hero', see Gareth Stedman-Jones's periodised typology, 'The "cockney" and the nation, 1780–1988', in David Feldman and Gareth Stedman-Jones, eds., *Metropolis. London* (London and New York: Routledge, 1989), pp. 272–324, pp. 284–8.

41. See Pierce Egan, *Life in London; or, the Day and Night Scenes of Jerry Hawthorn, esq., and his elegant friend Corinthian Tom, accompanied by Bob Logic, the Oxonian, in their Rambles and Sprees through the Metropolis* (London: Sherwood, Neely and Jones, 1821), p. 288.
42. Daniels, vol. 1, pp. 7, 8, vol. 2, pp. 58, 23–4.
43. See Harvey, 'Gender, space and modernity'.
44. Stallybrass and White, *Politics and Poetics*, pp. 198–9.
45. For a consideration of such critical commentary see Carol L. Bernstein, *The Celebration of Scandal: Toward the Sublime in Victorian Urban Fiction* (Pennsylvania State University Press, 1991).
46. Ibid., pp. 3–4. For comment on Egan's work as forerunning the Victorian urban novel, see Roger Sales, 'Pierce Egan and the representation of London', in P. W. Martin and Robin Jarvis, eds., *Reviewing Romanticism* (London: Macmillan, 1992), pp. 154–69, Deborah Nord, *Walking the Victorian Streets* (Ithaca and London: Cornell University Press, 1995), especially pp. 30–7, and Paul Schlicke, 'The Pilgrimage of Pierce Egan', *Journal of Popular Culture* 21.1, 1987, pp. 1–9.
47. Egan, *Life in London*, p. 291.
48. Mayhew's work appeared first in the *Morning Chronicle* and was collected into *London Labour and the London Poor* (London, 1861–2); Mearns, *The Bitter Cry of Outcast London* (London: James Clerke, 1883); Greenwood, *The Wilds of London* (London: Chatto and Windus, 1874), and other similar volumes. For a selection of material from the 'social explorers' see P. J. Keating, ed., *Into Unknown England, 1866–1913* (London: Fontana, 1976). Bernstein, *Celebration of Scandal*, p. 16, distinguished Egan from this tradition; his style and approach to the creation of a discourse of popular culture was shared with such low-life writers as Renton Nicholson, who, like Egan, existed on the fringes of the entertainment world and lived by publishing a rather scabrous periodical, *The Train* (1856–8), and by staging mock crim. con. trials in a Strand tavern. In 1838 he produced *Cockney Adventures and Tales of London Life* (London: William Clark, A. Forrester).
49. *Old Drury Lane* 1861, quoted in J. C. Reid, *Bucks and Bruisers: Pierce Egan and Regency England* (London: Routledge and Kegan Paul, 1971), p. 77.
50. Quoted in Reid, *Bucks and Bruisers*, p. 71.
51. Larpent no. 2262. The correspondence is included in the microfiche version of the text.
52. Quoted in Reid, *Bucks and Bruisers*, p. 81, see pp. 82–3 for details of the Adelphi run and reception.
53. 11 March 1822; quoted in Reid, *Bucks and Bruisers*, p. 82.
54. Letter to *The Drama, or Theatrical Pocket Magazine*, no. 7 (May 1822), pp. 321–2, from JLB of Chelsea Common.

55. *Mirror of the Stage*, vol. 1, no. 8 (18 November 1822), pp. 124–5; and vol. 1, no. 12 (13 January 1823), p. 192.

56. Quoted in Reid, *Bucks and Bruisers*, p. 82.

57. This is the tenor of the *Mirror of the Stage* criticism: that the stage should be 'an encouragement for wit and learning, and a school for morality, virtue, and good sense' – 'is such a piece [as Tom and Jerry] likely to improve our morals our virtue or our manners?' no. 8 (18 November 1822).

58. Reid, *Bucks and Bruisers*, p. 77.

59. All these appear in Charles Dibdin Jnr's version at the Olympic in November 1821; see Larpent no. 2257 and the very different printed version, John Lowndes, London 1822.

60. Vol. 1 (May–Nov. 1821), p. 380.

61. Published by Thomas Kelly; see p. 155 for an example of the Don's moral reflections.

62. Amateur, *Real Life in London*, 2 vols. (London: Jones and Co., 1821–2).

63. William Hone, *Ancient Mysteries Described, especially the English Mystery Plays* . . . (London: William Hone, 1823), p. 230.

64. *The Drama*, no. 6 (May 1822), p. 360.

65. See the Coburg playbills, 8 April to 2 May 1822.

66. W. T. Moncrieff, *Tom and Jerry; or, Life in London*, 2nd edn (London: Richardson, n.d. [1828]), pp. 32, 70.

67. Larpent no. 2257, Act 1 scene 3rd [actually scene 4] p. 24; Corinthian means a fashionable, brazen-faced idler, according to the dictionary of slang that Egan edited (*Grose's Classical Dictionary of the Vulgar Tongue*, 1823) and is applied by him to both Tom and Kate; Ephesian means 'boon companion' according to the *OED*, where a Shakespearean instance is cited.

68. Larpent no. 2257 1/3 p. 29.

69. Ibid., Act 2 scene 4.

70. Playbills in the Theatre Museum, London, 25 February 1822, 6/7/8 December 1821.

71. Moncrieff, *Tom and Jerry*, pp. 20–1.

72. *Mirror of the Stage*, no. 12 (13 January 1823), p. 191.

73. Olivia Smith, *The Politics of Language 1791–1819* (Oxford: Clarendon Press, 1984), pp. vii, 155.

74. Deborah Vlock, *Dickens, Novel Reading, and the Victorian Popular Theatre* (Cambridge University Press, 1998), pp. 81, 82.

75. Egan, sensitive to the commercial need to keep his representations up to date, included such a figure in his own work when he extended the Tom and Jerry saga in his last work, *The Pilgrims of the Thames in Search of the National!* 1837. He adds a retired merchant called Peter Makemoney – 'a bourgeois tourist rather than a dissipated idler': see Schlicke, 'Pilgrimage of Pierce Egan', p. 4.

76. Scene 4 in Larpent no. 2257, 5 in the printed edition.
77. Vlock, *Dickens, Novel Reading*, p. 113.
78. Larpent MS. 2262.
79. Reid, *Bucks and Bruisers*, p. 80.
80. Egan, *Life in London*, p. 290.
81. Larpent MS. 2257, Act 3, pp. 60–2.

7 CLAIMING KIN: AN EXPERIMENT IN GENEALOGICAL
RESEARCH

1. Jack Le White and Peter Ford, *Rings and Curtains* (London: Quartet, 1992), pp. 246–7.
2. Biographical particulars of eighteenth-century players used in this chapter are taken, unless otherwise specified, from their entries in Philip H. Highfill Jnr, Kalmin A. Burnim and Edward A. Langhans, *A Biographical Dictionary . . . 1660–1800*, 16 vols. (Carbondale and Edwardsville: Southern Illinois University Press, 1973–93); for later biographies and family links the reference works are *The Green Room Book*, ed. John Parker (London: 1907–9) and his continuation of that work, *Who's Who in the Theatre* (London: Pitman, 1912–1978).
3. Frances Ann Kemble, *Records of a Girlhood* (New York: Henry Holt, 1883), pp. 142–3.
4. See in this regard George Speight, ed., Henry Allen Whiteley, *Memories of Circus Variety etc as I knew it* (London: Society for Theatre Research, 1981) – a facsimile manuscript in which centuries of amazing family connections and convolutions, making up a history that covers all Europe and involves far more complicated relationships than the one Jack mentions, are detailed with unblotted lucidity.
5. Stanley Lupino, *From the Stocks to the Stars: An Unconventional Autobiography* (London: Hutchinson, 1934), pp. v, 34, 33.
6. Lupino Lane, *How to Become a Comedian* (London: Muller, 1945), pp. 55–6.
7. LeWhite and Ford, *Rings and Curtains*, pp. 1–4; the ill-treatment of children in training undoubtedly occurred – see for example the memoirs of the clown Frowde, ed. Jacky Bratton and Ann Featherstone, Cambridge University Press (forthcoming); but many memoirists dismissed it as an exaggeration, took pride in their own toughness and contested the middle-class concern that tried to legislate against the exploitation of children: see for example Charlie Keith, *Circus Life and Amusements*, serialised in the *Magnet*, 1875, Chapter 1 continued, week ending Saturday 3 July 1875, who asserts that MPs are outsiders taken in by the mythology used to scare aspirants to the profession, and that boys brought up to it make it 'their pride' to 'possess a good name in the public estimation'.
8. Oxberry, *Dramatic Biography*, vol. 1, pp. 1–2.

9. *Era*, 25 March 1866; a 'wanted' advertisement emanating from Price's circus, then touring in Yorkshire.
10. John R. Gillis, *A World of Their Own Making: Myth, Ritual, and the Quest for Family Values* (New York: Basic Books/HarperCollins, 1996), p. 53; the preceding paragraph draws on this source.
11. Tracy C. Davis, *Actresses as Working Women* (London: Routledge, 1991); see also her essay 'Questions for a feminist methodology in theatre history', in Thomas Postlewait and Bruce A. McConachie, eds., *Interpreting the Theatrical Past* (University of Iowa Press, 1989), pp. 59–81.
12. Leonore Davidoff and Catherine Hall, *Family Fortunes: Men and Women of the English Middle Class 1780–1850* (London: Hutchinson, 1987).
13. Ibid., pp. 272–320.
14. Ibid., p. 13.
15. *Examiner* review, 19 November 1815; reprinted in William Archer and Robert W. Lowe, *Dramatic Essays by William Hazlitt* (London: Walter Scott, 1895), pp. 70–3, p. 72.
16. For Faucit's family, see Carol Jones Carlisle, *Helen Faucit: Fire and Ice on the Victorian Stage* (London: Society for Theatre Research, 2000), pp. 3–13.
17. Helena Faucit, Lady Martin, *On Some of Shakespeare's Female Characters* (Edinburgh and London: Blackwood, 1885), p. 6.
18. Sir Theodore Martin, *Helena Faucit (Lady Martin)* (Edinburgh and London: Blackwood, 1900), pp. 4, 30.
19. Oxberry, *Dramatic Biography*, vol. 3, pp. 209–10.
20. Davidoff and Hall, *Family Fortunes*, p. 290.
21. Oxberry, *Dramatic Biography*, vol. 5, pp. 19–32, p. 28.
22. See, for example, the biographies of Maria Foote, vol. 1, Mrs Orger, vol. 2 and Emma Sarah Love, vol. 3.
23. Mrs Bland was found her first engagement by a theatrical hairdresser (vol. 1). Many girls in stage families also went by the apprenticeship route; see instances in the lives of Fanny Kelly (vol. 1), Amelia George (vol. 3), Ann Maria Tree (vol. 3) and Mrs Billington (vol. 3). The musical apprenticeship system was legally established and could be extremely exploitative, with masters taking large profits from the public appearances of young people bound to them with no control over their own lives. Anyone wanting training and needing an entrée to the profession had little choice but to enter into a sometimes very lengthy bond: Elizabeth Poole, for example, appeared at the Olympic and at Astley's in London from the age of seven with great success, but then was bound at the age of nine to the Drury Lane chorus master James Thomas Harris for seven years and immediately rearticled on the day her bond expired for five years more, an obligation from which she was finally released

by his death. *Actors by Daylight* no. 22, 28 July 1838, pp. 170. I am grateful to Tracy Davis for this reference.

24. Oxberry, *Biographies*, new series, vol. 1, p. 97.
25. See Davidoff and Hall, *Family Fortunes*, pp. 274, 286, 282–3, for the difference from the norm that this profile represents.
26. Ibid., p. 32.
27. Oxberry, *Biography*, vol. 7, pp. 20–1.
28. See Tracy C. Davis, 'Female managers, lessees and proprietors of the British stage (to 1914)', *Nineteenth Century Theatre* 28.2 (Winter 2000), 115–44.
29. Oxberry, *Biography*, vol. 4, p. 146.
30. These family details are derived from the *Dictionary of National Biography*.
31. Oxberry, *Biography*, vol. 5, p. 181, in the biography of her son James.
32. *Dictionary of National Biography*.
33. Herschel Baker, *John Philip Kemble: The Actor in his Theatre* (Cambridge, MA: Harvard University Press, 1942), p. 7.
34. Letter from Ann Hatton to J. P. Collier, 27 August 1832, Folger Shakespeare Library Yc 923(3a).
35. Ibid.
36. In a list preserved amongst his papers at the Garrick Club, London.
37. *The Thespian Dictionary; or, Dramatic biography of the eighteenth century* (London: T. Hurst, 1802). Unpaginated; entry for 'Eliza Kemble'.
38. Baker, *John Philip Kemble*, pp. 191–2.
39. J. S. Bratton, 'Working in the margin: women in theatre history', *New Theatre Quarterly* 10.38 (1994), 122–31.
40. Frances Ann Kemble, *Records of a Girlhood*, pp. 22–3.
41. Ibid., pp. 23, 19, 24.
42. J. C. Trewin, ed., *The Journal of William Charles Macready* (London: Longmans, 1967), entry for 27 August 1836, p. 75.
43. George Taylor, *Players and Performances in the Victorian Theatre* (Manchester University Press, 1989), p. 98.
44. See Maggie Gale, 'From fame to obscurity: in search of Clemence Dane', in Maggie Gale and Viv Gardner, eds., *Women, Theatre and Performance* (Manchester University Press, 2000), pp. 121–41.
45. Clemence Dane, *Broome Stages* (London: Heinemann, 1931), pp. 3–5.
46. See chapter 1, p. 9.

Index